£4.99
c2

Modernism

Stratified Modernism

The Poetics of Excavation from Gautier to Olson

Sasha Colby

PETER LANG
Oxford • Bern • Berlin • Bruxelles • Frankfurt am Main • New York • Wien

Bibliographic information published by Die Deutsche Bibliothek
Die Deutsche Bibliothek lists this publication in the Deutsche Nationalbibliografie;
detailed bibliographic data is available on the Internet at <http://dnb.ddb.de>.

A catalogue record for this book is available from The British Library.

Library of Congress Cataloguing-in-Publication Data:

Colby, Sasha, 1978-
  Stratified modernism : the poetics of excavation from Gautier to Olson
/ Sasha Colby.
     p. cm.
  Includes bibliographical references and index.
  ISBN 978-3-03911-932-5 (alk. paper)
  1. Archaeology in literature. 2. Archaeology and literature. 3.
Modernism (Literature) 4. Literature, Modern--19th century--History and
criticism. 5. Literature, Modern--20th century--History and criticism.
I. Title.
  PN56.A717C65 2009
  809'.93358301--dc22
                    2009013020

ISBN 978-3-03911-932-5

© Peter Lang AG, International Academic Publishers, Bern 2009
Hochfeldstrasse 32, CH-3012 Bern, Switzerland
info@peterlang.com, www.peterlang.com, www.peterlang.net

All rights reserved.
All parts of this publication are protected by copyright.
Any utilisation outside the strict limits of the copyright law, without the
permission of the publisher, is forbidden and liable to prosecution.
This applies in particular to reproductions, translations, microfilming,
and storage and processing in electronic retrieval systems.

Printed in Germany

*For the books
and those who opened them*

Contents

Acknowledgements	ix
Introduction	1
CHAPTER 1 The Spade and the Word: A Brief History of Archaeology and Writing	9
CHAPTER 2 Reverie and Revelation: The Textual Archaeologies of Théophile Gautier	37
CHAPTER 3 The Aesthetics of Excavation: Walter Pater's Stratified Text	61
CHAPTER 4 Dream, Delusion, and Dynamite: Freud as Literary Trace	87
CHAPTER 5 "Original in the right sense": Ezra Pound, Adrian Stokes, H.D., and the Archaeology of the New	115
CHAPTER 6 Urban Archaeologies of the French Surrealists	141
CHAPTER 7 The Rhetoric of Resurrection: Charles Olson in Meso-America	169
Conclusion: Archaeologies Past and Future	189
Works Cited	195
Index	209

Acknowledgements

No genuine repayment is possible for the debts incurred by an eight year project, particularly for the support and intellectual generosity I have received over the past several years. This project began as a doctoral dissertation at the University of Sussex under the expert supervision of Peter Nicholls, whose inspiring scholarship motivated the journey to Britain. He deserves tremendous thanks, not only for sharing his extensive knowledge and insight but also for maintaining confidence in me during a rather unusual, transnational course of study. Stephen Bann and Laura Marcus sat on the examining committee and provided many helpful suggestions for turning the dissertation into a book. I would particularly like to thank Laura Marcus for suggesting the addition of H.D., which led me to write the play, *H.D.: A Life*, in addition to the section on H.D. included here. During my time at the University of Sussex I received generous financial support from an Overseas Research Scholarship, administered by the British Council, a Social Sciences and Humanities Research Council of Canada Doctoral Fellowship, and language school funding in Rome, Florence, and Venice through the Italian Cultural Institute in Vancouver. At Simon Fraser University I received the support of friends and colleagues in English, Explorations, and World Literature as well as travel and publication funding provided by a President's Research Grant, the University Publications Fund, an Arts Research Incentive Grant, and a World Literature Research and Culture Grant. Librarians everywhere are the guardian angels of academics, and I would like to extend particular thanks to Joanne Whiting and Mary Wood at Vancouver Island University, to Vera Yuen at Simon Fraser University, and to the generally helpful librarians and staff at the British Library in London and the Bibliothèque Nationale in Paris. Nick Reynolds, Mary Critchley, and Shirley Walker Werrett at Peter Lang made publication pleasant and painless. Undergraduate and graduate students at Vancouver Island University and Simon Fraser University consistently re-ignited my enthusiasm for discussions about modernism and literature. Teachers, in the true sense, who initially set me on this path include Luke Carson, Evelyn Cobley, James Eadie, Ian Graham, Christopher Keep, Sheila Rabillard, and Maria Roberts. Brian Colby, Lucy Colby, and Irene Nikifortchuk made it possible to write this book and along with Sophia Forster and John Mallory provided welcome injections of fun, encouragement, and irony.

I would like to thank *Comparative Literature and Culture* for granting me permission to reprint an early version of the Gautier chapter, which appeared as:

"The Literary Archaeologies of Théophile Gautier." *CLCWeb: Comparative Literature and Culture* 8.2 (2006): <http://docs.lib.purdue.edu/clcweb/vol8/iss2/7/>.

I would also like to thank the following for permission to quote copyright material:

Archangel for Nuno Júdice's "Fragments" from *Meditation on Ruins*, trans. Richard Zenith, copyright ©1997 by Nuno Júdice, introduction and translation ©1997 by Richard Zenith.

Faber and Faber Ltd. and New Directions Publishing Corp. for Ezra Pound's "Papyrus" from *Personae*, copyright ©1926 by Ezra Pound.

University of California Press for Charles Olson's "The Distances" from *The Collected Poems of Charles Olson: Excluding the Maximus Poems*, ed. George Butterick, copyright ©1987 by the Estate of Charles Olson.

Every effort has been made to contact copyright-holders. In the case of inadvertent omission please contact the author.

Introduction

> We have often been asked how the victims in the royal graves met their death, and it is impossible to give a decisive answer. The bones are too crushed and too decayed to show any cause of death, supposing that violence had been used, but the general condition of the bodies does supply a strong argument. Very many of these women wear headdresses which are delicate in themselves and would easily be disarranged, yet such are always found in good order, undisturbed except by the pressure of the earth; this would be impossible if the wearers had been knocked on the head, improbable if they had fallen to the ground after being stabbed, and it is equally unlikely that they could have been killed outside the grave and carried down the ramp and laid in their places with all their ornaments intact; certainly the animals must have been alive when they dragged the chariots down the ramps, and, if so, the grooms who led them and the drivers in the carts must have been alive also; it is safe to assume that those who were to be sacrificed went down alive into the pit.
>
> (*Ur of the Chaldees* 59)

In this passage on his 1927 findings at the Royal Cemetery at Ur, Leonard Woolley acts as a pathologist of history, carefully reconstructing the circumstances surrounding the burial of a Sumerian king and the entourage that was to accompany him into his next life. Examining the bodies and gathering clues, Woolley, one of the first systematic archaeologists of the twentieth century, is our hero-detective, piecing together past events through material evidence, making connections and inductive inferences. Not just a scientific report, Woolley's account of the excavations is an imaginative reconstruction, one as crafted to appeal to popular audiences as *Murder in Mesopotamia*, Agatha Christie's adventure tale based on her own experience visiting the excavation site at Ur. Like Christie, Woolley foregrounds the elements of death and decay. Yet his account also identifies the past as a space of luxury and excess, the women wearing, "the gala headdress of lapis and carnelian beads ... great lunate earrings of gold, silver 'combs' ... inlaid with lapis, gold, and shell, and necklaces of lapis and gold" (50). A site of sacrifice, the pit is also a reminder of an age of lost plentitude.

Lost but not forgotten – and not completely impenetrable, either. For Woolley, the outlines of the Sumerian civilization, its customs and ideals, can be intuited from what remains. The retrospective mentalities of the men and women who entered the funeral pit alive are inferred from their frozen postures; their "good order and alignment" suggest they "took some kind of drug – opium or hashish" and lay down willingly, after which "the last touches were given to their bodies and the pit was filled in" (60). Through careful reconstruction, Woolley creates a vivid portrait of events that took place four thousand years before. The cemetery, as it appears in Woolley's written account, is not just the site of death. It is also a space where the victims, interred for centuries, are brought to life once more.

Human sacrifice, a lost dynasty, valuable treasure, reconnection with the distant past – here are some of the elements that made eighteenth-, nineteenth- and early twentieth-century archaeology an "open site" for the popular and poetic imagination. As Woolley's account illustrates, archaeology consistently exceeds material remains, the exhumed objects giving rise to imaginative reconstructions of their surrounding contexts. As such, archaeological objects can be perceived as translocationary talismans to another time in history, the site itself a rich repository of cultural memory. Full of dramatic potential, early archaeology offered the public a palpable *frisson* – ghostly reconnections, vicarious transgressions, a privileged voyeurism, and a host of bizarre scenarios that would become the subject of numerous archaeological fantasies.

This is to say that while archaeology was developing as a distinct discipline throughout the nineteenth and twentieth centuries, it also spawned a new imaginative arena. Beginning with the popularization of the excavations at Pompeii and Herculaneum toward the end of the eighteenth century, there came into being a series of cultural archaeological *mentalités*. These modes of thought were the shared precepts, suppositions, attitudes, associations, and imaginative configurations that shaped each generation's archaeological matrix. By the time archaeology reached the mid-nineteenth century it was not just a discipline: it was a series of imaginative templates – a sequence of methods or approaches enriched by the constant oscillations between the object and the civilization it evoked, the fragment and the totality it called into being, solid earth and the layers that belied it. Changing in dynamics, subtlety and emphasis but retaining a nexus or complex of ideas, archaeological modes of thought tunnel through nineteenth- and twentieth-century writing, where the texts themselves are the topographies of sedimented meanings and encrypted significances.

In this sense the archaeological site is a magnetic site, a site that drew in public and literary interest from the age of romanticism to that of the modernist avant-garde. A force-field that absorbed and recast anxieties about the present and future, archaeology was able to both create coherent narratives about the distant past as well as destabilize pre-established historical assumptions. In its ability to encompass a wide range of desires and intentions, the archaeological site existed as a cultural *combinatoire*, a space where variegated ideological and historical fragments were played and replayed in an endless combination of imaginative constructions and reconstructions. Adopted, absorbed, and translated from the archaeological, these excavational dynamics are contained within the vaults of the written. In turn, these pages can also be excavated for traces of authorial and cultural desire. Within the work of Théophile Gautier, Walter Pater, Sigmund Freud, Ezra Pound, Adrian Stokes, H.D. (Hilda Doolittle), André Breton, Louis Aragon and Charles Olson dwell some of the most powerful handlings of archaeological templates, tensions, and dynamics. Hailing from English, European, and American traditions, they are united by their susceptibility to archaeological fantasies and, in the works of the later writers, a tendency to embalm their literary predecessors' archaeological modalities into the structures of their own work. They are also united by a modern cosmopolitanism that precipitated keen interest in both ancient repositories and contemporary international trends. Through their distinctly divergent modes, from Freud's psychic excavations to Pound's social invocations, from Gautier's mummies to Breton's dreaming archaisms, revolution, and indecipherable objects, from Pater's hypnotic and diaphanous cadences to modernism's jagged appropriation of the fragment are the echoes, the resonance, the mark of the archae.

Rather than a discreet set of writers to whom archaeological dynamics apply, it is important to understand that these writers belong to a tradition, albeit an occluded one. Broadly speaking, two (sometimes intersecting) trajectories of archaeological thought have been pursued: the social archaeology which sought to reactivate templates from the distant past for future application, an archaeology often formally associated with a sculptural, emergent, and fragmented poetic; and the interiorized, psychic excavations of the archaeological self which, when adapted by literature, more often use dream images and softer tonal variations to coax the past into the margins of the text. Whether these archaeologies took on social or psychic form, the common denominator is that they gave rise to new imaginative order. The archaeological, like the literary, became a site of displaced fulfillment, absorbing desire often, on the surface operations of everyday life, obscured or condemned. In this sense, archaeology is modernity's double: the past that is the flip side of its newness, the dream that contradicts its supposed rationalism, the richness of existence which modernity holds cheap. The writers studied here deliberately inhabit the schism between these two spheres and as such represent an overlaying tradition which both draws upon and rejects various aspects of the work that has come before. Taken as a whole their work represents a rich cultural repository, a stratified modernism which spans from 1840 to 1955.

"The problem of the subject," wrote Foucault: "In distinguishing between the epistemological level of knowledge (or scientific consciousness) and the archaeological level of knowledge, I am aware that I am advancing in a direction that is fraught with difficulty" (xiii). Certainly Foucault's archaeology, particularly the underground forces that coalesce to create modern forms of knowledge, is relevant here – as are his warnings. To suggest that archaeology exerted certain effects on both the form and content of certain nineteenth- and twentieth-century texts is indeed "fraught." Archaeology as a mode of literary inquiry has its pit-falls, the most problematic of which is reading too much into a paradigm of "layers" and "depth." At the same time, the persistence of archaeological modalities in pan-European writing beginning from approximately 1840 (from the time archaeology gathered momentum in British, European and American consciousness) is undeniable; the archaeological summoned a series of circulating meanings:

the lure of the past, the search for origins, the aura of the object, the place of the fragment, the hidden erotic, the undulating feminine, the processes of writing and memory, the power of dream and fantasy, the encrypted and deciphered, the monstrous and the ideal. This convection of themes also manifested themselves through the structural effects of modern writing: sedimentation, occlusion, echo, compaction, fragmentation – all of which, when examined within the context of prevalent archaeological *mentalités*, support a rich line of cultural and textual archaeo-logic.

To write about a given set of themes and structural effects running from the mid-nineteenth to mid-twentieth century is to propose an archaeology the avant-garde would prefer to see as surface. According to most twentieth-century modernists, the beginning of the century signified a dramatic break with the writing of the *fin-de-siècle* decadents and aesthetes. The modern was a moment of rupture, an absolute break with the immediate past and a reconnection with the more visceral intensities of primal history. Apollinaire's credo "You cannot carry your father's corpse with you everywhere" is illustrative of the modernist desire to rid one's self of the past and begin again. Yet even this metaphor speaks persuasively of the presence of the past: for if you do not carry your father's corpse, you must bury him. The persistence of what is buried, its continuing force, preoccupied modern writers and found a correlative, physically and psychically, in prominent excavations. While it changes in accent and inflection, and despite modernist protestations, the consistent reappearance of the archaeological thematic illustrates how elements of Victorian and French Romantic writing exist as substrata of modernist literature, the buried inheritance – a heritage most modernists dismissed, but often encoded into their own practices and approaches.

And so the question becomes: Why did archaeology, in particular, exert such a powerful personal and cultural influence over nineteenth- and twentieth-century writers? Why did it become such a compelling space for imaginative reconstitution and displaced desire? As a starting point, and this illustrates the first contradiction in a discipline that is riddled by more than its fair share of paradox, archaeology was a late emerging science, which is to suggest that the study of the very old was very new. While in use in the 1600s signifying "ancient history generally," the earliest example of "archaeology" referring to a distinct discipline does not occur until D. Wilson's 1851 pronouncement: "The closing epoch of geology is that in which archaeology has its beginning" (*The Oxford English Dictionary: On Line Edition*). Julian Thomas has speculated that archaeology, tied to the nineteenth-century rise of the human sciences, could not have existed without modernity for it is: "... modern philosophy, modern forms of political organization, and modern social practices [that] represent the ground of the possibility of 'doing archaeology'" (17). Enmeshed in modern forms of organization, archaeology also elucidated modernity's temporal paradox. Prehistoric archaeology supplied a history of human evolution that reinforced a teleological world-view, a view that frequently cited the value of technology, including the advanced stratigraphic machinery that was employed on archaeological sites by the mid-nineteenth century. The advent of the underground in London in the 1860s and the first line of the Parisian Métro in 1900 created a heightened awareness of underground structures as the pathway of the modern. By association, archaeology was very much a science of the future, enabled by technology, interested in new underground worlds, and implicated in the evolutionary ideology of human progress. At the same time, archaeology fed a cultural hunger for origins by establishing concrete, material bonds with the distant past. This tension between evolution, progress, and technology on the one hand and the desire to heal the rift between modernity and the rest of history on the other characterizes a fundamental disjunction in nineteenth-century thought. In a similar manner, in the twentieth century, archaeology's perceived ability to tap into primal energies and intensities through disruptive modes of invasion – the destruction of the surface combined with the uncovering of something "new" from the rubble of the past – made the aesthetics of excavation powerful modes of modern expression.

This confluence of dynamics between archaeology and modernity was also shared by a modern conception of poetry and modern imaginings of the unconscious. Gaston Bachelard has noted that in its newness or originality "the poetic act has no past, at least no recent past" (xv). At the same time, Bachelard acknowledges the relation of the new poetic image to "an archetype lying dormant in the depths of the unconscious" (xvi). This flickering up of newness from the depths of an ancient source exists on the same plane

Introduction

as the archaeological pattern, tied to this complex temporality which is specifically modern. Twentieth-century modernist interest in the power of the archaic and its unpredictable ruptures into contemporary life would make poetic thinking about the patterning among epochs particularly susceptible to archaeological models. Similarly, and Bachelard draws on psychoanalysis to make his point, modern conceptions of the unconscious rely heavily on Freud's use of archaeological imagery, which was equally committed to the flash of consciousness rooted in buried events. The twinned idea that poetry, the originary language, and the subconscious, site of original desire, could be a recovered, reactivated, and the source of literary renewal, would present itself with particular attractiveness. New ideas, forms, and texts were penned to pull forward these original sources, just as new technologies were created to excavate their material equivalents.

While this book concerns itself mostly with the forms and fantasies generated by the archaeological project rather than the evolution of archaeology itself, it is useful to have a sense of the interrelated nature of this progression. As a result, Chapter 1 provides an introduction to archaeology's development and the imaginative realms that accompanied it. Chapter 2 on Théophile Gautier and Chapter 3 on Walter Pater examine late romantic handlings of the archaeological fantasy, the way in which it paved the way for their modernities, and the formal mechanisms it engendered. Chapter 4 on Sigmund Freud diverges from traditional accounts of Freud's excavational understandings by focusing on the way in which his archaeological preoccupations are underscored by the importance of the written. This path was subsequently followed by modernist writers H.D. and Adrian Stokes and in Chapter 5, their interiorized archaeologies of desire, which also borrow from Pater, are compared with Ezra Pound's explicitly social archaeology, which encrypts the work of Gautier. In Chapter 6, an alternate unification of social and interiorized archaeologies is considered in the writings of the French Surrealists, who transform Freud's archaeological paradigms into dream excavations of the modern metropolis. Finally, in Chapter 7, Charles Olson, versed in both Anglo-American and French traditions, an archaeologist on land as well as on the page, is read as a Poundian influenced poet of the post-atomic era who understood archaeology as central to the "postmodern advance."

CHAPTER 1

The Spade and the Word:
A Brief History of Archaeology and Writing

Archaeology and literature have a long history of similar preoccupations. Deriving from the Greek "arche," "the beginning" or "archaios" meaning "ancient," archaeology's precursors were the myths and legends of the ancients, the same narratives that generated the literary tradition. Archaeology, like literature, is a meaning-maker, a means to knowledge that seeks to answer fundamental questions about who we are and where we came from. As Philip Schwyzer notes in *Archaeologies of Renaissance Literature*: "Archaeology and literary studies share an unparalleled and unsettling intimacy with the vestiges and leavings of past life – with the words the dead wrote, sang, or heard, with the objects they made, held, or lived within" (19).[1] In order to contextualize this intimacy it is useful to sketch briefly the development of archaeology,[2] its most significant cultural manifestations, and its historical relationship with writing. This interwoven history provides a basis for understanding the archaeological *mentalités* that would exercise profound influence on the imaginative structure of the modern literary topos.

For a great deal of human history, the quest for origins was contained in the mythic. The compiling of detailed histories, both of the present

---

1   Other books that provide insight into archaeology and literature include Jennifer Wallace's wide ranging memoir/cultural-literary study, *Digging the Dirt*, Christine Finn's *Past Poetic* about archaeology in the work of W.B. Yeats and Seamus Heaney, and John Hines' more analytical study, *Voices in the Past*.
2   For more detailed analyses of archaeology's development see Bruce Trigger's *A History of Archaeological Thought* and Glyn Daniel's *One Hundred and Fifty Years of Archaeology*.

moment and of past events, did not begin until after 500 B.C.E. A conscious interest in the past is present in Egyptian, Classical Greek and Roman civilizations, for example, in the histories of Herodotus and Pausanias, but no systematized techniques were developed to disinter monuments or artifacts. As interest in the past was primarily contained in narrative form rather than in material pursuit and preservation, "archaeology" per se cannot be said to have existed. In Medieval Europe, there is even less documented enthusiasm for material remains than during the Classical period, as collections of antiquities were generally reserved for holy relics, an emphasis which did not promote any kind of systematic archaeological development. For most people, the desire for origins was satisfied by biblical narratives and Medieval scholars were generally unaware of material changes that had taken place from the times of the ancient Greeks and Romans; it was, therefore, by and large assumed that conditions in the past were very similar to the present moment.

The fourteenth century A.C.E. marked a change in cultural and political views of the past. In northern Italy, scholars rallied against feudalism and turned to earlier times as precedents for political innovations. Italian intellectuals looked to the art and literature of ancient Greece and Rome to illustrate the possibilities of artistic and political resurrection. As Thomas Greene notes, "[t]he image that propelled the humanist Renaissance and that still determines our perception of it was the archaeological, necromantic metaphor of *disinterment*, a digging up that was also a resuscitation or a reincarnation or a rebirth" (92). This figurative resuscitation was made material by an increasing interest in literally digging up the past from the ground. This grand scale exhumation was very much tied to literary accounts; Renaissance antiquarians generally referred to the works of Horace or Pliny before choosing to excavate a specific location. This method, now referred to as "text aided" archaeology, would continue to be the primary mode of deciding where to dig during the fifteenth, sixteenth, seventh, eighteenth, and even nineteenth centuries. Furthermore, once objects were exhumed, they were most often identified through literary sources. When the Laocoön was discovered on January 14, 1506, for example, antiquarians identified the statue through a passage from Pliny's *Historia Naturalis*.

The dynamics of disinterment were so pervasive during the Renaissance that they both penetrated and propelled literary activity. Greene suggests that Petrarch "found it natural to use the term *ruinae* for the lost or fragmentary literary remains of antiquity" as well as for "the material remains that were being pulled from the ground" (92). Italian patrons began not only to excavate their properties for antiquities but also actively sought to restore classical literature and requisitioned literary works that were consciously crafted in Greek and Roman styles. To briefly project ahead, when the Italian Renaissance was itself reclaimed by the Victorians, similar tropes of architectural and literary disinterment regained their cultural appeal.

Like the Victorians, Renaissance antiquarians were often more interested in a projected image of the classical past than the past as it had actually existed. In the Renaissance, the desire to fulfill this projection was enacted by antiquarians who frequently altered their records to match a preconceived ideal. Philip Jacks notes that when Renaissance architects objected to "the proportions and asymmetry of the interior of the Pantheon," they simply corrected "these shortcomings, as documented in their drawings" (7). Yet the growing understanding and appreciation of literary texts and ancient monuments of ancient Greece and Rome did foster a more vivid sense of the difference among historical periods. By the late fourteen hundreds, popes, nobles, and clergymen were collecting and exhibiting works of ancient art and laws were passed to prevent scavengers from taking stone blocks from ancient buildings. While not strictly adhering to an overall archaeological system or methodology, all of these developments demonstrated a growing valuation of material ruins and a more pronounced sense of their aesthetic, cultural, and historical appeal.

The Enlightenment witnessed increasing tension between the push toward the future and a pull toward the ancient past. Currents of neo-classicism were encouraged by the discovery of Pompeii and Herculaneum in 1738 and 1748. At the same time, a pronounced cultural mindset advanced particularly by the middle class in northwestern Europe propounded the idea of human amelioration over time. Confidence about human beings' ability to develop economically and socially led to an increased valuation of the present and future, an ideology which would pave the way for evolutionary archaeology. While the spirit of progress and science did not produce an archaeological discipline as such, antiquarians began to provide specific and accurate accounts of archaeological finds. Moreover, in the organization of these relics, antiquarians became more aware of the importance of establishing a relative chronology.

In 1857, Jacques Boucher de Perthes, a French civil servant and amateur archaeologist, discovered stone tools alongside the bones of extinct mammals in the Somme Valley. This discovery convinced him of a human history that stretched far beyond the four thousand year chronology established by the Book of Genesis. In other words, biblical narratives and archaeological evidence were entering into direct conflict. While Boucher de Perthes' claims were at first dismissed, Darwin's 1859 publication of the *The Origin of Species* prompted renewed interest in his discoveries. A team of scientists including John Prestwich and John Evans, well-established scholars of the time, visited the sites of the Somme Valley and concurred that the strata in which the tools were found predated 4000 B.C.E. This confirmation, compounded by the furor surrounding Darwin's publication, convinced most Western natural historians that the beginnings of humanity predated any previous speculation. The religious and secular consequences of these findings gave archaeology a heightened profile in academic circles as well as increased public visibility and prestige.

The advent of evolutionary archaeology spawned a series of ideological implications for both prehistoric and classical studies. On the one hand, archaeologically proven evolutionism was supported by members of the scientific establishment and liberal members of the middle class because it lent authority to the ideals of progress. At the same time, those wishing to prove the legitimacy of biblical claims were also turning to archaeological evidence. Mesopotamian archaeology gained worldwide attention in the 1870s when George Smith found and transcribed a clay tablet from the biblical city of Niveneh which related the story of the deluge. Newspapers across Britain seized on the story and *The Daily Telegraph* sent an expedition to find missing portions of the tablet. Archaeology's simultaneous ability to disprove the Book of Genesis while lending credence to scriptural claims placed it at the center of wide-ranging religious and philosophical debates throughout the nineteenth century. The archaeological dependence on writing was highlighted again when Europeans began to explore Assyria, convinced that they could not understand the ways of the ancients until the different types of cuneiform were deciphered. Meanwhile, in Turkey and Greece, Schliemann was excavating in order to prove the legitimacy of yet another set of texts: the work of Homer, to demonstrate to the world that Homeric Troy and the grave of Agamemnon existed just as the ancient bard had described.

The 1800s also saw the shift from antiquarianism to archaeology. As Kenneth Hudson notes:

> [The] archaeologist is a nineteenth-century innovation, a product of the new wish to study the evidence of the past in an organized manner ... If antiquarianism was a natural and appropriate expression of the spirit of the eighteenth century, then archaeology, with its much greater emphasis on order, method and conformity, is a true child of the nineteenth.
>
> (18–19)

This distinction between antiquarian and archaeologist is an important one, as it demonstrates the ways in which the collection and display of artifacts was becoming more professional as well as perceived to be more important to public history. From today's perspective, the most significant difference between an antiquarian and an archaeologist is that while an antiquarian is concerned with his own private collection and study, usually in the form of a "cabinet of curiosities," the archaeologist is generally affiliated with either a university or museum and deals with the presentation of history to the public. As Susan Crane summarizes, the transition from antiquarianism to archaeology is the "shift from stories to histories, from fragments to totalities, from cabinets to museums" (187). As we will see, archaeologists' attempts to delineate professional archaeological activity from the "dilettantism" of private study was often defeated by popular conceptions of the past-fetishizing antiquarian/archaeologist, a composite figure who most often appears as either humorously disjointed from contemporary life or more menacingly as a threat to innovation and "the new," exemplified by numerous modernist diatribes against the repressed, unhygienic nature of antiquarian collecting. According to Jeffery Schnapp, Michael Shanks, and Matthew Tiews, this rancor against antiquarians and archaeologists is a key posture in modern thought, as the archaeologist, "whether amateur or professional, has routinely been dismissed as an intransigent and acritical worshipper of the past, and as an adversary of the new, the unexpected, and the unknown" (3). Similarly, Crane comments:

> ... antiquarians became figures of ridicule and contempt from the nineteenth century onward, their status reduced to that of "dilettante." Writers such as Sir Walter Scott and the poet Annette von Droste-Hülshoff caricatured the older type of historical collector as one hopelessly behind the times, in an era when the passions of historical collecting had shifted from personal, idiosyncratic and elite networks to nationalist, collective and representative ones.
>
> (186)

"The older type of historical collector" reappears frequently in nineteenth-century literature, not only in Scott and Droste-Hülshoff but also in the works of Hugo, Balzac and James. In James' *Portrait of a Lady*, Osmond appears as the sinister embodiment of the antiquarian impulse, one who is both reified with antique objects and intent on adding a human dimension to his collection through the psychological domination of his wife.

The move from the antiquarian cabinet of curiosities to the public museum was mirrored by an equal professionalization of archaeological fieldwork. If nineteenth- and early twentieth-century archaeology consisted largely of amateur endeavors, sponsored by wealthy scholars and undertaken by adventurers, then the second decade of the twentieth century marked a transitional moment as the training of professional archaeologists became more common in Europe, the Middle East and North America. These professional teams moved much more slowly than early discoverers, employing a few well-trained professionals as opposed to hundreds of unskilled laborers. Woolley's excavations at Ur are a prime example of the successes of this slower-moving method that would become common place in post-World War I archaeology. Howard Carter's discovery of King Tutankhamun's tomb is another example of more assiduous and scientific methods, characterized by five fruitless seasons of careful searching followed by the discovery of the missing tomb in November of 1922. Yet, despite more careful searches, better stratigraphic techniques, and ameliorated context and dating strategies, Woolley and Carter retained the tradition of producing popular accounts of their discoveries. Passages of Carter's *The Tomb of Tut-ankh-amen* (1923), for example, are as crafted to be read by popular audiences as the earliest archaeological adventure tales:

> At first I could see nothing, the hot air escaping from the chamber causing the candle flame to flicker, but presently, as my eyes grew accustomed to the light, details of the room within emerged slowly from the mist, strange animals, statues, and gold – everywhere the glint of gold. For the moment – an eternity it must have seemed to the others standing by – I was struck dumb with amazement, and when Lord Carnarvon, unable to stand the suspense any longer, inquired anxiously, "Can you see anything?" it was all I could do to get out the words, "Yes, wonderful things." ...
>
> I suppose most excavators would confess to a feeling of awe – embarrassment almost – when they break into a chamber closed and sealed by pious hands so many centuries ago. For the moment, time as a factor in human life has lost its meaning. Three thousand, four thousand years maybe, have passed and gone since human feet last trod the floor on which you stand, and yet, as you note the signs of recent life around you – the half filled bowl of mortar for the door, the blackened lamp, the finger marks upon the freshly painted surface, the farewell garland dropped upon the threshold – you feel it might have been yesterday. The very air you breathe, unchanged throughout the centuries, you share with those who laid the mummy to its rest. Time is annihilated by little intimate details such as these, and you feel an intruder.
>
> (95–7)

This passage is clearly intended to induce readers to imaginatively partake of Carter's sense of wonder and discovery. It is interesting to note the ways in which Carter highlights the humanity of the Egyptians – the "half filled bowl of mortar," the "blackened lamp," "the finger marks upon the freshly painted surface" which give the scene a strong sense of human presence. This power of the artifact, its almost mystical qualities and ability to invoke an entire civilization – in effect, its auratic presence, were standard features of fictional archaeological literature as were the tropes of voyeurism and transgression Carter enacts.

The blurring between fictional and supposedly non-fictional archaeological accounts was frequently noted by archaeological scholars, including this assessment by H.V. Hilprecht who suggests that the excavation of ruined cities:

> ... is so full of dramatic effects and genuine surprises, and at the same time so unique and far-reaching in its results and bearing upon so many different branches of science, that it will always read more like a thrilling romance penned by the skillful hand of a gifted writer endowed with an extraordinary power of imagination than like a plain and sober presentation of actual facts and events.
>
> (3)

In Carter's account, exceeding "actual facts and events" is achieved through a series of literary devices – the building of suspense, the careful inclusion of telling details, the sensuous attention to "the very air you breathe" – which suggest the ways in which he was tuned into the public's taste for romantic accounts. From a theoretical point of view, Carter's sensitivity to the Egyptians *as they lived* as well as his own sense of himself as "an intruder" is in sharp contrast to the accounts of early tomb-raiders, who generally only concerned themselves with valuable artifacts and gave little thought to either the damage they caused or the violation their actions might represent.

In addition to operating within fictional paradigms, Carter's account also illustrates the ways in which the twentieth century produced new archaeological views of the past. Nineteenth-century evolutionary archaeology, with its emphasis on creating systematized theories of history, had largely ignored questions pertaining to the ways in which various people had lived over time. As Bruce Trigger suggests, British and French "evolutionary archaeologists had become more interested in artifacts than in their makers" (173). In the 1920s, V. Gordon Childe championed the idea that artifacts be treated as expressions of living societies rather than fossils. This method, called cultural-historical archaeology, became a focal point of archaeological theory for the remainder of the Twenties, Thirties, and Forties and generated a significant amount of information on the living patterns of ancient societies. Cultural historical archaeology, with its emphasis on recreating the conditions of extinct peoples through an interpretive analysis of material remains, in many ways parallels various types of archaeological fiction, such as Gautier's fantastical archaeological romances, or reconstructive aesthetic criticism, such as the works of Pater and Stokes, which attempt to imaginatively recreate the processes and conditions surrounding the production of a given work of art based on a reading of material traces.

While archaeology moved away from the cultural-historical paradigm during the course of the twentieth century – the "New Archaeology" of the 1960s, for example, emphasized a data-based approach to artifacts – Childe's methods have remained a cornerstone of archaeological thought and current archaeological methodology takes its lead from the emphasis on living societies advocated by cultural historians.

Currents in contemporary archaeological theory have also been inclined to recognize and address the literariness of archaeology. Emphasizing the role texts play in reconstituting the archaeological site, William Calder and David Traill note that: "Archaeology is the only discipline in ancient studies which to attain its ends is required to destroy its evidence. Once excavated, a site must be reconstructed from literary evidence, letters, notebooks, diaries, and published reports" (9). Here, archaeology's fundamentally destructive process is counter-balanced by literature's generally reconstructive mode – a productive relationship between excavation and re-creation, materiality and textuality that highlights the symbiotic nature of text and site. Moreover, as Michael Shanks and Christopher Tilley have argued in their work in post-processual archaeology, the very process of drawing history from archeological objects is in effect an exercise in re-creation and narration:

> Archaeology attempts to forge a linguistic expression of the past congealed in objects and their relationships. The words used in the texts remain concepts substituted for the objects. There is always a gap or difference (a distance) between the words and that to which they refer. This flaw in every concept, its non-identity to what it refers, makes it necessary to cite others, to construct structures, constellations, narratives or "stories" in order to make sense or produce a meaningful representation of the past.
> (*Re-Constructing Archaeology* 19–20)

But archaeology as the stories about "objects and their relationships" is only one strand in the tapestry of tales inspired by the discoveries of ancient remains. Narratives of all kinds are mobilized by the inability of archaeological objects to explain themselves. They invited interpretation and fantasy. They required words to complete them. As John Baines has suggested, in many ways writing and archaeology are inextricable as they "complement each other's silences" (209).

Deriving from common origins in the mythic and the biblical, archaeology has consistently existed in a state of tension with the written: from text-aided archaeology to the processes of encryption and decipherment, from narratives of exploration to the archaeological finds that are inscribed into written history. The nature of archaeology's narrative invitation was transfigured, however, by the excavations at Pompeii, Egypt and Greece. The "Great Discoveries" of the eighteenth, nineteenth, and twentieth centuries and the proliferation of material surrounding their unveiling – in academic journals, first-hand archaeological publications, popular fiction, world fairs, paintings, operas, and guidebooks – produced a new level of archaeological consciousness. The speculation of what might be dredged from these sites gave rise to a new order of fantasy, one that exceeds the on-going relationship between archaeology and writing and extends into the reaches of the modern literary text.

The Great Treasure Hunt: Herculaneum and Pompeii

The discovery of Herculaneum in 1738 and Pompeii in 1748 prompted one of the first grand-scale cultural waves of interest in the recovery of lost civilizations since the Renaissance. Early excavation of the two cities, which had been buried by the eruption of Mount Vesuvius in 79 A.C.E., was commissioned by the Bourbon Court and was rudimentary. Classical reproductions were seized, while the site itself was assigned little cultural value and many fragments of native Pompeiian art were destroyed. A change in method, along with the production of the first accurate plans, did not occur until 1812, when Queen Caroline commissioned qualified antiquarians to restore three houses in Pompeii and to leave their furnishings and decorations *in situ* to demonstrate the actual outlines of Pompeiian life. The fall of Napoleon thwarted these plans but after 1815 continuing interest and repeated calls for systematization from the European intellectual community began to produce a more careful and methodical approach to the ancient cities.

Certainly the lack of a precise archaeological methodology in the eighteenth century did not deter writers from adopting Pompeiian motifs. As Caroline Springer observes:

> No one could dispute the importance of archaeology to the romantic imagination. The revival of interest in the ruins of classical antiquity that characterized neoclassicism remained a primary component of the romantic experience. Italy, which for generations of eighteenth-century travelers had been a paradigm of picturesque decay, in turn became a privileged ground for the emerging romantic sensibility and the preferred setting for a "poetry of ruins" that reached its climax in the early decades of the nineteenth century in poets like Byron and Shelley. (1)

Sections of the excavations that had been cleared to show the houses of Pompeiian citizens, for example, provided the public immediate contact with the daily domestic objects of the lost civilization and literary material for Lamartine, de Staël, Bulwer-Lytton and Leopardi. In 1816, Shelley produced one of the most popular "Pompeiian" poems, "Ode to Naples," which begins: "I stood within the City disinterred / And heard the autumnal leaves like light footfalls / Of spirits passing through the streets" (qtd. in Leppmann 123).

The English romantics present an interesting case of the early uses of archaeology as both methodology and poetic modality.[3] Thomas McFarland, in a formative example of what has become the wide-spread analysis of the romantic fragment poem, writes that "... the pervasive longing of the Romantics for an absent reality was at the same time an index to a prevailing sense of incompleteness, fragmentation, and ruin" (11). Certainly the romantics turned to the landscape of ruins to express a mood of emotional desolation, just as Shelley would look to the statue of Ramesses II

---

[3] In addition to those titles listed below see Laurence Goldstein, *Ruins and Empire*; Marjorie Levinson, *The Romantic Fragment Poem: A Critique of a Form*; and Christopher Strathman, *Romantic Poetry and the Fragmentary Imperative*.

in Egypt to convey a feeling of political disillusionment in "Ozymandias."[4] Anne Janowitz, who makes the connection between ideology and form in *England's Ruins*, notes that fragmentary models are often the reflection of a national political moment, particularly evident in romanticism and modernism:

> The image of the ruin ceases to be poetically fecund once the secure grounding of national identity has been accomplished. Mythically stable, the equivalent poetry of the Victorian period enacts a pure idealization of the past ... The image of ruin is not poetically central again until the poems of Rosenberg and Sassoon describe, and then Eliot attempts to repair, the crisis of European imperialism in the opening decades of the twentieth century.
>
> (19)

For Janowitz, the image of the ruin and its adaptation as a poetic form of indeterminacy during the national political instability of the English romantic period finds an equivalent in an English modernity that sees itself torn by the dissolution of Empire in the twentieth century. As we will see, the factors that play into modernism's preference for the fragment are many, including but not limited to ideas of nationhood, and reflective of the ruins of two world wars, an interest in shattered psychological realities, and a new set of archaeological aesthetics engendered by the major discoveries. Yet Janowitz is intuitive in pointing out that particular forms are reflective of political and ideological moods, and also, importantly, that the image of ruin is a latent one, a specter that assumes embodied form in the poetry of periods that have a particular need for it.

Historically speaking, Johann Winckelmann (1717–68), the so-called "father of classical archaeology," was among the first scholars to draw pan-European attention to Pompeii and Herculaneum. Winckelmann visited Pompeii twice, once in 1758 and once 1762. On his first visit, Winckelmann was discouraged from participating in the excavations as the Bourbon Court feared that he might object to the state of archaeological activities. As a

---

4   It is likely that Shelley's preoccupation with the statue resulted from the heightened publicity around Giovanni Belzoni's acquisition of the Ramesses II figure for the British Museum.

result, Winckelmann spent most of his time in the Naples museum, deciphering papyri with Camillo Paderni, the museum's director. His second visit, four years later, confirmed his suspicions that the excavations were being mishandled. Work gangs were largely made up of captured pirates and convicts chained together while the excavations themselves were generally random efforts to loot the site of potentially valuable antiquities. Winckelmann published his "Open Letter on the Discoveries made at Herculaneum" later that year. While the letter addresses various matters surrounding Pompeii and Herculaneum, including an overview of Vesuvian topography and the artifacts in the museum, the letter is essentially a public castigation of the bureaucrats in charge.

In the midst of his assault against antiquarian incompetence, however, Winckelmann also includes passages that draw the reader's attention to the charm and value of objects from Pompeii. For example, in a passage on some pitchers and vases disinterred at Herculaneum, he writes:

> These vessels owe their beauty to their gently curving lines, which as in beautiful young bodies are not fully grown but still maturing, so that the eye neither exhausts itself in beholding perfectly shaped semispherical outlines nor comes up against corners or points. The sweet sensation conveyed by such lines can be likened to a soft, tender hand. In the presence of such harmony, our very thoughts become light and palpable.
>
> (qtd. in Leppmann 74)

In the context of the open letter, the attention to the quality of the artifacts both draws in the interest of the reader and serves to highlight the loss the destruction of Pompeiian antiquities represents. But the sensuousness of the language also highlights the way in which archaeological disinterment was giving way to a new kind of imaginative empathy that takes off from the reality of the dig.

Winckelmann's references here to the "gently curving lines" reminiscent of "beautiful young bodies" cannot help but summon the connection between Pompeii and the sensual representations of homoerotic relationships in Greek art. These pieces, once exhumed, were most often closeted in the backroom of the museums at Herculaneum and Naples.[5] This process of disinterment followed by a metaphoric reburial gave the Pompeiian excavations the aura of the forbidden, reinforcing the sense of possibility veiled beneath the earth's surface. In the case of Winckelmann, as Whitney Davis argues, encounters with ancient art provided "archaeological" evidence for modes of desiring that could be ushered into the present:

> Winckelmann's imagination of the sexual history of the ancient world enabled him to reconfigure his own erotic imagination. Winckelmann's vision of erotic possibilities, ancient and modern, later became a crucial point of reference for an emerging modern sexuality – what came to be called, in the later nineteenth century, "homosexuality." To retrace Winckelmann's steps is to explore how a distinctively modern sexuality was partly constituted in an engagement with ancient art.
> (262)

For Davis, Winckelmann's "reconstruction of ancient practices and concepts" was unmatched by anything in the "immediate social world." This gap represents a period of suppression which Winckelmann believed might be followed by a period of reemergence as he began to "identify ... [the] reappearance [of particular predispositions] in the constitution of certain modern young men" (262–3).

Winckelmann's engagement with Pompeii was, therefore, multi-fold and complex. On the one hand, Winckelmann was responsible for bringing attention to the importance of the excavations and legitimizing the disinterred artifacts by including them in one of the first comprehensive art-historical systems. He was also a pioneer of text-aided archaeology in that he consistently referred to ancient sources, particularly Pliny, in order to reconstruct the Pompeiian milieu and the nature of Pompeiian art. In

---

5   See David Gaimster's "Sex & Sensibility at the British Museum": "In 1795 we read for the first time in the Herculaneum Museum of a room, number XVIII, the first 'secret museum,' reserved for 'obscene' antiquities which could only be visited by those in possession of a special permit" (11). Gaimster notes that a similar room, the "Secretum," or "secret museum," created to house "obscene" objects, was created by the Department of Antiquities at the British Museum early in the nineteenth century.

this sense, we can perceive Winckelmann to be a pioneer of "imaginative reconstruction," the careful, logical creation of contexts for material remains that we see in Woolley's approach to the cemetery at Ur, a systematic reconstitution that becomes the basis of an art criticism that is socially and historically responsive. Working from the shape, textures, and forms of Pompeiian objects in relation to documentary texts, Winckelmann situates art within its historical context. In this sense, the art of Pompeii acts as a fingerprint from which Winckelmann attempts to construct the body of an entire civilization.

Yet in Winckelmann's work there is a point at which imaginative reconstruction gives way to fantasy – the projection of desire onto the canvas of the past. The material remains of the lost epoch give rise to a utopian realm with which the writer imagines himself to be much more compatible than the present. Hence Winckelmann's claim: "I have come into the world and into Italy too late," a line that Walter Pater quotes with empathy in *The Renaissance* (121). In this sense, archaeological reconstitution makes of the past both a reconstructed landscape of logical deductions as well as a topographical fantasy that embodies the desires of its imaginer. Frequently, archaeological portraits are every bit as aesthetic as the remnants which are the subjects of imaginative interrogation.

In terms of popular appeal, it was Edward Bulwer-Lytton's novel, *The Last Days of Pompeii* (1834) that set the standard for the interweaving of archaeological facts and imaginative additions. As the title suggests, the novel is a re-creation of Pompeiian life days before the eruption of Mount Vesuvius, an exercise that was partly drawn from archaeological evidence but is mostly fictional in its characters and events. In addition to the reanimation of the daily lives of the Pompeiians, the novel also provides a dramatic re-enactment of the eruption of Mount Vesuvius, a detailed narration of carnage and despair that would give the event an aura of palpable public *frisson*:

> In other places, cinder and rock lay matted in heaps, from beneath which emerged the half-hid limbs of some crushed and mangled fugitive. The groans of the dying were broken by wild shrieks of women's terror – now near, now distant – which, when heard in the utter darkness, were rendered doubly appalling by the crushing

sense of helplessness and the uncertainty of the perils around; and clear and distinct through all were the mighty and various noises from the Fatal Mountain; its rushing winds; its whirling torrents; and, from time to time, the burst and roar of some more fiery and fierce explosion.

(397)

This description would remained fixed in the imagination of the British reading public, and reassert itself with particular force in the moment when the Blitz in London would seem an eerie re-enactment, as illustrated in the war poetry of H.D.

In addition to attaching images of horror to the archaeological site, Lytton, like Woolley and Carter, was also interested in its associations with luxury and plentitude, both in terms of material wealth and sensuous excess. Like these archaeologists, too, Lytton is intent on conveying the immediacy of the disinterred city in the novel's epilogue, its proximity to the present through the dynamics of disinterment:

Nearly Seventeen Centuries had rolled away when the City of Pompeii was disinterred from its silent tomb, all vivid with undimmed hues; its walls fresh as if painted yesterday, – not a hue faded on the rich mosaic of its floors, – in its forum the half finished columns as left by the workman's hand …

(408)

Lytton continues by describing how in the house of Diomed, in the subterranean vaults, twenty skeletons were discovered among jewels, coins, and candelabra. Exceeding the importance of this material splendor is Pompeii's libidinous remnant, the calcified impression of the heroine: "The sand, consolidated by damps, had taken the forms of the skeletons as in a cast; and the traveler may yet see the impression of the female neck and bosom of young and round proportions – the trace of the fated Julia!" (409). The image of this hollow impression would gain a great deal of cultural currency in the archaeological tradition, summoning fantasies that would, inevitably, seek to complete the empty cast with supplementary narratives, as we will see dramatized in the work of Gautier and the writings of the French Surrealists. Overwhelmingly, Lytton's novel and Winckelmann's art history acted together to create a visual imaginary of Pompeii as the site of historical resurrection and a space for reconnection and communion with classical and sensual intensities. The popularity of these texts contributed to a healthy tourism industry in the Italian south. But it also created a densely layered field of possibility for nineteenth- and twentieth-century literature and thought.

Eastern Treasures: Egypt and the Foundations of Egyptology

The origins of Egyptology demonstrate how early archaeology was enmeshed in another formative aspect of modernity: European colonialism. The first thorough and systematic study of ancient Egypt was undertaken by the French scholars who accompanied Napoleon on his 1789 invasion of Egypt. In the late eighteenth century, very little was known about the ancient cultures of Egypt and the Near East; most notably, the inscriptions that would become a source of debate among European intellectuals were by and large still undiscovered. During Napoleon's campaign, the French studied and measured the pyramids, recorded the size and location of various monuments, and most importantly, accidentally discovered the Rosetta Stone while digging fortifications. While Napoleon eventually lost the campaign to the joint British and Ottoman forces and was forced to surrender the Rosetta Stone and other antiquities, the twenty-four-volume record of French scholarship was published beginning in 1809 under the title *Description of Egypt*.

Despite the state of war that existed when the Rosetta Stone was first discovered, Napoleon himself recognized the stone's historical significance and had plaster casts of the inscription made and distributed to scholars across Europe. The reason the stone generated so much excitement was that the decree of the Egyptian priesthood of 199 B.C.E. inscribed into the stone is written three times over: once in hieroglyphics, once in demotic (a cursive Egyptian script) and once in Greek. It quickly became clear that the Rosetta stone was the key to deciphering Egyptian hieroglyphs. By 1822, Jean-François Champollion, a young French linguist, had created a summary of the inscription.

The popularization of the Egyptian past through *Description of Egypt* brought an onslaught of scholars, antiquities agents and treasure hunters into the country. Egypt's Macedonian governor-general facilitated the process of shipping ancient Egyptian art to Europe by maintaining an open door policy to European visitors. Both the British Museum and the Louvre hired on-site antiquities agents to supervise the excavation and export of Egyptian artifacts. The most influential of these officials was Henry Salt, the British consul-general, and Bernardino Drovetti who acted in the same capacity for the French. The stand-offs between British and French antiquities teams digging and tomb-raiding along the Nile Valley were legendary and often violent.

The most famous of these archaeological adventurers was Giovanni Belzoni, a former Italian circus performer whose strength, agility, and familiarity with hydraulic devices made him an invaluable asset to Salt's excavating teams. Throughout his employment for the British in Egypt, Belzoni excavated in the Valley of the Kings and the Giza Plateau and was the first person in recent history to enter the Pyramid of Khafre, where he left his name emblazoned on the ceiling of the funeral chamber. This act is emblematic of the proprietary attitude of the European treasure-hunters as they amassed antiquities and shipped them to museums across Europe as well as to private collectors. In turn, the excavators often became living legends as they frequently published popular accounts of their exploits and were often celebrities in their own right. In Belzoni's *Narrative of the Operations and Recent Discoveries in Egypt and Nubia* (1820), we can sense the adventurous spirit that made this book so popular along with the hopelessly careless and unscientific approach to the exploration of a mummy cave:

> In such a situation I found myself several times, and often returned exhausted and fainting, 'til at last I became inured to it, and indifferent to what I suffered, except from the dust, which never failed to choke my throat and nose: and though, fortunately, I am destitute of the sense of smelling, I could taste that the mummies

The Spade and the Word

were rather unpleasant to swallow. After the exertion of entering into such a place, through a passage of fifty, a hundred, three hundred, or perhaps six hundred yards, nearly overcome, I sought a resting place, found one and contrived to sit; but when my weight bore on the body of an Egyptian, it crushed in like a bandbox. I naturally had recourse to my hands to sustain my weight, but they found no better support; so that I sunk altogether among the broken mummies, with a crash of bones, rags, and wooden cases, which raised such a dust as kept me motionless for a quarter of an hour, waiting 'til it subsided again. I could not remove from the place, however, without increasing it, and every step I took I crushed a mummy in some part or another. Once I conducted from such a place to another resembling it, through a passage of about twenty feet in length, and no wider than a body could be forced through. It was choked with mummies, and I could not pass without putting my face in contact with that of some decayed Egyptian; but as the passage inclined downwards, my own weight helped me on: however I could not avoid being covered with bones, legs, arms, and heads rolling from above. Thus I proceeded from one cave to another, all full of mummies piled up in various ways, some standing, some lying, and some on their heads. The purpose of my researches was to rob the Egyptians of their papyri; of which I found a few hidden in their breasts, under their arms, in the space above the knees, or on the legs, and covered by the numerous folds of cloth that envelop the mummy.

(156–8)

Belzoni's account, while clearly crafted to entertain popular audiences in the same way as Carter's *The Tomb of Tut-ankh-amen* one hundred years later, bears the marks of its archaeological period. Overridingly, Belzoni's narrative resounds with aggressive object-lust. Where Carter confesses to feelings of awe, which he assumes most excavators feel, Belzoni is in rugged pursuit. Moreover, where Carter is impressed with the "signs of recent life" in the tomb and comments on the air that is shared with the living souls who "laid the mummy to its rest," Belzoni's emphasis is on the sensual dynamics of death: the "decayed Egyptian" who is "rather unpleasant to swallow." It is clear that Belzoni does not feel like Carter's "intruder," but rather like an adventurer come to claim his rightful prize from the hands of the dead. The fact that Belzoni caused irreparable damage to the mummies whose "bones, legs, arms, and heads" came "rolling from above," can also be contrasted with Carter's painstaking progress or Woolley's careful reconstructions.

The plundering of Egyptian monuments was only officially halted thirty-eight years after Belzoni published this account of his exploits. In 1858, Auguste Mariette was appointed Conservator of Egyptian Monuments by the French and declared the cessation of all harmful and unauthorized excavation in Egypt. Mariette also set up the Boulaq Museum, the first national museum in the Middle East. While both these steps signaled a more systematic and careful approach as well as an end to the frantic export of Egyptian artifacts, treasure-hunters continued to operate without licenses and Mariette's own excavation teams often did more harm than good in their pursuit of national antiquities.

The continuing popularity of Egyptian archaeology in Europe soon prompted the organization of large-scale public exhibitions. Shortly after publishing his account, Belzoni organized an exhibit of antiquities in the Egyptian Hall, Piccadilly, in 1821. This small exhibition was a precursor of the great Egyptian exhibitions, which would become part of almost every world's fair after London's Crystal Palace Exhibition of 1851. At the Crystal Palace, the Egyptian pavilion featured enormous reproductions of the Abu Simbel colosoi of Ramesses II – two giant statues which almost reached the glass ceiling of the exhibition hall. The French also participated in the propagation of the past as spectacle. Mariette, the impresario of French archaeology, organized the Egyptian displays for two of the universal exhibitions in Paris.

The pervasiveness of Egyptian antiquities in the French sphere led to a concomitant evolution in archaeological epistemology. Donald Reid notes that the word "*égyptologue*" first appeared in 1827, the same year that Champollion created the Egyptian section of the Louvre. "*Égyptologie*" gained popular use in the 1850s. Reid further notes that it was not until the 1860s that similar words evolved in English, demonstrating French pre-eminence in the battle for Egyptian antiquities. Once started, however, "Egyptomania," which first gained a toehold in France, quickly spread to other Western nations including Britain, Germany, Italy, and America. The Egyptian theme, like the Pompeiian, had a significant impact on British and French art, culture, and fashion. Reid suggests the Egyptian rage influenced: "Western painting, photography, clothing styles, travel literature, novels, popular songs, classical music, world's fairs, guidebooks, postcards, and postage stamps" (12).

In addition to its sway over popular culture, Egyptian archaeology also exercised considerable influence over "high" art. Romanticism, with its emphasis on death and beauty, horror and eternity, found imaginative correlatives in archaeological imagery. As we will see in Chapter 2, it was Théophile Gautier who established one of the first bodies of fictional accounts about archaeology in the East and essentially popularized Egyptology the way Winckelmann and Bulwer-Lytton contributed to the reputation of Pompeii. Gautier's adoption of archaeological themes to illustrate fantasies of escape and the pleasures of pantheism made the Egyptian archaeological space an imaginary antithesis to the confines of a Western, Christian modernity. Equally appealing to romantic writers were the images of ruins, cemeteries, death, and decay implicit in the archaeological landscape. Yet the most fundamental tension in early Egyptological writing is found in its epistemological dynamics. On the one hand, ancient Egypt represented a means to knowledge, a fantasy of what could be discovered and uncovered, and in this regard was an idealized landscape of unending desire. On the other hand, euphoric searching that results in the attainment of knowledge frequently also results in dissatisfaction, a depression generated by the anticlimax of deciphering unknown scripts or successfully retrieving objects and artifacts.

This "will to know" coupled with the desire for the unknown that characterizes the archaeological romance is in many ways tied to the invasive imperialism that was the precursor to Egyptology. Napoleon's mission in Egypt, for all its scholarly trapping, was a military invasion. Between 1858 and 1908 when the French established four national museums in Egypt, they were equally searching for natural resources, foreign investments, overseas markets, as well as colonial power to combat inter-European threats. Treasure-hunting imperialism spread to other Middle Eastern and African nations with similar results: "national" museums in the control of the colonizers, and more often than not the best of the archaeological spoils shipped to Europe for sale or display.

In addition to acting as a treasure-trove for European antiquities agents, overseas archaeology also provided the West with a racial rationale for colonial interference. Nineteenth-century evolutionary archaeology began to produce theories of romanticized national, ethnic, and racial differences. According to conservative members of the scientific establishment, different ethnic groups possessed divergent biological make-ups, which resulted in varying physical and behavioural characteristics. Less "successful" civilizations were considered to have a diluted racial composition and would eventually become extinct. Some scholars advanced the idea of divine polygenesis, meaning that various races had been created separately and inequitably. In its most insidious form, this belief led to the idea that "less civilized peoples" were emotionally, intellectually, and morally inferior to Europeans, a view that was frequently expressed by Darwin. These precepts were largely accepted and integrated into archaeological textbooks of the late 1800s.

These ideological adaptations of prehistoric archaeology had a significant impact on the attitudes surrounding classical archaeology in the Middle East. Modern day Arabs were perceived to be in an advanced state of cultural degeneration and unable to appreciate and protect the material legacies of their ancestors. Western intervention was "required" in order to ensure the survival of the great monuments of Egypt and Mesopotamia. The institutionalization of racist evolutionary archaeological ideology created a hegemony which legitimized Western interference in classical archaeology. Tourism, too, adopted the archaeological myth of Eastern degeneration. The Baedeckers of the 1890s warned European tourists of Egyptians' "lower grade in the scale of civilization" and advised the Western traveller to "make due allowances" for the natives while treating them with "consistent firmness" (qtd. in Reid 77).

According to Edward Said, the relationship between East and West was in itself "archaeological": "European culture gained in strength and identity by setting itself off against the Orient as a sort of surrogate and even underground self" (3). For Said, archaeology not only informed the dynamics of the West's imagining of its other, it also provided practical and ideological premises for invasion:

> To restore a region from its present barbarism to its former classical greatness; to instruct (for its own benefit) the Orient in the ways of the modern West; to subordinate and underplay military power in order to aggrandize the project of glorious

knowledge acquired in the process of political domination of the Orient; to formulate the Orient, to give it shape, identity, definition with full recognition of its place in memory, its importance to imperial strategy, and its "natural" role as an appendage to Europe; to dignify all the knowledge collected during colonial occupation with the title "contribution to modern learning" when the natives had neither been consulted nor treated as anything except as pretexts for a text whose usefulness was not to the natives; to feel oneself as a European in command, almost at will, of Oriental history, time, and geography; to institute new areas of specialization; to establish new disciplines; to divide, deploy, schematize, tabulate, index, and record everything in sight (and out of sight).

(86)

Within this schema of political and epistemological domination, archaeology represents important ground. Its object was the former "classical greatness" which must be "restored," and most often it was the pyramids, tombs, and hieroglyphs that were "schematiz[ed], tabulat[ed], index[ed] and record[ed]." Moreover, the desire "to record everything in sight (and out of sight)" speaks to excavation as the consistent pursuit of what lurks beneath the surface, the hunt for the unknown that must be unveiled, analyzed and quantified. But the "full recognition of [the Orient's] place in memory" is also linked to the archaeological imagining of the unknown other as a representation of the unknown self. To dig into the East embodied a desire to reclaim the cradle of civilization. Yet this desire for origins was counteracted by the rejection of Eastern races; conquering Eastern soil amounted to a simultaneous connection with the originary and denial of the racial composition of this primary source.[6] The co-existing impulses of desire and destruction are built into the aesthetics of Egyptology; accounts depicting the excavations reflect a sense of frantic seeking counteracted by an equally frenetic desire to bury and destroy.

---

6   In *Black Athena*, Martin Bernal argues that the conception of Classical Greek culture endured even more rigorous editing, as the Afroasiatic roots of Classical Greece were systematically disregarded in favour of an "Aryan Model" as the result of nationalist and racist sentiment. This included deliberate mis-readings of archaeological evidence, a practice that would become commonplace in both Hitler's Germany and Mussolini's Italy.

In a similar manner, even while establishing archaeological ways to knowledge in Egypt was a prime rationale for European presence, there were ways in which the decipherment of Egyptian "secrets" also led to Europe's disenchantment with the East. It is with an air of disappointment that in 1877 Amelia Edwards, who supplied Britain with travelogues of the Egyptian scene, wrote of the decipherment of the hieroglyphic code: "So the old mystery of Egypt, which was her literature, has vanished. The key to the hieroglyphs is the master-key that opens every door ... The Sphinx has no secret now, save for the ignorant" (xii, xv). In a time when mystery and inscrutability were the pillars of Eastern appeal, the attainment of knowledge frequently resulted in dissatisfaction. As Cambridge Egyptologist John Ray has pointed out in a documentary interview, much of the English speaking world echoed Edwards' unhappiness with the translations of ancient Egyptian inscriptions:

> The decipherment of hieroglyphs was like discovering a new planet and finding that the planet did not behave like planets you were used to. So, suddenly we could read hieroglyphs and what we expected to find was something like Greek philosophy or we expected to find the secrets of the universe laid out in very plain language. It didn't happen like that. The preoccupations of the Egyptians are not the ones that we would like them to have; so there was a reaction very strongly, particularly in the English speaking world: The Egyptians were not intellectuals; they were not philosophers; a well known novelist has described them as merely craftsman, not artists; that idea dies rather hard because even while we could read the hieroglyphs we didn't understand the preoccupations behind them. We're beginning to but it's taken a long time. So there was a strong reaction, particularly in English, that the Egyptians were mystic but basically a bit thick. So it rapidly becomes the world of the chattering mummy, the strange unexplained phenomenon, the weird script, everything that leads to the Egyptian mummy film.

This tension between the simultaneous and paradoxical volition for unending mystery and epistemological resolution in many ways embodies the same dynamics as narrative desire. This similarity was not lost on writers traveling in Egypt and the opposition between the desire to know and the fear of knowing, frequently represented by the ubiquitous hex or "mummy's curse," became a fundamental theme in romantic archaeological accounts of the East.

Greek Studies: The Elgin Marbles, The Aegina Marbles, and finding Homer's Troy

If Egypt witnessed some of the most devastating pillaging of antiquities, it was Greece that incurred some of the earliest instances of British and French appropriation. In 1803, Lord Elgin, the British ambassador to Constantinople, had hundreds of workers remove the central frieze from the Parthenon. The reliefs were then shipped to London and sold to the British government, who after storing them in sheds for months, displayed them in the British Museum. Interestingly, the immediate reaction to the marbles was tepid, as some of the rough carving did not fit in with the British ideal of Greek workmanship. This did not prevent others from following Elgin's lead, however. On a trip to the island of Aegina in 1811, Charles Robert Cockerell and three other men found a series of sculptures at an ancient temple. Cockerell bought the marbles from the islanders for forty pounds and smuggled them out of Greece, only to resell them in a bidding war among the British, French, and Germans.

The interest in Greek antiquity was to a great extent propelled by the nineteenth-century classical education, rooted in Homer's *Iliad* and *Odyssey*. In many ways, it seems inevitable that this sort of immersion would spawn speculation as to whether Homer's accounts could be proven through archaeological exploration. Academic debate surrounding the possibility began in universities in earnest in the early 1800s. However, it took the resources of Heinrich Schliemann (1822–90), a German-born millionaire, to illustrate to the world that Homer's epics were literal historical fact. With the help of the American Frank Calvert, Schliemann dug at Hissarlik in northwestern Turkey from 1871 to 1873, in 1879, and again in 1882–3 and 1889–90, convinced that the mound was the site of Homer's Troy. Schliemann's project of disinterment was massive, creating one of the biggest messes in archaeological history. Despite his employment of several expert engineers, the sheer area covered in such short periods of time resulted in a chronic lack of precision. Yet Schliemann (and the newspapers that celebrated him) claimed he had made the most stunning archaeological discoveries of all time: Homeric Troy, the citadel of Priam, and a hoard of gold cups, diadems, jewelry, and silver vases, which Schliemann proclaimed to be "Priam's Treasure."

Between digs at Hissalirk, Schliemann also excavated Mycenae, the legendary city of Agamemnon. There, he disinterred several graves, two of which he claimed were the sepulchers of Agamemnon and Clytemnestra. Scholars immediately disputed his claims, insisting that the graves predated Homer. Later researches confirmed this, showing that the excavated graves must have predated the Trojan War by three hundred years. However, more press was showered on Schliemann's initial "discovery" than on any subsequent refutation. In a similar manner, recent scholarship has shown that Frank Calvert had begun digging into the mound at Hissarlik before Schliemann's appearance on the scene. Yet Schliemann continues to be the subject of biographies and fictionalized accounts, where Calvert is a relative unknown.

One of the reasons for Schliemann's popular success was his prolific writing about his excavations. Casting himself as the hero, Schliemann created readable narratives "written down by me on the spot while proceeding with my works" (12). These accounts, of which *Troy and Its Remains* (1875) is the most enduringly popular, contain autobiographical anecdotes about Schliemann's rise from rags to riches, his long-standing love of Homer, and the wedding of his third wife, Sophia, a Greek woman whom he married in order to inspire him in Greek archaeology. All of these elements were repeated in books and newspapers, creating a mythos that Schliemann was happy to perpetuate. Nonetheless, these accounts make for dramatic reading, as the following passage about finding "Priam's Treasure" demonstrates:

> While the men were eating and resting, I cut out the treasure with a large knife. This required great exertion and involved great risk, since the wall fortification, beneath which I had to dig, threatened every moment to fall down upon me. But the sight of so many objects, each one of which is of inestimable value to archaeology, made me reckless, and I never thought of any danger. It would, however, have been impossible for me to have removed the treasure without the help of my dear wife, who stood at my side, ready to pack the things I cut out in her shawl and to carry them away.
>
> (185)

Schliemann's self-depiction as the intrepid adventurer working almost single-handedly, despite the "great risk" and aided by his loyal wife held significant sway in European popular culture, despite later evidence which suggested that Sophia may not even have been present during this phase of the excavations. Through skillful self-promotion and a writer's bent for narrative, Schliemann became one of the brightest celebrities in the pantheon of hero-archaeologists.

As Hugh Kenner has discussed at some length, Schliemann's impact on literature stretched far beyond his own accounts. According to Kenner, Schliemann's discovery of Troy represented a complete topographical and imaginative shift in literature: "'Troy' after Schliemann was no longer a dream, but a place on the map. As his discoveries persisted, more and more Homeric words came to mean something producible, something belonging to the universe of the naturalistic novelist" (42). That Homer's accounts could be regarded in the same vein as the realist novel had a significant impact on emerging modernists. For Kenner, Ezra Pound, who had always been "susceptible to the magic of time," could now imagine all times on the same plane, "'in the timeless air' and ... archaized accordingly" (30). James Joyce believed that if Dublin were ever destroyed, archaeologists could read *Ulysses* to uncover its secrets in exactly the same way Schliemann had appealed to Homer. Joyce even visited Hissarlik to photograph what he believed to be the walls of Troy that Schliemann had discovered (47). Kenner also suggests that the fragments discovered by Schliemann at Troy, compounded by the fragments of papyrus regularly uncovered by archaeological investigations in Egypt and Greece, contributed to the modernist aesthetic of fragments, from Cubism and collage to H.D.'s Greek poems, to the cuts of Gaudier-Brzeska's statues:

> There was virtue in scraps, mysterium in fragments, magical power in the tatter of a poem, sacred words biting on congruent actualities of sight and feeling and breath. This sensibility lasted one poet's lifetime. "Oak leaf never plane leaf," we read at one point in the *Cantos*, and at another, "Le Paradis n'est pas artificiel / but spezzato apparently / it exists only in fragments unexpected excellent sausage, / the smell of mint, for example."
>
> (51)

It is this aesthetic of fragments, drawn from Troy and the consequent interest in papyri, half-deciphered hieroglyphs, missing parts of manuscripts that Kenner sees as central to the tradition of nineteenth-century decadence that: "hyperaesthesia prizing and feeding on ecstatic instants, fragments of psychic continuum" (60), a "Romantic quest for purity" that in Pound's generation "took the form of a tracing backward" (69).

As we will see, the evolution of disciplinary archaeology, which is made up of many co-existing, often combating currents and moments, from treasure hunts to classical resurrection, from exotic oriental fantasies to radical nationalist and racial archaeology, from strict empiricisms to cultural historicism, was both paralleled and undermined by contemporaneous literary production. Within this web of intersecting ideologies, the following chapters seek to draw out how the archaeological site became a focal point for the concentration of nineteenth- and twentieth-century energies, fantasies, and anxieties – how both disciplinary archaeology and nineteenth- and twentieth-century literary appropriations of the archaeological run beneath the ground of literary modernism.

CHAPTER 2

Reverie and Revelation:
The Textual Archaeologies of Théophile Gautier

The French interest in Egypt sparked by Napoleon's 1798 invasion and the subsequent publication of his scholars' *Description of Egypt* gathered momentum throughout the nineteenth century, reaching its peak with the colossal display of Egyptian monuments and antiquities at the Parisian universal exhibition of 1867. Throughout the 1800s, publications, exhibitions, and salons propelled the rage for all things Egyptian: members of archaeological and tourist expeditions published articles and books; luxury and antiquarian imports from Egypt commanded top price on the European market; hairstyles, clothing, home decorating and architecture defined the look of the "Egyptian vogue"; intellectuals and artists attended the Louvre's exhibitions of Egyptian antiquities and read Champollion's *Monuments of Egypt and Nubia* and Denon's *Voyage in Upper and Lower Egypt*; Paris' celebrated "*peintres-voyageurs*," Alexandre Decamps, Eugène Delacroix, Eugène Fromentin, Prosper Marilhat, Adrien Dauzats and Théodore Chassériau created a visual imaginary of the Orient as the locus of the feminine erotic, the festive and the vibrant as well as the cruel and sadistic through scenes of Egyptian harems, baths, festivals, dances, seductions, and slaves. At the center of it all, an enormous obelisk from Egypt's Luxor Temple was erected at la Place de la Concorde in 1836.[1] This symbol of colonial

---

[1] The Obelisk of Luxor was presented to Charles X in 1829 by the Viceroy of Egypt. It was not erected until 1836 under the reign of Louis-Philippe. The obelisk dates back to the thirteenth century B.C.E. and is engraved with hieroglyphs celebrating the reign of Ramesses II. Gautier wrote two pieces about the Obelisk of Luxor, the first a humorous article published in *La Presse* in 1838 and the second a poem entitled "Nostalgie d'Obélisques" published in *La Presse* in 1851.

and archaeological interaction standing at the crossroads of the modern metropolis was emblematic of the ways in which archaeology was imbedded in the very heart of an emerging modernity.

Egyptomania held equal sway in the literary sphere. Chateaubriand and Lamartine published two of the foundational Egyptian travelogues with *Itinerary from Paris to Jerusalem* and *Impressions, Thoughts, and Memories during a Voyage in the Orient*. Gerard de Nerval also published an account of his Egyptian adventures, *Voyage in the Orient*, the definitive version of which was published in 1852. Perhaps the most notorious literary adventurers in Egypt, Maxime du Camp and Gustave Flaubert, toured around the country for du Camp's government commissioned mission, taking calotypes of ancient Egyptian monuments. While Flaubert was more interested in the daily bustle of Egyptian life than in its artifacts, even he was disturbed by modernity's intrusion into an antique oasis and by the sense that the texture of ancient Egypt was corroding in the face of the modern Western invasion: "It is time to hurry," he wrote in a letter to his friend, Théophile Gautier: "Before very long the Orient will no longer exist. We are perhaps the last of its contemplators" (qtd. in Reid 87).

Gautier did not arrive in Egypt until 1859, when he was commissioned to report on the Suez Canal ceremonies for the *Journal Officiel*. Even then, he saw very little of the country as he dislocated his shoulder boarding the ship in Marseilles and was mostly hotel-bound during his stay in Cairo. Before this ill-fated foray into the "land of dreams," however, Gautier had written extensively on Egypt and Egyptological themes in, among others, *One of Cleopatra's Nights* (1838), *The Mummy's Foot* (1840), *The Thousand and Second Night* (1842), "Nostalgia of the Obelisks" (1851), and most famously, *The Mummy's Romance* (1857). Considered to be some of the most influential archaeological texts of the nineteenth century and often accurate in their most minute descriptions of ancient sites, Gautier wrote them before ever seeing Egypt. Yet the fact that these Egyptological works are imaginary, drawn from archaeological records and accounts, salon paintings, world exhibitions, travels in Spain, Algeria and Constantinople and from conversations with du Camp, de Nerval, and Flaubert, is perhaps more telling than if Gautier had written on the shores of the Nile. More than any other writer of the time, Gautier's writings are illustrative of a

French *mentalité* of Egyptology, a world-view constructed through the web of archaeological texts and images of Egypt that flooded mid-nineteenth-century Paris.

Egyptology, as a discipline, was still relatively unknown when Gautier began writing about it in the 1830s evidenced by the etymological appearance of *égyptologue* in 1827. While it had spawned an entire genre by the end of the century, Gautier was one of the first literary writers to broach the archaeological project in the East. A blending of fact gleaned from emerging archaeological texts and blatant imaginative exoticism, Gautier's Egyptian antique is the deepest stratum of what would become the layered folds of the Western archaeological imagination, a configuration that would become increasingly dense and complex as time went on. In this sense, Gautier's work can be considered the stone age of archaeological modalities, containing some of the most basic implements for probing archaeological motifs, tools that would, nonetheless, create templates for subsequent evolutions in archaeological approaches. These fundamental themes include the auratic importance of the archaeological relic, the parallel between archaeological regressions and dreams, the reclamation of the lost pantheistic landscape, and the mummified woman who embodies a conception of woman-as-earth and woman-as-past that pervades the modern literary topos. Additionally, and perhaps because Gautier's archaeology was so thoroughly a text-learned archaeology acquired through exposure to archaeological written accounts, writing itself is foregrounded, with particular attention to hieroglyphs, codes, and encryptions. Texts that are literally about archaeology, Gautier's scripts within scripts and sedimented significances also create a veritable archaeology of the text.

At once an exotic dream world and an increasingly excavated, charted, and quantified location, Gautier's renderings of ancient Egypt vacillate between decadent aesthetic fantasy and historical exactitude. As Luc Vives has aptly stated, in writing his archaeological romances, Gautier was enmeshed in a double preoccupation: "maintaining the Egyptian phantasm (l'Égypte rêvée) and egyptological erudition (l'Égypte textuelle) ... in sum, dreaming knowledge and disciplining the imagination" (54). Jean Carré notes that most of Gautier's archaeological education came from books and his ability to accurately depict ancient landscapes increased in accordance with the growing availability of archaeological texts. In 1838, when Gautier composed *One of Cleopatra's Nights*, only the first volumes of Champollion's posthumous *Monuments of Egypt and Nubia* had been published. The works of D'Avennes, Lepsius, and Rosellini that would create an archaeological paradigm for the nineteenth-century reading public were not yet available. As a result, Carré observes that Gautier's early archaeological novels are full of historical flaws and Greek and Roman substitutions, anachronisms that disappear in Gautier's later work as accurate Egyptological texts became increasingly available on the popular market.

It wasn't until 1852, during the writing of *The Mummy's Romance*, that Gautier claimed that he was finally able to make Egypt "amusing" without sacrificing "rigorous exactitude" in all "historical and archaeological details" (qtd. in Carré 151). Most of this newly acquired knowledge of archaeology came through access to the library of his friend Ernest Feydeau, a respectable Egyptologist, whose main contribution to archaeological scholarship was *History of the Funeral Customs and Burial Practices of Ancient Peoples*, a volume on the funeral practices of the Egyptians in the eighteenth and nineteenth dynasty (1500 B.C.E.). In Feydeau's library, Gautier came into contact with some of the most important archaeological texts of the mid 1900s: *Travels in Ethiopia* by Hoskins, *The Manners and Customs of the Ancient Egyptians* by Wilkinson, Belzoni's *Researches and Operations in Egypt and Nubia*, plus the collected works of Champollion, Rosellini, Lepsius, and d'Avennes. *The Mummy's Romance* is dedicated to Feydeau, and the wording of the dedication is indicative of the ways in which Gautier valued the scholarship imparted to him by his friend:

> I dedicate this book to you, which is your due; in opening up to me your erudition and your library, you made me believe I was a scholar and that I knew enough about ancient Egypt to describe it; in your footsteps I walked in temples, in palaces, in hypogeums, the city of the living and the city of the dead; you lifted the mysterious Isis before me and resuscitated a giant disappeared civilization. The history is from you; the novel is from me; all I had to do was reunite through style, like through the cement of a mosaic, all of the precious stones that you brought me.
> (*The Mummy's Romance*)

Reverie and Revelation

The most interesting line of this dedication is perhaps the last one, where Gautier suggests that "style" is the unifying "cement" that allows the author to create a historical novel from archaeological sources. In essence, this suggests that archaeological details are fragments which must be pieced together through the artist's talent. This reconstructive act of piecing fragments together to create a coherent narrative is one of the ways in which Gautier seems to be suggesting that writing, too, is an inherently reconstructive and, therefore, "archaeological" act. Yet this posture is also illustrative of early archaeological aesthetics, where it is assumed that fragments must be narrated into coherent wholes. The aesthetic of the shard, unadulterated and unornamented, was a later development in modern poetic adoptions of archaeological remains.

The Mummy's Romance, Gautier's most accurate narration of archaeological fragments, is in fact a double narrative, as it is a text within a text, a story encased within another story. The prologue features two British explorers, the scholar Rumphius and his patron, Lord Evandale, who follow their Greek guide into the Valley of the Kings and discover an unviolated Egyptian tomb. Contrary to their expectations, the tomb belongs to an Egyptian queen, Tahoser, rather than to one of the pharaohs. While examining the mummy, the adventurers find a papyrus. The second part of the novel is ostensibly Rumphius' translation of the hieroglyphs, which tell the story of Tahoser, a young woman, who falls in love with an Israelite but marries the Pharaoh, who also desires her, in order to prevent him from massacring the Israelites. When the Pharaoh dies, Tahoser rules over Egypt, and it is her body that is entombed along with the papyrus that describes the course of her life.

The motif of a deciphered papyrus within a text was a theme that had been written into French literature before. In Baudelaire's translation of the short story, "The Young Enchanter," a scholar cannot unroll a newly discovered papyrus and read the story written on it without another part of the tale disintegrating. This material difficulty is echoed in *The Mummy's Romance* through Rumphius' concern that all of the hieroglyphics on the Tahoser papyrus are not completely legible. This occlusion, a distance, or an inability to achieve perfect translation are suggestive of the ways in which texts themselves were increasingly perceived as material sites that conceal.

Partly metaphorical, the challenges of disintegration and decipherment literally correlate with the acknowledged difficulties of the nineteenth-century archaeological enterprise. Antonio Piaggio, a custodian of the Vatican library, was well known across Europe for building a complicated machine of pigs' bladders, thread, and winches precisely for the purpose of unrolling papyri without having them disintegrate. Similarly, the agonies of decipherment were disseminated through tales of the thirty-year process of decoding the Rosetta Stone. A daily concern in archaeology, the labours of unearthing, deciphering, decoding, and translating became processual metaphors for literary pursuits. Vives points to Victor Hugo's comment: "… we arrive at the truth that everything is hieroglyphic, and we know that symbols are only relatively obscure … What is a poet (I use this word in its largest sense), if not a translator, a decipherer?" (64). In Gautier, the role of the poet as translator is compounded by a sense of writer as archaeologist: a stylistic cementer of archaeological erudition, an adventurer, decoder, and encryptor in one.

In addition to highlighting the material nature of the textual, or the archaeological depths of the text, Gautier's archaeological tales are also elaborately inter-textual. Most of his archaeological storylines, for example, derive from various non-fictional accounts of excavation. Gautier's inspiration for *The Mummy's Romance* came from one of Champollion's anecdotes in *Letters from Egypt and Nubia 1828–1829*, which makes note of the legend of Tahoser and the tomb of a queen who had exercised sovereign power. However, according to Gautier's daughter, Judith, details for the novel came from a variety of sources, literary and painterly, which were strewn across the Gautier living room during the composition process (Carré 150). Quite often archaeological verisimilitude in Gautier's texts was achieved either through transcriptions of archaeological accounts or descriptions of archaeological plates and paintings. Carré has documented the ways in which various scenes from *The Mummy's Romance* are pulled directly from the pages of archaeological texts: the doors, corridors, and depths of the tomb, for example, follow the exact details of the hypogeum of Seti I, discovered and described by Belzoni (153); the point by point description of details, colours, and decorative motifs are taken from illustrations in Feydeau's book (154–6) and the fictional party's approach to the mummy's tomb are drawn from Mariette's 1851 account of his entry into the Serapeum of Saqqara (157). In addition, descriptions of Tahoser's lifestyle and daily activities can be traced to Wilkinson, while the passages on musicians and costumes are taken from d'Avennes. Carré also speculates that the funeral dinner is transcribed from Feydeau (159) while the Pharoah's physical characteristics mirror Belzoni's description of the head of Ramesses II (59).

In addition to supplying Gautier with precise historical detail, archaeological accounts also often provided him with plot outlines. *The Mummy's Foot*, for example, is derived from Vivant Denon's *Voyage in Upper and Lower Egypt* (1802). In this account of traveling with Napoleon in Egypt, Denon includes the anecdote of snatching "a little mummy's foot ... without doubt the foot of a young woman, a princess, a charming being" in the Valley of the Kings (278). Denon's description provides the basis for Gautier's central object, the foot of the embalmed Egyptian Princess Hermonthis. In Gautier's tale, it is a dandy who is struck with object-fetish and who purchases the foot in a *bric-à-brac* store in Paris. The dandy selects the foot from among a number of other antique items and once home uses it as a paperweight. From here, the story progresses in a humorous sort of way and greatly elaborates on Denon's original anecdote: After dining out with friends, the dandy returns home and falls asleep, only to be awakened by the incarnated princess, who is trying to reattach the foot to her body. The narrator gallantly returns the foot to the princess, who in turn offers to take him back to her father's house. The Pharaoh, relieved that the princess's foot has been returned, instructs the dandy to choose his reward. The dandy asks for the princess's hand in marriage in exchange for the return of the foot – a request the Pharaoh refuses, mocking the dandy's young age in contrast with the princess's three thousand years of immortality. The dandy awakes in his own room and finds the mummified foot gone, replaced by an iconic figure of "green paste."

Both *The Mummy's Foot* and *The Mummy's Romance* are inspired by textual archaeology in that they both draw on archaeological texts for plot and details. But an archaeological mode of creation, a hieroglyphics of inscription, is also implicit in the creation of these two texts. In *The Mummy's Romance*, Rumphius is said to have "translated the papyrus" after "long study," thereby gaining a place alongside Champollion in such a way that would make Lepsius "die of jealousy" (38). Here, Gautier interpolates fictional characters into the story of archaeology by invoking some of its best-known characters. Through the ritual of textual translation, Rumphius gains his own place in the historical documentation of an unfolding discipline. Moreover, the papyrus itself is the key to the story, the heart of the tomb. While the (dead) mummy is an object of interest and desire, there is no interpreting the significance of her life without an entry into her story through language. It is the text that preserves her life, just as embalming preserves her form or as Rumphius seeks to be preserved by the text of archaeological history. This tension between mortality and immortality, which drives the story, is mediated by text; without the papyrus the explorers would not know Tahoser, and without the story of Lord Evandale and Rumphius the reader would not know of their adventures. Life is, therefore, infinitely preserved through the artistic processes of textual production and decipherment, procedures the reader both reads about and participates in.

Likewise, in *The Mummy's Foot*, the foot is purchased for the very specific purpose of "paper weight." Before he goes to sleep, the narrator sets the foot on a pile of papers and half-written stories. It is easy to infer that the object, which lends weight or veracity to the tale, is secondary to the stories themselves, which come to encompass the object and generate an entire narrative around it. When the narrator awakens, our attention is again drawn to the texts as the idol left by the princess as proof of her presence also sits on the pile of papers. As Sima Godfrey notes, "… the real fetishes of the tale, the incomplete poems, unfinished articles, misplaced letters and censored words that speak in differing and displaced codes … utter no less persuasively the permanence of a dream" (311). And while the dream may be of archaeological or hallucinogenic inspiration (as the green paste idol suggests), it is through the text that the image becomes real, material, and lasting. Despite the Pharaoh's disdain for the narrator's mortality, ultimately it is the narrator who tells the story and gains artistic permanence through the text.

Within this textual archaeologizing, in which the word is of primary importance, material objects also have a central role. As Edna Epstein has

Reverie and Revelation

noted, the most common pose for Gautier's heroes is "'transfixed' before objects" (7). The talismanic quality of the object, its own outstanding properties as well as its ability to evoke an entire civilization is a theme that runs throughout archaeologically influenced literature. The closest we might come to understanding the quality of these objects is Walter Benjamin's description of "aura": that "unique phenomenon of distance, however close it may be" ("The Work of Art in the Age of Mechanical Reproduction" 1109). In Gautier's texts the object always retains the quality of distance that is particular to the vanished civilization. Moreover, because these objects are originals, which as Benjamin notes is the "prerequisite of the concept of authenticity" (1107), they are the guarantors of another time, the bridge between past, present and future. Like auratic objects, archaeological fragments remain "imbedded in the fabric of tradition" (1109) and are symbolic of a wholeness and completeness that exceeds a shattered modernity. The mummy's foot, for example, is not just the surviving fragment of another age; it is also a metonymic emissary that carries with it the full presence of its original time and place.

While a variety of objects hold magnetic appeal for Gautier's heroes, there is none as compelling as the figure of the mummy. This is true not only for Gautier's heroes, but for Gautier himself, who declared that the unwrapping of a mummy, which he witnessed at the 1867 universal exhibition, was in fact a truer experiencing of the Orient than his actual voyage to Egypt. Part of Gautier's literary interest in mummies seems to derive from their ability to encapsulate several themes and ideas at once; in some sense, the mummy is Gautier's ultimate hieroglyph, at once object and a series of infinitely shifting and translatable meanings. At its most basic level, the mummy is the ideal in art, a symbol of immortalized beauty, a metaphor that is consistently compounded by comparisons to Greek statues and the Venus de Milo, which also highlights Gautier's preoccupation with the parallels between archaeology and sculpture. But the mummy is also emblematic of the unfolding narrative and narrative desire. In *The Mummy's Romance*, for instance, the drawn out hunt for the tomb's entrance, the search through its lavish interior, and the opening of the coffin culminate in the act of removing the mummy's wrappings:

> The doctor removed the wrappings of the body, and, the last obstacle removed, the young woman was seen in all the chaste nudity of her beautiful form, guarding, in spite of the centuries, all the roundness of her former contours and the supple grace of her pure lines of breed.
>
> (34)

In this moment of discovery, Rumphius, the guide, and Lord Evandale issue a "cry of admiration." This experience of privileged voyeurism, of seeing the unobtainable without her "veil" is a suspended moment of both scopophilic and epistemological importance. In essence, it is the climactic narrative moment in a journey that has been motivated by the desire to see and know. The tale of Rumphius and Evandale ends shortly after with Rumphius' promise to translate the papyrus and the narrator's suggestion that Evandale will always remain retrospectively in love with the figure of Tahoser – a double posture which is illustrative of the two responses to the past Gautier considers to be correct: the love of antiquity which results in assiduous scholarship and the passionate identification which is the cornerstone of the historical imagination.

While there are several ways in which the violation of the tomb and the stripping of the mummy suggest a sexualized overcoming of the past, of the feminine, and of the Other, there is also a persistent parallel between the unwrapping of the mummy and the reader's unraveling of the text. In "The Unbinding Process," André Green suggests that "unbinding" is one of the most fundamental mechanisms of reading. Recognizing the text as "textile," Green argues that threads of meaning, propelled by narrative desire, at once bind the text and unbind it as readers follow the thread provided by the author and unbind it with meanings of their own. Seen in these terms, the unwrapping of the mummy reveals itself as another processual metaphor for the literary event, as the reader enacts the unwrapping of the text in order to reach some fundamental kernel of authenticity at the centre of the reading experience. Rather than following a set pattern of unveiling, though, Green's version of unbinding illustrates how the reader's experience is woven into the patterns of unwrapping. In this sense, the mummy is representative not just of the untangling of the narrative's mystery, but also the liberation of bound meaning from fixed parameters. Like the hieroglyph, which must be deciphered and translated, the unbinding of the mummy contributes to the proliferation of meaning. Assuredly the mummy's core is the object of desire, but it is the process of unraveling, deferment and suspense – in other words, the mechanisms of narrative – which create the climate of desire, both for the mummy's body and within the body of the text.

While the mummy metaphor stands for both the ideal in art and narrative desire, she is also symbolic of a glorified and unobtainable pantheistic past. The Orient Gautier presents is not the modern Orient, which he himself professed to be illusory and disappointing, but an archaic and exotic counterpart to Western modernity. Within this temporal topology, the elements of Otherness associated with the East are combined with the temporal Otherness of the past. The Ancient Orient, removed from the aesthetic hideousness of Modern Europe, is a double-ideal; it is a *paradis artificiel* built out of an Otherness that is at once Other-place and Other-time. As Elizabeth Dahab has noted, the Orient has "several precise functions in Gautier's imagination": it "served as an alternative to the West," as "the elsewhere where [he] could find beauty and escape from the ugliness of ... society" and as an exit from "mediocrity" and "usefulness" (1). In this game of affinities, the Orient is inevitably the locus of dream, the erotic, the subconscious – the reverse of Western rationalism and self-awareness. Within Gautier's archaeological topos, the elements of Otherness associated with the East are combined with the temporal Otherness of the past to create a utopian ideal of the Oriental antique.

In Gautier's mummy novels, the Oriental *femme fatale* is emblematic of this rarified past. Just as the lexicon for Egyptology evolved in accordance with exposure to the East, so the so-called "hidden treasures" of the East, its veiled and occulted women, were subject to an epistemological web of shifting associations. It has been speculated that the term "Oriental woman" was in fact synonymous with "unobtainable" in mid-nineteenth century France. Madelaine Dobie clarifes this definition by suggesting that the Oriental woman signified "desire intensified by the obstacles placed in its way" (1). For Dobie, this connotation, which began to conglomerate around the Oriental feminine in the travel literature of the 1600s, coalesced in the expression "*la femme orientale*" which by the early nineteenth century had become: "a figure of speech denoting a determinate set of characteristics, a mystery, an enigma, a promise." In Gautier, consistently deferred desire for the unreachable past attaches to the figure of the mummy, the ultimate obscured embodiment of the Oriental woman, veiled both by material wrappings and by the past itself. Yet the mummy also provides a metaphorical equivalent for the earth, a feminized landscape which veils its treasures beneath layers of historical accumulation.

This acute desire to find a kind of feminized home, a return to the earth, or pre-Oedipal bliss is another dominant feature of Gautier's archaeological writing. In an 1843 letter to de Nerval, Gautier expresses this desire for the past through his own sense of having an imaginary affinity with the East:

> We are not always from the country where we are born ... and so we keep searching for our real homeland. Me, I am a Turk, not from Constantinople but from Egypt. It seems as though I have lived in the Orient, and that during the carnival, when I disguise myself with ... a few authentic baubles, I feel as though I have put on my real clothes. I am frequently surprised by not understanding Arabic. It must be that I have forgotten it. In Spain, everything reminiscent of the Moors interested me as vividly as if I were a child of Islam, and I took up my part for them against the Christians.
> (qtd. in Carré 130)

Here we have an enactment of the historical empathy which Hayden White has described as crucial to the romantic experience of the past.[2] Gautier's empathy is so complete, however, that we begin to see how the archaeological can act as a tunneling mechanism which turns empathy, the momentary intellectual identification or vicarious experience, into a sustained nostalgic identification which becomes a new form of identity. Within this archaeology of self-identification, the goal of scholarly study or textual excavation is not to find the object but to recover the subject: to find one's own self in the rubble of the past, to pull it from the debris of antiquity and present it as a more authentic version of the self than

---

2 In *Metahistory: The Historical Imagination in Nineteenth-Century Europe*, White argues that the romantics: "believed in 'empathy' as a method of historical inquiry, and they cultivated sympathy for those aspects of both history and humanity which the Enlighteners had viewed with scorn or condescension" (38).

that generated by one's own time. For Gautier, his "real self" belongs not to mid-nineteenth century Paris or even the modern Orient, the "mirage éblouissant" (blinding mirage) that dissipates on contact, but rather to the fictive past, an imaginative realm that is constructed through fantasy interwoven with the pages of archaeological texts.

The French Romantic sense of alienation from the modern and an imagined affinity with the past is perhaps most vividly described in Huysman's manifesto of French decadence, *Against Nature*. Pitted against nature, Huysman's anti-hero, Des Esseintes, is also against the real – present time, present place, and present circumstances. Harboring himself in a decadent world of the most refined aesthetic making, Des Esseintes speculates that the true artist does not exist in the present, but rather creates for himself an exquisite fantasy of distant times:

> Unable to attune himself, except at rare intervals, to this environment, and no longer finding in the examination of that environment and the creatures who endure it sufficient pleasures of observation and analysis to divert him, [the artist] is aware of the birth and development in himself of unusual phenomena. Vague migratory longings spring up which find fulfillment in reflection and study ... He recalls memories of people and things he has never known personally, and there comes a time when he bursts out of the prison of his century and roams about at liberty in another period, with which, as a crowning illusion he imagines he would have been more in accord.
>
> In some cases there is a return to past ages, to vanished civilizations, to dead centuries; in others there is a pursuit of dream and fantasy, a more or less vivid vision of a future whose image reproduces, unconsciously and a result of atavism, that of past epochs.
>
> (181–2)

This description is an apt diagnosis of both Gautier and his narrators' malaise in the modern world that provokes a desire to "return to past ages, to vanished civilizations." However, Huysman's recognition that the sensation of having been more in tune with a past epoch is a "crowning illusion" is relatively unexplored by Gautier, who seems to approach the past with an unambiguous reverence that dissipates in the work of later modernists. Gautier's heroes, as representatives of the modern, rarely recover from their brushes with the phantasmagoric past; they remain transfixed by the memory of an idealized and generally feminized landscape and taunted by the vulgarity of the present. Rather than painting this as a retrospective posture, however, for Gautier this backward glance is half of the definition of the modern. In an article for the *Moniteur*, Gautier defined modernity as "on the one side, the most extreme modernity; on the other, an austere love of antiquity" (qtd. in Lehmann 10). This twinned and paradoxical definition would plague the modern: the extreme modernity that would become an exacerbated quest for the new spurred by this "austere love" which like most loves would become infinitely more complex as it turned to passion, to hate, to ambivalence, to aggression, to nostalgia, to desire in various stages of modern writing. What remains is the inescapable sense that modernity is tied to its other: eternality is the shadow innovation can never outstrip.

While it may be tempting to ascribe Gautier's "archaeological mode" and its thematic trappings: writing, Otherness, objects, dreams, to a particular type of Orientalism, it is important to recognize that these preoccupations also exceed Gautier's Egyptian oeuvre. Published in the *Revue de Paris* in 1852, *Arria Marcella* belongs to a line of Pompeiian fictions produced in the eighteenth and nineteenth centuries, yet also surpasses these works in its conglomeration of archaeological motifs. Beginning with Goethe's *Italian Journey 1786–1788*, Pompeii had become a thematic landscape for meditations on the brevity of life, fate, and the eternality of art. Of the archaeological novels that followed, Bulwer-Lytton's *The Last Days of Pompeii* is the most well known. But in Gautier, the Pompeiian motif shifts to include a more full-bodied reclamation of the archaeological object, the archaeological gateway to the pagan past, and the archaeological nature of the human subconscious.

Arria Marcella begins in a museum in Naples in the nineteenth century with three young Parisian friends touring the archaeological artifacts. One of them, Octavian, becomes transfixed by the relic first encountered in Bulwer-Lytton's Pompeii: a petrified lava cast of a woman's breast and hip, "a piece of coagulated black ashes, bearing a hollow impression ... the curve of a beautiful breast and of flanks as faultless in outline as those of a Greek statue" (*Théophile Gautier's Short Stories* 106). Later that day, the friends take a tour of Pompeii, including the villa of Diomedes Marcellus,

Reverie and Revelation 51

where the guide informs the three friends that the body of "the lady whose mold is shown in the museum at Naples" was found: "She had gold rings on her fingers, and pieces of her fine tunic were found stuck to the mass of ashes which retained her shape" (122). Octavian responds empathetically and emotionally to the scene: "his bosom swelled, his eyes glistened with furtive moisture; that catastrophe, effaced by twenty centuries of oblivion, affected him like a disaster of recent occurrence" – a testament to the emotive possibilities of the archaeological fragment. That evening, after dinner, Octavian wanders back to the excavation site in a somnambulant state where he is transported to the Pompeii of 79 A.C.E. He is possessed by the idea of finding the woman whose calcified figure he had admired at the museum. He finally finds her at the theatre and Arria Marcella sends her maid to summon Octavian back to her villa. Arria Marcella tells Octavian that the force of his passion on seeing her archaeological cast brought her back to life. They embrace. The scene is interrupted by a Nazarene, who chastises Arria Marcella. Arria Marcella protests that the Nazarene should not subject her to the doctrines of a religion that was never hers, for she believes in the ancient gods who love life, youth, beauty and pleasure (161). The Nazarene utters an oath and Arria Marcella disintegrates into ash and bones. Octavian wakes up to his friends shaking him in the ruins of the Marcellus villa. That evening, he returns to the archaeological site but is unable to return to the Pompeiian epoch. He resigns himself to marry and leads a typical bourgeois life in Paris, though his wife always suspects him of harboring a hidden love.

In this particular short story, Gautier explicitly refers to a theme that pervades his work, the "incurable homesickness" (110), a retrospective longing that is particular to archaeological modes of desiring and which also appears in the work of Winckelmann and Pater. Sensuous and immediate, Octavian's experiencing of the past is a fevered reverie that in all senses seems more real than the present. Indeed, Gautier's archaic reversions are the locus of desire, and the talismanic objects that transport the narrators to imaginative locations are only useful insofar as they provide entry into another realm. Unlike the "antiquary" who would have been driven "mad with joy" by the sight of a restored Pompeii, Octavian "saw naught but the deep, black eyes of Arria Marcella, and that superb bosom, triumphant over time, which even universal destruction had chosen to preserve" (156). Passion, not pottery or possessions is the past's seduction, and the subtle incorporation of the antiquarian figure is a sly dig at the difference between the repressed archaeology of collecting artifacts and the highly erotic archaeology of filling the hollow impression of an antique relic with completing fantasies of reconnection, transforming an aesthetic of absence into an erotically charged full-presence.

In *Arria Marcella*, then, we can discern all of the themes that characterize Gautier's Egyptological tales: the fetishistic object that gives rise to another reality, the beautiful, unobtainable woman to whom it belongs, the remote pantheistic landscape, and the dream or period of unconsciousness. In that *Arria Marcella* takes place at Pompeii instead of in Egypt, however, it is possible to discern that these themes for Gautier are not simply part of an Orientalist mode but also central to an archaeological mode, which borrows from the exoticized ambience of Orientalist discourse. Just as the phenomenon of Orientalism can be said to define Western modernity, the past seems to provide Gautier with another Other: feminine, pagan, antique. Hence, in so far as totalities invoke their opposite, the archaeological past underwrites Gautier's project of masculine, modernist literary production.

Another aspect that differentiates *Arria Marcella* from the Egyptological tales is that Gautier had in fact visited Pompeii before writing his archaeological romance. This fact challenges the idea that Gautier's textual encryptions are the result of textually mediated archaeological experience. Yet in *Arria Marcella* as well writing stands out as a primary theme. For F. Schuerewegen, for example, the lava from Vesuvius creates an "écriture naturelle" on the flanks of the mountain (Schuerewegen 326). The idea of a natural writing produced by the volcano opens up a suggestive line of thinking into the ideas of "trace" that become prominent in later archaeological works. Additionally, Gautier deliberately likens the character of Arria Marcella to textually produced heroines, citing Octavian's preference for the ideal in history and art rather than its incarnation: "Like Faust he had loved Helen ... He had formed for himself an imaginary harem, with Semiramis, Aspasia, Cleopatra, Diane de Poitiers, and Joan of Aragon" (*Théophile Gautier's Short Stories* 130). At once material trace come to life and literary creation, we can infer that Arria Marcella, while tied to the physical cast of her hip and breast, is essentially an archaeological fantasy, a "retrospective ideal" (131) whose resurrection is brought about by a desire for the past that is projected onto the written page.

The dominating feature of Gautier's tale, therefore, remains the unrequited desire for the past as embodied through the unobtainable woman. Fundamentally, Tahoser, the Princess Hermonthis and Arria Marcella are ghostly embodiments of the pantheistic past, the loci of generative poetic power. Ancient Egypt and archaic Pompeii, in their subscription to sensuous, material-based religion, are also the root of culture, an assumption Gautier illustrates through significant detailing of the artisanship of Egyptian tombs as well as the craftsmanship of the theatre at Pompeii. This idealization of the pagan past as the core of the artistic is a theme that runs throughout Gautier's critical writings. In a remarkably Paterian passage on Leonardo da Vinci, for example, Gautier elaborates a theory of Renaissance regeneration that references the pagan spirit, decipherment, and archaeology as the basis of creative resurrection:

> The Greeks had attained beauty in everything... Without seeking to be unjust to the efforts and attempts of later civilizations, one may affirm that a long night followed that brilliant day, and that the feeling for beauty disappeared for many a century amid the cataclysms of empires and the chaos of the Middle Ages. Sculpture and painting, borne down by the fall of polytheism, wholly vanished... But at last comes that marvelous sixteenth century, when the mind of man awakes as from a long dream and regains possession of itself... A few manuscripts deciphered in spite of the obstacles presented by the Gothic, monkish handwriting, a few fragments of antique marble unearthed as if by a miracle, sufficed to bring about this revolution.
> ("Leonardo Da Vinci" 253–4)

Here, the Greek ideal, exemplified by sculpture and painting inspired by a polytheistic world-view, disappears during the Middle Ages, until "the mind of man" reawakens, in part through the translation of Gothic manuscripts and the disinterment of "antique marbles." This dense accumulation of themes which forms the nexus of archaeological modalities is reminiscent of Heinrich Heine's philosophy of pagan resurrection, which we will examine in the following chapter, and it is not surprising that Gautier and

Heine were friends and mutual literary admirers. In Gautier, it is clear that the creative pagan forces that fuel artistic production can be reclaimed. In the Renaissance, this reclamation took place through decipherment and excavation; hence, Gautier draws on decipherment and archaeology to usher these primal, generative forces into modernity. Nor was Gautier alone in this attempted resuscitation. As we will see, Pater, Pound, H.D., Breton, and Olson perform similar excavations in order to extricate artistic energies from the bedrock of a lost, but consistently present, pantheistic past.

In addition to consolidating Gautier's appreciation for the pagan world-view and his desire to retrieve it, *Arria Marcella* is also Gautier's most extensive elaboration of the connection between archaeology and the subconscious. As Jean Pierrot has pointed out, while in some sense "'dream' in this period had become merely a synonym for escape from the real" (183) dream is also a gateway to the forgotten past as well as the entry point into a more creative state of mind. As a result, Octavian's journey from Paris to Pompeii is paralleled by a movement from north to south, modern to ancient, Christian to pantheistic, surface to subterranean. Of all of these associations, Gautier draws dream to the forefront from the beginning of the tale. On seeing Arria Marcella's petrified cast, Octavian retreats from consciousness; all of Naples appears to him as a dream world where he falls into a "somnambulant state" (120), the regression to Pompeii in 79 A.C.E. is said to be "the accomplishment of his dearest dreams" (125) and at the theatre he finds himself "face to face with his chimera" (131). Moreover, ancient Pompeii disappears for him at the moment where his friends shake him awake at the excavation site. For Gautier, the archaeological site is, therefore, not just illustrative of the relationship between past and present, it is also a powerful metaphor for the relationship between unconscious and conscious mind, between dormant creative energies and rational thought, and between a repressed memory of pre-oedipal fulfillment and adult fetishism and anxiety. While there have been few psychoanalytic readings of *Arria Marcella*, fifty years later Wilhelm Jensen published *Gradiva: A Pompeiian Fantasy*, a very similar short story that would become the basis for Freud's archaeological metaphor for repression and the mind.

Gautier's fiction consolidates a series of themes characterizing archaeological modes of imagining: the archaeological object, the *femme fatale*, the pantheistic past, the reanimating dream, and various forms of encryption and decipherment. However, to gain a fuller sense of archaeological modes of writing, it is useful to briefly turn to Gautier's poetry. While the themes explored above also appear in Gautier's verse, it is in the poetry that there is a more pronounced sense of play surrounding archaeology's formal possibilities, a more detailed intermarrying of the sculptural and the archaeological, and a more ambiguous approach to the past's erotic potential. Published in 1852, the same year as *Arria Marcella*, *Enamels and Cameos* enacts many of the archaeological structures Gautier forged in his short fiction. But these poems are also illustrative of the ways in which the idea of the archaeology of the text gives rise to a poetic mode of composition.

Egyptologically loaded in both form and content, "Nostalgia of the Obelisks" is a clear starting point for poetic archaeological analysis. This pair of poems is written from the perspective of the two Luxor Obelisks: one in Luxor, one transplanted to Paris, with each obelisk professing a desire to inhabit the space of the other. Yet the archaeological motif is not limited to the invocation of hieroglyphically inscribed objects. An archaeological resonance formally reinforces the themes of nostalgia and memory and evokes the ambience of the tomb, as illustrated by this stanza uttered by the obelisk in Paris:

> Sur l'échafaud de *Louis* seize,
> Mon*oli*the au sens ab*oli*,
> On a m*is* mon secret, qui pèse
> Le poids de cinq m*ille* ans d'oub*li*.
> (*Émaux et Camées* 72, italics added)
>
> On the scaffold of Louis the Sixteenth,
> Monolith, the meaning abolished
> They placed my secret that weighs
> Five thousand years of oblivion.

Here, in the French, the repeating "i" sound in "Louis," "monolithe," "aboli," "mille," and "oubli" creates a wandering echo through the solid confines of the quatrain. This chambered sound is made explicit later in the poem when the Obelisk of Paris refers to the sacred soil of Egypt where underfoot "sounds the crypt" (74). In this stanza, the crypt is literally "sounded-out" through the reverberating syllable. That the words for "abolished" and "forgetfulness" both contain the repeating sound contributes to the sense that the past – here the execution of Louis XVI or the eroded memories surrounding the obelisk – is only heard or remembered through a kind of play of resonance and distorted repetition. The layering of sound also contributes to Gautier's sense that historical topographies are sites of overlap and sedimentation: where Louis XVI was executed now stands the symbol of Egyptian civilization, which in its transposed location is also a symbol of the history of French colonialism. As a result, the obelisk is not only heavy with its own ancient Egyptian history but also saturated by the weight of its new place in French culture.

In contrast, the Obelisk of Luxor laments that he is left in an antiquated Egypt, unappreciated, unnoticed, while the obelisk in Paris is surrounded by curious spectators who attempt to decipher the hieroglyphics carved into the stone:

> Là-bas, il voit à ses sculptures
> S'arrêter un peuple vivant,
> Hiératiques écritures,
> Que l'idée épelle en rêvant.
> (*Émaux et Camées* 76)
>
> Over there, he sees for his sculptures
> A living people stopping,
> Hieratic writings,
> That the idea spells through dreaming

Again, and this time to reinforce ideas of encryption and decipherment, Gautier uses the repetition of syllables and sounds to emphasize the archaeological aspects of the poem. The word "écriture" could be spelled phonetically with the letters in the word "hiératique," an encryption which underlines the ways in which writing is a site where words and letters are combined to both reveal and conceal. The only other words in the stanza which use the "é," are "épelle," meaning to spell, and "idée," which creates a synthesis of sound that joins the words for writing, hieratic, spelling, and thought. This syntactical structure is situated right next to the articulation of a hieroglyphic mode of reading where an idea is spelled through dreaming. A decipherment where understanding takes place within a dream evokes all of Gautier's archaeological fictions, where epiphany occurs through a subconscious reunion with or animation of the distant past. This concept of an urban population set into motion through reverie induced by decipherment is picked up again by H.D., who sees understanding of the archaic as taking place in the "dream parallel," and by the French surrealists, who perceive the world to be hieroglyphic, most explicitly in Louis Aragon's *Paris Peasant*, where the surrealists run across a column and make Champollion-like attempts to decode the "incomprehensibility and indecipherability of the cuneiform darkness" (179). The surrealists, in other words, apply the concepts of deciphering an Egyptian obelisk to an everyday monument inscribed in French. But it is Gautier who forges this idea of the Parisian crowd standing and decoding, attempting to grasp "[h]ieratic writings, / That the idea spells through dreaming."

The motif that is generally considered to hold *Enamels and Cameos* together, however, is not the archaeological but the sculptural. As Russell King notes, almost every poem in *Enamels and Cameos* contains at least one specific reference to sculpture, whether it be through statues, obelisks, marble, Carrara, or Paros (82). King further argues that the direct referencing of sculpture is reinforced through certain "stylo-linguistic" effects (84). For King, the way in which Gautier distances himself from the poems in *Enamels and Cameos* gives the poems an object-like status, an "impersonalized independence" where the "syntactical structures of each verse and each strophe organize themselves into regularized 'blocks' that suggest masonry" (85). This analysis reinforces the position that Gautier's leit-motifs are illustrated both through direct reference as well as through more occluded formal effects. But it would be wrong to suggest that the sculptural and the archaeological motifs are distinct. For Gautier, there is a strong set of correspondences between sculpting and exhumation in the sense that chipping away stone to reveal a statue is mirrored by the archaeologist's reclamation of statues from the earth. In this sense the archaeologist, belatedly, performs the same task as the original sculptor: removing a surplus to reveal the hidden aesthetic object. In combining these motifs in the poems of *Enamels and Cameos*, Gautier suggests a kind of poetic dialectic where the act of unveiling, of revealing inner form, becomes an intention that supersedes the literal acts of excavation and sculpting to become a mode or reflex appropriate to composition. This thematic nexus of archaeology, sculpture, and writing, with the associated affiliations of stone, emergence, removal and resurgence, is a complex of ideas that, as we will see, consistently recur in Pater, Pound, H.D., Olson, and the surrealists.

As a final point of analysis on the differences between Gautier's archaeological fictions and the archaeological resonance in his poetry, it is interesting to note the ways in which the poetry presents a shift in the gendering of the past and the nature of memory and desire. Where the narratives always present the past in the form of a curvaceous young woman, Gautier's poetic invocation of the sculptural aesthetic also draws on the homoerotic associations of ancient art. As for Winckelmann, antique sculpture opens the door to alternate forms of desire, which can safely be cited in the historic ideal. In "Contralto," Gautier evokes the completeness of the past through the description of the ancient sculpture, *Hermaphrodite Sleeping*:

> On voit dans le musée antique,
> Sur un lit de marbre sculpté,
> Une statue énigmatique
> D'une inquiétante beauté.
>
> Est-ce un jeune homme? est-ce une femme,
> Une déesse, ou bien un dieu?
> L'amour, ayant peur d'être infâme,
> Hésite et suspend son aveu.
> (*Émaux et Camées* 60)
>
> We see in the museum of antiquity,
> On a bed of sculpted marble,
> An enigmatic statue
> Of a worrying beauty.
>
> Is it a young man? Is it a woman?
> A goddess, or yet a god?
> Love, afraid of infamy,
> Hesitates and suspends its desire.

The statue, which had been exhumed from near the Baths of Diocletian shortly before 1620 and displayed in the Palazzo Massimo, presents an interpretational conundrum. Is the "enigmatic sculpture / [o]f a worrying beauty" male or female? Viewers, inscribed and prescribed by their own time, are thrown off balance by their inability to distinguish a gender and, therefore, to determine if the statue is an appropriate object of desire. This poem, more than any of Gautier's archaeological fictions, presents the possibility for an archaeological escape from social and sexual rules. In its ambiguity, the statue, like the past, is semi-obscured and indistinguishable, becoming a ready canvas for varied fantasies and projections.

In citing the body's ambiguous potential in an encounter with ancient art, Gautier employs the past as a screen for the projection of possibilities deemed immoral in his own time. In 1835, at the age of twenty-three, Gautier had published *Mademoiselle de Maupin*, a frank contemporary discussion of androgyny and bisexuality, to public outrage. Amid the young male narrator's meditations on his love for Théodore, the ambiguous figure who is in fact a woman disguised as a man, Gautier includes a passage on the *Hermaphrodite Sleeping*, the same statue that inspired "Contralto," highlighting the ways in which the statue's bodily dialectic enchants the viewer:

> For someone who worships form exclusively, can there possibly be a more pleasing state of uncertainty than the one you are thrown into upon seeing that ambivalent rear view and those legs which are so fine and strong that you don't know if they belong to Mercury about to take flight or Diana emerging from her bath? ... The belly is a little too flat for a woman, a little too round for a man, and the whole body has something vague and indeterminate about it which is very difficult to convey and which has the most peculiar attraction.
>
> (182)

Moving the description of this "pleasing state of uncertainty" into its present application, the narrator notes, "Théodore would be undoubtedly an excellent model for this type of beauty."

In opting to describe a similar state of uncertainty in "Contralto," while leaving the source in the ancient past, Gautier chooses to semi-reinter the hermaphroditic ideal that he excavated and brought to life in *Mademoiselle de Maupin*. In this sense, "Contralto" is the novel's double, operating on a subterranean, classical level, probing French morality on a much more subtle plane, retaining a position of social safety that the examination in *Mademoiselle de Maupin* precluded. A "peculiar attraction" arises from the immediacy of the relic, yet the thousands of years separating the viewer from the statue's context create a distancing effect which allows discussion to take place uncensored. The archaeological, in its abilities to usher the past forward, equally provides the mechanisms for a consideration at arm's length. This pattern of citation, emergence, and reburial would find many equivalents in the nineteenth-century aesthetic text, not least of all in the work of Walter Pater.

CHAPTER 3

The Aesthetics of Excavation: Walter Pater's Stratified Text

In the postscript to *Appreciations*, Walter Pater expresses a theory of romanticism which does not limit the romantic spirit to a particular time and place, but rather sees it as an archaic and imbedded impulse in culture which consistently returns under the right conditions:

> ... the romantic spirit is, in reality, an ever-present, an enduring principle, in the artistic temperament; and the qualities of thought and style which that, and other similar uses of the word *romantic* really indicate, are indeed but symptoms of a very continuous and widely working influence.
>
> (539)

For Pater, romanticism is not a peculiar or isolated phenomenon but part of a larger force or influence which finds its beginnings in Greek culture and re-emerges at particularly fertile moments in the history of art. This theory of cultural return which pervades Pater's oeuvre is, in this particular work, affiliated with a group of French writers: Stendhal, Hugo, Murger, and notably, as his name appears six times in the course of this short essay: Théophile Gautier.

On some counts Pater's interest in Gautier is unsurprising. Both were aesthetic critics and both, at various points, were proponents of *l'art pour l'art*. In poetic method as well, we can discern similarities, Gautier's sculptural/archaeological method of unveiling and revealing mirrored by Pater's view of the elimination of surplus as a precondition for the production of good art.[1] As John Conlon has observed: "Gautier appealed to Pater as

---

1 For Pater's views on surplus see *Appreciations*: "For in truth all art does but consist in the removal of surplusage, from the last finish of the gem-engraver blowing away

a conscious artist in search of *le mot juste* who had a predilection for the bizarre rendered into gemlike words" (85). Indeed, Pater's famous invocation of the "hard, gem-like flame" bears certain resemblances to the chiseled inflections of *Enamels and Cameos*. But Gautier's most important influence on Pater may have not been directly, but in exposing him to the theories of pagan return espoused by Heinrich Heine. Hence, in the Da Vinci essay, Pater suggests that Saint John's resemblance to the *Bacchus* in *Saint John the Baptist* hanging in the Louvre, "... set Théophile Gautier thinking of Heine's notion of decayed gods, who, to maintain themselves, after the fall of paganism, took employment in the new religion" (*The Renaissance* 75). It is on this point, the return of pagan sensuousness in art, that Pater and Gautier are most closely aligned and it is, therefore, fitting that in the romanticism essay Pater should perceive Gautier to be a central figure in the most recent wave of pagan cultural resurrection.

It is within this intellectual tradition of cultural revival, which for Pater is comprised of a chorus of voices as varied as Winckelmann, Coleridge, Wordsworth and Morris as well as the ancient Greeks and Renaissance artists, that Pater posits a "mind latent in nature, struggling for release, and intercourse with the intellect of man through true ideas" (*Appreciations* 437). The image of the "mind" in nature is at once expressive of Pater's animistic sense of the natural world as well as indicative of his belief in a latent human dynamical flux, which conceals itself beneath the surface of civilization. The idea of a deistic or human intelligence in nature, and more specifically, embedded in earth, runs throughout Pater's criticism and suggests an archaeological *mentalité* specific to his sympathies for the Hellenic ideal yet also relates to his apprehension of a subterranean antinomian force that would become central to the modern *geist*.

Pater's understanding of a "mind" "struggling for release" has clear affiliations with the Victorian era of Hellenic cultural disinterment, a period

---

the last particle of invisible dust, back to the earliest divination of the finished work to be, lying somewhere, according to Michelangelo's fancy, in the rough-hewn block of stone" (402).

The Aesthetics of Excavation

that literally sought to excavate the Greeks from the ground. As Carolyn Williams observes:

> Pater's own age was experiencing a second wave of the classical revival, more "scientific" than the Renaissance and provoked by archaeological findings that graphically demonstrated how much of the cultural past lay hidden beneath the surface of the earth. His modern sense of geographical strata hiding the impressions of the past (fossils of organic life pressed into rock, fragments of ancient sculpture in repose underground) is evident throughout *The Renaissance*.
>
> (161–2)

Williams' description of a culture "experiencing a second wave of the classical revival" usefully identifies Pater's place within a nineteenth-century archaeological context, where the Greek and Latin bent of Pater's Oxford, in particular, resulted in regular discussions of archaeological recoveries: Lord Elgin had brought the Panathenaic frieze to London early in the century, the Aegina marbles had been shipped from Greece in 1811 and Pater's beloved Venus of Melos had been uncovered by a Greek farmer in 1820 and purchased by the French government shortly thereafter. Moreover, while Schliemann did not attempt his first dig at Hissarlik until 1871, two years before the first edition of *The Renaissance* was published, speculation as to whether Homer's Troy could be archaeologically validated had been debated in English universities for decades.

Given Pater's place in the second classical revival, his obsessive interest in both the arts and hermeneutics of the Renaissance as well as the elusive ideal of Hellas and the archaeologically favorable climate of the university, it seems worthwhile to subject Pater's work to an investigative "subreading" for archaeological optics and overtones. This term belongs to Thomas Greene, who has suggested that within the Renaissance paradigm of disinterment, artworks themselves came to assume "subterranean outlines" and "emergent presences" (93). This template is fully at play in Pater's writing and the mind in nature represents the most important of these "emergent presences." Theories of poetic "possession" are another. The old gods and the idealized world of homosocial Greece constitute a third. Moreover, within Pater's style there is enough layering of sedimented meanings, concealments, and nostalgia for origins to make an excavational reading rewarding.

The difference between the classical revival in Pater's age and the classical revival of the Renaissance was, as Williams notes, a matter of science. Even between Gautier's romantic archaeological landscapes and Pater's late nineteenth-century ones, we can sense the ways in which the application of science had become more prominent in the popular imagining of archaeological processes. The type of underground reading that Greene proposes for unearthing archaeological themes in Renaissance production must be modified by considerations of cultural and temporal difference, science and technology when applied to the late Victorians. This is particularly important when speaking of Pater, who was deeply influenced by science and its advances, first through his readings as an undergraduate and later as an independent researcher. We will, therefore, begin by "subreading" Pater's scientific views conditioned and formulated in reaction to a nineteenth-century British context, before examining the ways in which Pater's imaginings of aesthetics, culture, and poetry contain echoes of an archaeological mode.

The "suspicion of a mind latent in nature, struggling for release, and intercourse with the intellect of man through true ideas, has never ceased to haunt a certain class of minds" (*Appreciations* 437). The quotation appears in the essay on Coleridge, and the approbatory if uncanny view of nature that Pater expresses here also extends to his appreciation for scientific study:

> For many years to come [literature's] enterprise may well lie in the naturalisation of the vocabulary of science ... for after all the chief stimulus of good style is to possess a full, rich, complex matter to grapple with. The literary artist, therefore, will be well aware of physical science; science also attaining, in its turn, its true literary ideal.
> (399)

The sympathetic and reciprocal relationship Pater envisages between science and "style" is in evidence in several passages of his own writing. In the famous "Conclusion," for example, it is science that gives rhetorical power to the brevity of existence: "What is the whole physical life in that moment but a combination of natural elements to which science gives their names?" (*The Renaissance* 150). Beyond the stylistic possibilities inherent in

The Aesthetics of Excavation

scientific discovery, many have suggested that nineteenth-century science shaped Pater's most significant contributions to aesthetic theory. Philip Appleman, for example, has persuasively argued that Pater's insistence on the subjective ("What effect does it really produce on me? Does it give me pleasure?") was influenced by Darwin and the events of 1859 (82). For Appleman, Pater's supposition that: "the philosophical conception of the relative has been developed in modern times through the influence of the sciences of observation" is a direct statement of the impact of evolutionary archaeological theory on Pater's most important critical stance. In a similar vein, Frank Turner suggests that Pater's grounding in science makes his scholarship much more vibrant than those of his predecessors, arguing that Pater's reading in geology, archaeology, and anthropology renders his Hellenism "far more complex, rich, and dynamic than that of Winckelmann, Arnold, and the Victorian critics of Greek art" (74).

Pater's integration of scientific precepts is certainly a pervasive if subtle characteristic of his prose style. In making his argument against the Arnoldian credo to "see the object as in itself it really is" on the first page of *The Renaissance*, for example, Pater not only suggests, as Appleman argues, that science inspires the "philosophical conception of the relative," Pater also borrows from the *vocabulary* of science to make his point:

> To define beauty, not in the most abstract but the most concrete terms, to find, not its universal formula, but the formula which expresses most adequately this or that special manifestation of it, is the aim of the true student of aesthetics.
> (1)

The use of the word "formula" here is almost unnerving in a passage devoted to the advancement of a pure aestheticism. But it is a trope that Pater continues as he progresses into the passage on art's effect on the individual:

> How is my nature modified by its presence, and under its influence? The answers to these questions are the original facts with which the aesthetic critic has to do; and, as in the study of light, of morals, of number, one must realise such primary data for one's self, or not at all.

Here, aestheticism is presented as a self-inflicted experiment, a careful observation of factors and reactions and the assiduous accumulation of "data." Aestheticism, Pater seems to be suggesting, is also a kind of science, the science of the beautiful – a subjective, reflective science of the self.[2]

While it is clear that Pater borrows from science to extend his knowledge, theoretical grasp and stylistic range, it is equally plain that Pater's vision of science is neither conventional nor restricted to the boundaries of observable fact. In Pater's scientific borrowings there is an alchemic quality – the addition of mystical elements and the rhythms of incantation. When Pater asks: "What is the whole physical life in that moment but a combination of natural elements?" (*The Renaissance* 150) it is with the knowledge that the reader has absorbed the tributes to supra-natural imagination in the preceding nine chapters of *The Renaissance*. Therefore, while Pater's aestheticism is presented in scientific terms, it is no less true that Pater's science is more than somewhat aesthetic – hence the reciprocal relationship Pater envisions between "style" and science's "true literary ideal."

Pater's scientific approach, then, is deliberately distinct from the nineteenth-century norm. Rather than fostering objectivity, science, for Pater, inspires a model of subjective relativism *in the arts*. Aestheticism is not a-scientific but a particular manifestation of science which finds its complement in science-as-aesthetic. The blurring of these categories is a direct challenge to nineteenth-century categorization and the professionalization of an archaeology that sought to transform "stories into histories" (Crane 187); typically for him, Pater refers to the historical to find a more integrated ideal of the spiritual and the material, the intellectual and the aesthetic. Not only does this ideal surface in the melding of artistry and science in passages on Da Vinci, for example, it also latently appears in Pater's multi-layered view of a science which is not simply a product of

---

2 In Pater's stance on a subjective understanding of the object, we begin to see the development of a pattern of archaeological thinking where the object is less important in and of itself than as the key to some subjective understanding of the inner workings of one's own mind and being. This posture would become particularly important to the French surrealists, whose reclamation of abandoned objects correlated with an inward-oriented pattern of recognition.

The Aesthetics of Excavation

rational methodology but the most recent manifestation of an ancient reverence for nature.

To understand science as distinct from an objective and progressive epistemological category, let alone as the inspiration of the subjective and the relative in aesthetic criticism, is odd if not outright rebellious in the context of the nineteenth-century ordering of knowledge. To this extent, Pater's definition of science is as subversive as the one he sympathetically assigns to Coleridge: "Science, the real knowledge of that natural world, is to be attained not by observation, experiment, analysis, patient generalisation, but by the evolution or recovery of these ideas directly from within, by a sort of Platonic 'recollection'" (*Appreciations* 437). The dynamics of this definition are fascinating; "science" is not a matter of outward observation but rather an inner directed reminiscence of an earlier ideal. This inner directed recovery is particularly resonant with Pater's idea of the buried mind. "Recollection" as a mode of scientific recovery also supposes latent information within the mind or in the earth, distant repositories of knowledge which can be animated through reconnection. More than a "literary ideal" the Coleridgean angle of Pater's science is the miraculous *rapprochement* of humanity and the mind in nature – a fusion that results in the uncovering and reactivation of lost knowledge. Indeed, science-as-recollection is less reminiscent of nineteenth-century disciplinary sciences than of the anecdote in *Appreciations* of the young student who visits Thomas Browne expecting Browne to demonstrate the chemical theory of "*Palingenesis*, resurrection, effected by orderly prescription" and turn an incinerated violet "to freshness, and smelling sweet again, out of its ashes, under some genially fitted conditions of the chimeric art" (485).[3]

This particular mystical quasi-scientific process is paradigmatic of Pater's archaeological imaginings. Archaeology, for Pater, involves not only the scientific unveiling of ancient objects but some kind of palingenic process of "recollection" where the past rises from its incinerated form to "freshness," whole and alive. Archaeological science uncovers the matter.

---

3   Thomas Browne was himself a writer and antiquary. See Chapter 6 of Schwyzer's *Archaeologies of Renaissance Literature*.

Art supplies the missing element that lifts lifeless remains to their former freshness or imaginatively restored state. The fusion of artistic temperament with the literal excavation of buried repositories or the metaphorically excavated scholarly fragment makes for unending combinations of recovered memory. The "chimeric art" as archaeology is neither pure art nor pure science but rather a blending – a scientifically based aestheticism which breathes life into dead worlds. The "remains" of Charles Lamb, Pater suggests, are "full of curious interest for the student of literature as a fine art" (457). But it is Pater's selections and additions to the Lamb essay that recreate a world and reactivate a life. Each of Pater's portraits is this kind of reconstruction, a careful reconstitution and reanimation of what is left behind, a tapping into the secrets of the buried mind.

In "Hippolytus Veiled," Pater presents his rationale for adding imaginative embellishment to the archaeologist's fragmented recoveries:

> Centuries of zealous archaeology notwithstanding, many phases of the so varied Greek genius are recorded for the modern student in a kind of shorthand only, or not at all. Even for Pausanias, visiting Greece before its direct part in affairs was quite played out, much had perished or grown dim – of its art, of the truth of its outward history, above all of its religions as a credible or practicable thing. And yet Pausanias visits Greece under conditions as favourable for observation as those under which later travellers, Addison or Eustace, proceed to Italy ... Had the opportunities in which Pausanias was fortunate been ours, how many haunts of the antique Greek life unnoticed by him we should have peeped into, minutely systematic in our painstaking! How many a view would broaden out where he notes hardly anything at all on his map of Greece!
>
> (*Greek Studies* 152)

The dismay in the last two sentences is almost palpable. "Had the opportunities in which Pausanias was fortunate been ours ..." but the gap of two thousand years to a time when these faint tracks were still perceptible has passed. What is left is a "kind of shorthand only" – available to the average reader only through translation into modern prose. For Pater, as for Gautier, these fragments do not stand on their own but require some kind of narrative reconstruction. The logic is straightforward: The threads that connect one civilization to another become more attenuated as time passes; the "shorthand," which is barely legible to the modern critic will eventually

The Aesthetics of Excavation

either fade away or become a kind of undecipherable hieroglyphic code. Therefore, while what "remains" is the student of literature and fine art's consolation, to flesh it out with imaginative detail is the critic's duty – a preventative measure against time's ongoing erasure of uncollected traces.

While the archaeological resonance of Pater's scientific-aestheticism is ascertainable faintly, as though emanating from a distant source, the excavational contours of his historicism are directly felt. Throughout *The Renaissance*, Pater alludes to "absorbed, underground" forces within culture, which lie dormant until they are rediscovered. The archaeological metaphor enables Pater to suggest a mode of historical progression which allows for the sudden re-apparition of latent forces: "With [Michelangelo] the beginning of life has all the characteristics of resurrection; it is like the recovery of suspended health or animation, with its gratitude, its effusion, and eloquence" (48). This paradoxically suggests that "beginnings" do not have their points of origin in the present but at some point in the remote past. Artistic development, here, is not elaborated in an organic metaphor of continuous growth, but rather through the recuperative strategies of the archaeologist. The "resurrection" or "recovery" is dependent on existing materials pressed beneath the earth, beneath conscious perception. Like the archaeologist, the artist can, in certain semi-divine moments, tap into a pre-existing culture and bring it to the surface of civilization.

While absorbed underground forces speak most pervasively of Pater's archaeological theories of cultural latency and recovery, the motifs of "survival" and "surfacing" are equally relevant. Wordsworth's "sympathetic animism," for example, is perceived to be the "survival" of an earlier feeling. The Wordsworth essay is a good example of Pater's sense of surviving elements in culture; for Pater, some of Wordsworth's best passages are the result of a "primitive condition" – "that mood in which the old Greek gods were first begotten, and which have many strange aftergrowths" (*Appreciations* 419). It is interesting to note that Heidegger associates a similar primitive condition with the poetic or "naming of the gods" and this is, essentially, Pater's point. For Pater, Coleridge's finer poetic passages, for instance, are produced when the "Greek mind ... [is] ... vibrating strongly in him" (437). This consistent resurfacing of the animistic spirit, which is the core of the poetic, presents itself for Pater in "successive periods by enthusiasts on the antique pattern." Set against the rationalizing principles of modernity, this kind of poetic knowledge "may ... [seem] paler and more fantastic amid the growing consistency and sharpness of outline of other ... forms of knowledge" as naming is now accomplished by other "more positive forms," the world a "combination of natural elements to which science gives their names" (*The Renaissance* 150). For Pater, however, it is always this primitive condition, the originary language, which is the heart of the poetic and which consistently returns under the right conditions: "wherever the speculative instinct has been united with a certain poetic inwardness of temperament ... there that old Greek conception, like some seed floating in the air, has taken root and sprung up anew" (*Appreciations* 437).

While Pater identifies the conditions under which this creative element of culture surfaces, he is less positive on the nature of the spirit itself. Primarily of "Greek" origin, it is also the core of the "romantic spirit" when romanticism (such as that of Gautier) is defined as a key element of the Renaissance and coincident with a thirst for beauty which can be traced back to Sophocles. In addition to the speculative instinct and poetic inwardness of the artist – which brings us back to the idea of science as "recollection" – the historical period must be one of those "special epochs" after "a long *ennui*, or in reaction against the strain of outward, practical things" (543). In other words, the surviving element only surfaces after prolonged periods of dormancy, such as in the Renaissance after the "dark ages" or, it would seem, during the romantic period after too harsh an insistency on neoclassical taste. This sense of cultural latency, of cultures existing within cultures, is consistent not only with the idea of the mind in nature but also with Pater's view of the old gods dwelling just beneath the surface, prepared to take up their place in the garment of a new culture under appropriate conditions.

This brings us back to Heine's notion of the decayed gods taking up employment in the new religion, a concept which Pater is believed to have first assimilated through Gautier.[4] Heine writes explicitly on this theme in *The Gods in Exile* and to an equally detailed extent in "Concerning the

---

4   See John Harrison's "Pater, Heine, and the Old Gods of Greece" (655).

History of Religion and Philosophy in Germany." The stance he adopts embraces the pre-Christian sensuousness of poetic possibilities and, consequently, decries the role of the church in suppressing the pleasures of the material:

> Christianity, unable to annihilate matter, has always denounced it. Christianity has degraded the noblest pleasures, the senses were forced to play the hypocrite, and the result was deceit and sin ... Thus, the immediate aim of all our new institutions is the rehabilitation of matter, its restoration to dignity, its moral recognition, its religious sanctification, its reconciliation with the spirit.
> (*The Prose Writings of Heinrich Heine* 148)

Despite the cultural dominance of the Christian faith and its enforcement of a period of creative "dormancy," there is for Heine a strong sense in which the old gods either dwell just beneath the surface of culture or, contrastingly, disguise themselves in elements of the new religion. Certainly, this train of thought would appeal to Pater, who sought to reinstate an appreciation of material culture to the level of spiritual valuation and never deviated from his belief in the supremacy of Greek art. Moreover, there are elements of Paterian thought which are very much aligned with the ethos propounded by Heine's "nature philosopher," the poet/idealist who:

> ... allies himself with the primitive powers of nature, can conjure up the demonic forces of ancient ... pantheism, and there awakens in him that lust for battle ... Christianity – and this is its finest merit – subdued to a certain extent that brutal Germanic lust for battle, but could not destroy it, and if some day that restraining talisman, the Cross, falls to pieces, then the savagery of the old warriors will explode again ... This talisman is decaying, and the day will come when it will sorrily disintegrate. The old stone gods will then arise from the forgotten ruins and wipe the dust of centuries from their eyes, and Thor will at last leap up with his great hammer and smash the Gothic cathedrals.
> (176)

Here, the resurrection of the gods necessarily involves the death of God – the medieval Christian ideal will perish as the mythological "old stone gods" reclaim their place as rulers of the human realm. In essence, Heine's metaphors promulgate the return of the pagan sensuousness and earth as opposed to a Christian valuation of pure spirit. Certainly, this heretical pagan impulse is present in Pater. As David DeLaura writes, however, Pater's "relation with Christianity varied significantly through the years, and the precise relationship in [his] work between the classical deposit and 'Christianity' fluctuates in important ways" (169). Pater's admiration for Pico della Mirandola's attempt to reconcile the Christian faith with pagan impulses, and to a certain extent Pater's own bid for Christian-pagan reconciliation in *The Renaissance*, in addition to a recurrent theme of the merging of the pagan and the Christian into a dialectically superior category, suggests a profound desire for an aesthetic that accommodates both the spiritual and the material.

In terms of the pervasiveness of Hellenism and its power to reassert itself in privileged cultural epochs, though, Pater's thinking does mirror Heine's credence in the endurance of the gods. Thus, in *The Renaissance*, Pater identifies the Hellenic force as "antinomian," the "rival religion" with its strange, cultic beauty:

> One of the strongest characteristics of that outbreak of the reason and the imagination, of that assertion of the liberty of the heart, in the middle age, which I have termed a medieval Renaissance, was its antinomianism, its spirit of rebellion and revolt against the moral and religious ideas of the time. In their search after the pleasures of the senses and the imagination, in their care for beauty, in their worship of the body, people were impelled beyond the bounds of the Christian ideal; and their love became sometimes a strange idolatry, a strange rival religion.
>
> (16)

For Pater, as for Heine, the "outbreak of the reason and the imagination" has far from died out. The old gods persist, if buried, as the "mind latent in nature, struggling for release, and intercourse with the intellect of man through true ideas" (*Appreciations* 437). The emphasis on "release" is particularly important in Pater, where a Christian orthodoxy is likened to repression and introversion while the classical pagan is linked to an exteriorizing expressionism, an archaeological vein of emergence versus submergence which persists in the writing of Pound and Stokes.

The idea of a surviving element, an old force struggling to find expression in the new, is most explicitly drawn in Pater's Michelangelo essay. It is

The Aesthetics of Excavation

also here that we find Pater's affinities for Gautier's equivalence of the sculptural and the archaeological. The creation of life which comes as "recovery" or "resurrection" is the channeling of old energies into new forms. Within Michelangelo's sculpture dwells the "brooding spirit of life," the "summer" which "may burst out in a moment," a force which struggles "for liberty" (*The Renaissance* 49). Pater ties Michelangelo's "survivals" into discussions of earth by dwelling on Michelangelo's love of the quarries of Carrara, meditating on "*live stone*" and, as the pre-eminent symbol of resurrection born of earth, mentioning the "morsel of uncut stone" on the "crown of the head of the *David*" as the "one touch to maintain its connexion with the place from which it was hewn." Here, we are particularly struck by Pater's attention to the material nature of sculpture, its connection to the ground in the one place where the stone is uncut. For Pater, much of Michelangelo's ability to maintain a "connexion" with antique forces is dependent on his sensuous appreciation of earth. In addition to a pagan sensualism, Pater also ascribes Michelangelo's empathy for the old gods and his ability to draw them from the stone to his own condition as a kind of ghost, a "*revenant*" lingering beyond his time (58). As an artist who must be approached "not through his followers, but through his predecessors" and as one who also believes in lingering souls, Michelangelo exists in a heightened condition which permits him to empathize with and carve out lingering spirits.

The idea of a latent pagan force existing within the earth or as Pater writes in the essay on style: "the ... divination of the finished work to be, lying somewhere, according to Michelangelo's fancy, in the rough-hewn block of stone" (*Appreciations* 402) is not an unfamiliar concept in literary modernism. Later, it is Ezra Pound who becomes a prime proponent of this idea of plasticity, of latent shapes existing in full form beneath the surface. In *Literary Essays*, in a piece on Cavalcanti, for example, Pound meditates on the idea of sculptural poetics:

> Out of these fine perceptions, or subsequent to them, people say that our Quattrocento, or the sculpture of the Quattrocento, discovered "personality." All of which is perhaps rather vague. We might say: The best Egyptian sculpture is magnificent plastic; but its force comes from a non-plastic idea, i.e. the god is inside the statue.
>
> I am not considering the merits of the matter, much less those merits as seen by a modern aesthetic purist. I am using historic method. The god is inside the stone,

vacuos exercet aera morsus. The force is arrested, but there is never any question about its latency, about the force being the essential, and the rest "accidental" in the philosophic technical sense. The shape occurs.

(*Literary Essays* 152)

"The god is inside the stone." "The shape occurs." Here, in one of the more radical treatise on the formation of modern art, Pound acknowledges the latent forces present in the rough material of the *objet-d'art*, forces, be they sculptural, archaeological, or poetic, which must win their way to the surface in order to achieve a fully released expressionism.

For Pater, like Gautier and Pound, then, the idea of the old gods dwelling under the earth, inside the stone, is not just a matter of sculpture but also the core of the poetic. The Michelangelo essay, after all, is called "The Poetry of Michelangelo" and the artistic process of excavation which Pater originally elaborates as a part of Michelangelo's masonry is extended to his literary production. Reading Michelangelo's sonnets is not just an exercise in appreciating, as with his sculpture, its outward strength but also in seeking an inward quality, "recovering, touch by touch, a loveliness" (*The Renaissance* 47) This tactile recovery of loveliness requires a mode of attentive reading where inner meaning unveils itself layer by layer: "Beneath the Platonic calm of the sonnets," Pater suggests, "there is latent a deep delight in the carnal form and colour" (52). This latent vibrancy, hidden in the prosaic exterior of the standard sonnet form, is, for Pater, the treasure of Michelangelo's poetry, its animation and connection to the "Greek mind." Here, Pater interpolates Michelanglo's use of language into a discourse of sculptural recovery. The core of the poetic, emerges, like Michelangelo's statues, as a "recovery" or "resurrection." The sculptor's stone, therefore, is not only emblematic of earth but also of language. For Pater, a writer's language "is no more a creation of his own than the sculptor's marble" (*Appreciations* 397).

The idea that a writer's language is not his own, that, in essence, no art truly belongs to or is generated by one person, is consistent with Pater's understanding of the tradition. In the essay on style, for example, Pater suggests that language itself is a "product of myriad various minds and contending tongues, compact of obscure and minute association ... abundant

The Aesthetics of Excavation

and often recondite" – laws which have been formed by the use of language over time. It is this sense of tradition as consistently operating on the present that gives Pater's work some of its most expressive archaeological resonance. For Pater, all good art is essentially a dense condensation of the history of art, each aesthetic object possessing within it a multi-layered accumulation of human thought and emotion. The most vivid illustration of this art of sedimented significance is, of course, the famous passage on the Mona Lisa:

> The presence that rose thus so strangely beside the waters, is expressive of what in the ways of a thousand years men had come to desire. Hers is the head upon which all "the ends of the world are come," and the eyelids are a little weary. It is a beauty wrought out from within upon the flesh, the deposit, little cell by cell, of strange thoughts and fantastic reveries and exquisite passions. Set it for a moment beside one of those white Greek goddesses or beautiful women of antiquity, and how would they be troubled by this beauty, into which the soul with all its maladies has passed! All the thoughts and experience of the world have etched and moulded there, in that which they have of power to refine and make expressive the outward form, the animalism of Greece, the lust of Rome, the mysticism of the middle age with its spiritual ambition and imaginative loves, the return of the Pagan world, the sins of the Borgias. She is older than the rocks among which she sits; like the vampire, she has been dead many times, and learned the secrets of the grave; and has been a diver in deep seas, and keeps their fallen day about her; and trafficked for strange webs with Eastern merchants; and, as Leda, was the mother of Helen of Troy, and, as Saint Anne, the mother of Mary; and all this has been to her but as the sound of lyres and flutes, and lives only in the delicacy with which it has moulded the changing lineaments, and tinged the eyelids and the hands. The fancy of a perceptual life, sweeping together ten thousand experiences, is an old one; and modern philosophy has conceived the idea of humanity as wrought upon by, and summing up in itself, all modes of thought and life. Certainly Lady Lisa might stand as the embodiment of the old fancy, the symbol of the modern idea.
>
> (*The Renaissance* 79–80)

Here we see Pater attempting to instill a collective sense through the aesthetic, beating down monadic isolation by releasing himself and his readers from the confines of the present moment into the imaginative realm of other ages through the act of writing. Throughout the passage, we sense Pater's ongoing archaeological tropes: the exteriorizing impulse of "beauty wrought out from within," the accumulation of the strange and rare: the "fantastic" and the "exquisite." Yet, in terms of formal effect, Pater exceeds himself in creating a densely sedimented site of historical significance: "All the thoughts and experience of the world," the "animalism of Greece, the lust of Rome, the mysticism of the middle age ... the return of the Pagan world, the sins of the Borgias" are layered one on top of the other. The painting is literally an embodiment of the "animated instant" Pater describes in "The School of Giorgione," the moment where: "all the motives, all the interests and effects of a long history, have condensed themselves, and which seem to absorb past and future in an intense consciousness of the present" (95). But in expressing this depth-charge of accrued tradition Pater himself creates a condensed, multi-layered, highly cadenced site of historical overlay. An accumulated history, "Lady Lisa" is paradoxically the sum of the ages and the symbol of the modern, and it is the texture of the writing as much as the history it invokes that creates a densely concentrated vision of the forces of the past acting on the present moment.

If Pater's metaphorical survivals, resurrections, and rhythmical incantations speak softly of a tonal *emprunt* from the archaeological field, then it is his penchant for literal exhumations which make it manifest. In *Pater and the French*, Conlon points to the exhumation theme as another of Pater's metaphors for the survival theory. It is to this end, Conlon argues, that Pater reproduced a tale from Infessura that J.A. Symonds had found in the course of researching his own study of the Renaissance. Within the legend we find the recurring archaeological trope of the resurrection of untouched pagan beauty, which can be retrieved and exist on the surface of everyday life:

> On the 18th of April 1485, a report circulated in Rome that some Lombard workmen had discovered a Roman sarcophagus while digging on the Appian Way. It was a marble tomb, engraved with the inscription, "Julia, daughter of Claudius," and inside the coffer lay the body of a most beautiful girl of fifteen years, preserved by precious unguents from corruption and injury of time. The bloom of youth was still upon her cheeks and lips; her eyes and mouth were half open, her long hair floated round her shoulders. She was instantly removed, so goes the legend, to the Capitol; and then began a procession of pilgrims from all quarters of Rome to gaze upon this saint of the old Pagan world. In the eyes of those enthusiastic worshippers her

The Aesthetics of Excavation 77

> beauty was beyond imagination or description; she was far fairer than any woman of the modern age could hope to be. At last Innocent VIII feared lest the orthodox faith should suffer by this new cult of a heathen corpse. Julia was buried secretly and at night by his direction, and naught remained in the Capitol but her empty marble coffin ... What foundation for the legend may really have existed need not here be questioned. Let us rather use the mythus as a parable of the ecstatic devotion which prompted the men of that age to discover a form of unimaginable beauty in the tomb of the classic world.
>
> (J.A. Symonds, qtd. in Conlon 76)

For Conlon, "[t]he story's importance for Pater is obvious; it calls to mind his reveries on the *Mona Lisa*, his references to Heine's 'old gods' and his interest of the old religion surfacing to the medieval and Renaissance ages" (77). Another interesting parallel is the similarity between this passage and Gautier's *The Mummy's Romance*: the corpse of a woman of unsurpassable beauty exhumed and found in perfect condition. This survival of the sensuous, unscathed emissary of the pagan world which can be accessed in some concrete, material form seems to be a myth that is repeated in archaeologically influenced literature. Somewhere, somehow, the past survives in "unimaginable beauty," not living, but still perfect and infinitely retrievable.

The tale also brings to mind the perfection of the concealed, a running motif in Pater's work, as evidenced by the consistent exaltation of the vision within. The mysterious and the arcane receive a higher valuation in Pater than that which is superficial or evident to the eye. Anthony Ward has noted Pater's "dissatisfaction with the present and, importantly, 'the *hiddenness* of perfect things' ... [a] taste for the arcane and mysterious which often provokes Pater into cloaking his meanings, into making it more ambiguous or inexplicit that the complexity of the subject matter demands" (133). In this elaboration on the attraction of the concealed, Ward notes Pater's habit of reinforcing a conceptual preference for the occluded with a stylistic mode of "cloaking his meanings" in veils of language. Yet in interesting himself in the gothic and the mysterious, Pater's archaeological paradigm also closely intersects with the romantics, and when attempting to elaborate on the exquisiteness of the strange unseen, Pater defers to Gautier's tribe and their "*bizarrie* of motive." After all, says Pater, it is:

> ... to minds in this spiritual situation, weary of the present, but yearning for the spectacle of beauty and strength, that the works of French romanticism appeal. They set a positive value on the intense, the exceptional; and a certain distortion is sometimes noticeable in them ...
>
> (*Appreciations* 545)

The desire for escape from the modern world is in evidence here – the sense that the strange and the arcane, the remote and the exotic, are the properties of a lost world. And, through some reciprocal relationship with the arcane, it is by reaching for the deeply buried impulse that the "shadow of approaching humanity" will gradually deepen, the "latent intelligence winning a way to the surface" (438).

If the truly wonderful and exotic is somehow a property of the lost world, however, the forbidden and the macabre also exist beneath the surface, frequently concealed in the depths of the text. When Ward equates Pater's nostalgia with a desire for "home," he also marks it as a final reconciliatory desire: "Death and 'home' often seem similar to him" (Ward 23) or as Pater himself expresses it: "It is with a rush of home-sickness that the thought of death presents itself" (*The Renaissance* 129). The longing for origins runs throughout Pater's texts, an impulse which Sophie Gilmartin describes as the Victorian need for "roots or solid foundation" (16) which manifests itself partly, as Gilmartin argues, in an obsession with pedigree and partly, as we see in Pater, in the melancholic realization that there is no return to a mythic point of origin, that the gap can never be bridged. Death, origins, and desire all linger beneath the surface of the Paterian text, the underworld accessed only through dense sedimentations, recesses where the underbelly of "exquisite" perfection is hidden.

This combination of longing for and the impossibility of achieving the Greek ideal find their culmination in the essay on Winckelmann. According to Pater, Winckelmann did not feel the gaps that separated Pater from the past:

> To most of us, after all our steps towards it, the antique world, in spite of its intense outlines, its perfect self-expression, still remains faint and remote. To [Winckelmann], closely limited except on the side of the ideal, building for his dark poverty "a house not made with hands," it early came to seem *more real* than the present. In the

> fantastic plans of foreign travel continually passing through his mind, to Egypt, for instance, and to France, there seems always to be rather a wistful sense of something lost to be regained, than the desire of discovering anything new.
>
> <div align="right">(<i>The Renaissance</i> 115, emphasis added)</div>

For Pater, Wickelmann's ability to emotionally and intellectually co-exist with the Greeks transcends temporal boundaries, an imaginative capacity that may extend from Winckelmann's direct contact with the archaeological ruins of lost dynasties. For Pater, working only with words except for his exposure to the remains stored in the Ashmoleon collection at Oxford, the past always exists as something "faint and remote." The veil in "Hippolytus Veiled" acts as a sort of hermeneutic key here, and Pater's experience is that the past always shimmers behind the veil of time, inaccessible if dimly perceptible. As we will later explore, Pater develops his aesthetic theory from the idea that the past *should* be remote, the boundaries of time left intact, that, in fact, to think differently is a form of self-delusion. It is not without envy, however, that Pater views Winckelmann's reification with Hellenism.

Pater's essay on Winckelmann in *The Renaissance* is, of course, somewhat oddly placed, a peculiar addition in the space of a volume otherwise devoted to Renaissance artists and their precursors. Yet the inclusion of Winckelmann is an important aspect of Pater's Hellenism and, more broadly, of his archaeological imagination. For Pater, Winckelmann's ability to transcend the barriers of time was not so much an intellectual feat or one of willed self-delusion so much as a particular manifestation of character:

> That his affinity with Hellenism was not merely intellectual, that the subtler threads of temperament were woven in it, is proved by his romantic, fervent friendships with young men. He has known, he says, many young men more beautiful than Guido's archangel. These friendships, bringing him in contact with the pride of human form, and staining his thoughts with its bloom, perfected his reconciliation to the spirit of Greek sculpture.
>
> (123)

Here, it is Winckelmann's "temperament" which brings him into alignment with the Greek ideal, a temperament directly affiliated with a predisposition for intense friendships with men. The sense of recollection that permeates Pater's writing is here subliminally linked to the memory of a time when homo-sensual behaviors went uncensored. For Pater, Winckelmann "seems to realise that fancy of the reminiscence of a forgotten knowledge hidden for a time in the mind itself" (125). The apologia for Winckelmann's preferences at the end of the essay not withstanding, Pater's elaboration of Winckelmann's affinity for Greek art as a matter of character and temperament are as close as Pater ever comes to directly declaring his own preference for a homoerotic domain, an expression which is, nonetheless, occluded by the citation of these preference in another person (Winckelmann) or another time (Classical Greece). Within the circulating meaning of Pater's passages on Winckelmann, archaeological metaphors figure prominently, perhaps more persistently than in the rest of *The Renaissance*. Richard Dellamora observes, "Winckelmann's erotic affinity with the classical past enabled him to bring its culture, then being quite literally uncovered at Herculaneum and Pompeii, to life again" (52). Pater, too, directly acknowledges archaeological repositories as the site of Winckelmann's artistic and personal realizations, citing the moments where Winckelmann gains greatest insight into Greek art as a time when "Pompeii had just opened its treasures; Winckelmann gathered its first-fruits" (*The Renaissance* 125). But it is in the Winckelmann chapter, too, that Pater refers to the "buried fire of ancient art" rising up "from under the soil" (118) and to an "absorbed, underground life" (123). Like a classical text, the archaeological site is, for Pater, a space for the displacement of the self, a place to engage in a hidden or buried set of terms that are vicariously pursued. In the distant past, Pater seems to project a legitimized homosocial mode, a Hellenic landscape, which like one of Giorgione's paintings becomes a "country of the pure reason or half-imaginative memory" (87). This complex dynamic of overt aesthetic and covert personal interest in the resurrection of Greece is deeply ingrained in Pater's writing and strongly contributes to a convection of surface and concealed meanings within the texts themselves.

While Pater's naturalization of archaeological concepts influences aspects of his style, approach, and subject matter, there are also ways in which Pater is also vehemently anti-passéism. In contrast with the embracing attitude Pater adopts toward Winckelmann's fevered attachment to the

Hellenic mode, Pater deliberately rejects any kind of historicism affiliated with the object-mongering figure of the antiquarian. For Pater, antiquarian historicism is to fetishize the musty remnants of the past without evoking the aesthetic world to which they belong. In "Aesthetic Poetry," Pater suggests that the proper approach to the past is to "throw it up into relief" and examine a given historical period through the lens of distance that separates past from present, in other words, to dig up past worlds while still retaining cognizance of the sedimentations of earth and meaning that separate disparate historical existences: "anything in the way of an actual revival must always be impossible ... to come face to face with the people of a past age, as if the Middle Age, the Renaissance, the eighteenth century had not been, is as impossible as to become a little child, or enter again into the womb and be born" (*Appreciations* 526). Despite the nostalgic tenor of much of Pater's writing, which suggests he had at times desired all three of these transformations, as a critic he insists that the "actual revival" is impossible. The acknowledgement of the impassable chasm between past and present in many senses makes Pater a transitional figure in archaeological thought. In Gautier, we see characters moving freely into the past through the vehicle of the subconscious. For Pater, however heated the impression of antiquity may be and however freely the conversations between great minds may continue through art, the actual reinstatement of the past in the present is impossible due to the layered sedimentations separating one epoch from the next.

Pater repeats the theme of anti-antiquarianism through many of his writings. In "Two Early French Stories" Pater suggests that: "To say of an ancient literary composition that it has an antiquarian interest, often means that it has no distinct aesthetic interest for the reader of to-day" (*The Renaissance* 12). Here, Pater is opposing a dry antiquarianism with the bringing-to-life of fragments represented by "aesthetic" criticism. The archaeological approach that aestheticism represents is, therefore, antithetically opposed to the morbidity of an earlier antiquarian interest. Likewise, Pater demonstrates a marked dislike for the museum; thus, in the portrait of Browne, Pater likens Browne's unhygienic fantasy of death with the atmosphere of the museum space: "A museum is seldom a cheerful place – oftenest induces the feeling that nothing could ever have been young;

and to Browne the whole world is a museum" (*Appreciations* 474). For Pater, Browne's redemption lies in his "wonderful genius for exquisitely impassioned speech," which elevates these dusty remnants of the dead to a "miraculous saintly" ardency. The museum, dry and dull, fails to reassert the animation of its objects. Hence Pater's empathy for Joachim du Bellay, who sees literature written in Greek and Latin with presumptuous disdain for the "vulgar" tongue as "relics which one may only see through a little pane of glass, and must not touch with one's hands" (du Bellay, qtd. in *The Renaissance* 103). This repressed antiquarianism is perceived within the Paterian text as both unhygienic and undesirable, a historical method that lacks the reanimating qualities of palingenesis and is antithetical to archaeological and aesthetic routes of imagining. In Pater, the aura of introversion circulates around the figure of the antiquarian, a repressed force which contradicts a more natural and sensuous expressiveness.

In this sense, Pater's views on antiquarian historicism are reminiscent of Nietzsche's. To say so seems like an outright contradiction. As Williams remarks, Pater's "ruthful remembering may ... be seen as a nostalgic opposite of Nietzsche's 'ruthless forgetting'" (167). And yet, on the subject of antiquarianism, there seems to be some commonality between the two. In Nietzsche's formulation of the three approaches to history – monumental, antiquarian, and critical – the antiquarian method belongs to the "person who preserves and admires" (10). This seemingly admirable trait quickly degenerates. Soon, the antiquarian, whom Pater describes as arbitrarily substituting himself for the soul of the historical, for Nietzsche indulges in the delusion of an "instinctively correct reading of ... erased and reused parchments (which have, in fact been erased and written over many times)" (14). According to Nietzsche, this misguided identification with the past escalates into a maniacal passion where the antiquarian's "possession of his ancestors' goods changes the ideas in such a soul, for those goods are far more like[ly] to take possession of his soul." Moreover, Pater's muted passages on unhealthy obsessions with the past resonate with Nietzsche's condemnations of the antiquarian:

The Aesthetics of Excavation 83

> Then we get a glimpse of the wretched drama of a blind mania for collecting, a restless compiling together of everything that ever existed. The man envelops himself in a mouldy smell. With the antiquarian style, he manages to corrupt a significant talent, a noble need, into an insatiable new lust, a desire for everything really old. Often he sinks so deep that he is finally satisfied with that nourishment and takes pleasure in gobbling up for himself the dust of biographical rubbish.
>
> (16)

While Pater is the much more nostalgic of the two writers, there is nonetheless a correspondence between them in the rejection of both a complete identification with the past and with too passionate a consumption.

If Pater rejects the model of passionate antiquarianism, however, he is nonetheless attuned to a different, positive sort of overcoming: the past's possession of the poet. Here we might look to a different philosophical text, "Hölderlin and the Essence of Poetry" for an elaboration of this theme. For Heidegger, man's affirmation of his belonging "to the earth" (565) is concretized through poetic language, the "naming of the gods" (568). Heidegger's view that poetry is the "essence" of language points to the poetic as a point of origin. In this analysis, Heidegger proceeds to bring up the question of communication with the gods, whose naming is the inception of language, thought, being, and the essence of the poetic. The answer comes as a surprising form of possession of the poet-intermediary, who interprets the "signs" "from antiquity" which are "the language of the gods" into poetic speech: "The speech of the poet is the intercepting of these signs, in order to pass them on to his own people." For Heidegger, the poet "stands between gods and men" and is "exposed to divine lightnings."

For Pater, too, the poetic emerges both as a point of origin and a source of "mania," a materially, archaeologically derived force. This connection is most clearly elaborated in the Wordsworth essay, where Wordsworth's use of the "unconscious mysticism of the old English language ... and the not wholly unconscious poetry of the language" of "the simplest people under strong excitement" is a demonstration of "language ... at its origin" (*Appreciations* 415). Here we see poetry as "the primitive language of a historical people" – "the simplest people" resorting to the poetic, or to the gods, to explain the world around them. Wordsworth himself, however, is not portrayed as one of these spontaneously poetic people. In fact, much of Pater's essay focuses on the weak and prosaic elements of Wordsworth's verse. Those lines in which Wordsworth demonstrates poetic genius, Pater suggests, are composed in the moments when he is "taken over" by some other force:

> ... the mixture of his work, as it actually stands, is so perplexed, that one fears to miss the least promising composition even, lest some precious morsel should be lying hidden within – the few perfect lines, the phrase, the single word perhaps, to which he often works up mechanically through a poem, almost the whole of which may be tame enough. He who thought that in all creative work the larger part was *given* passively, to the recipient mind, who waited so dutifully upon the gift, to whom so large a measure was sometimes given, had his times also of desertion and relapse; and he was permitted the impress of these too to remain in his work. And this duality there – the fitfulness with which the higher qualities manifest themselves in it, gives the effect in his poetry of a power not altogether his own, or under his control, which comes and goes when it will, lifting or lowering a matter, poor in itself; so that the old fancy which made the poet's art an enthusiasm, a form of divine possession, seems almost literally true of him.

"A form of divine possession" – Pater elaborates on this theme as one of Plato's two higher forms of "divine" mania with an "incidental insanity" which follows a "vivid poetic anthropomorphism ... [an] almost grotesque materializing of abstractions." This phenomenon of momentary poetic overcoming is reminiscent of Benjamin's "*profane illumination* – a materialistic, anthropological inspiration" ("Surrealism" 209). The primacy of the material here in forms of "divine possession" emphasizes both the concrete nature of the poetic as well as the animistic force from which it seems to derive. "Survivals" from an earlier age, in Pater, are not always latent forces; at times they are active inhabitants of the present, particularly in the minds of artists where "bold trains of speculative thought" encounter "venturesome, perhaps errant, spirits" (*Appreciations* 423).

"Divine possession" is perhaps the closest Pater comes to modernist appropriations of archaeology where primal energies are extracted to replace the outworn models of the present. The idea of the zeitgeist, which appears repeatedly in Pater, is also conspicuous in the work of modernists compelled by ideas of perpetual personality or virtù, notably Pound. According to Wendell Harris: "Retrospective *zeitgeists* are reconstructions of an earlier spirit known through fragmentary evidence" (173). This definition permits us to understand how the archaeological artifact might function within *fin-de-siècle* culture as the "fragmentary evidence" of earlier spirits. Certainly in Pater the Hellenic impulse reappears as a *force* more than as a memory, which is evidenced by survivals, surfacing, and possessions.

The idea of possession by earlier spirits brings Pater into closer contact with Ruskin and later, as we will see, with the modernists than we would generally expect. A similarity exists between Ruskin and Pater's archaeological reconstitution of their chosen epochs; in *The Stones of Venice* Ruskin extracts the character traits of the builders from a "dramatic presentation of fragments" (Austin 1) and in *The Renaissance* Pater draws complete "portraits" of the artist from miniscule details of art. Despite their disparate critical approaches, moreover, both believe the spirit of past ages acts on the modern milieu. The zeitgeists they invoke are primitive forces of earlier epochs – be it "the strange *disquietude* of the Gothic spirit" – "that restlessness of the dreaming mind, that wanders hither and thither among the niches, and flickers feverishly around the pinnacles, and frets and fades in labyrinthine knots and shadows along wall and roof, and yet is not satisfied, nor shall be satisfied" (Ruskin 383) or the demanding paganistic impulses of Hellenism – the "spirit of rebellion and revolt" (*The Renaissance* 16) a "taste for what is *bizarre* or *recherché* in landscape" (71), the "buried fire" of ancient energies (118).

In desiring to connect with primal intensities or in believing that good art is a kind of channeling of these archaic energies, Pater and Ruskin prefigure modern invocations of the archaeological. Frances Connelly, in one of remarkably few articles that make the connection between the nineteenth-century zeitgeist and twentieth-century primitivism, notes that Ruskin's medievalism bears a striking resemblance to modern usages of ancient intensities. For Connelly:

> The arguments developed by nineteenth century advocates, the call for the rejuvenation of artistic expression, for feeling over beauty, for the relativism of stylistic expression, anticipated those advanced for primitivism in modern art decades later. It is those arguments made for the "primitive" in medieval imagery which move the definition of medievalism beyond a limited historical revival, and locate it at the inception of a significant shift from the classical to the modern.
>
> (184)

According to Connelly, "primitive" is not so much a matter of "specific styles" as "fundamental visual elements, such as the grotesque" (182). However, it might be added that it is not only just a matter of visual elements but of function – the retrospective force, whatever it may be, which seeks to purge contemporary models and act as a "youthful antidote" (181).

The Paterian zeitgeist presents itself in this form as well; the recurring spirit, the "survival," is not a benign presence but rather the "spirit of rebellion and revolt against the moral and religious ideas of the time" (*The Renaissance* 16). In Pater's archaeological recoveries we sense not only retrospective portraiture but also the advancement of the "rival religion" – a tapping into the primal energies of the Renaissance in order to perpetuate "strange" and wonderful "aftergrowths" (48). Through the language of science and the spirit of aestheticism, Pater's own mind struggles with the mind in nature and presses for its release. What endures in Pater's criticism is the belief that the spirit of Greek animism and the old poetic gods will continue to erupt through the sedimentations of modernity.

CHAPTER 4

Dream, Delusion, and Dynamite: Freud as Literary Trace

> Freud re-created the classical world. The colonial Third World was not there. There was no Africa, Brazil, or America. What is remarkable here is the absence of the Third World when compared to other revolutionary studios at the turn of the century. Picasso's studio in Paris at the same time was filled with African masks and artifacts from around the world. In Freud, the new Third World doesn't exist except in the residues of cocaine and the mention of a chocolate bar in a dream or in the dust that covers his office like the fog coming off the Niger in Conrad's *Heart of Darkness*. Add these elements into the scheme and the part the proper Viennese landscape played in ordering the mapping of the unconscious is exposed. Freud was part of that landscape in what he experienced, how he dressed, and how he marked his patients. Rearrange his marks and Freud himself is uncovered as another landscape, another layer of marking.
>
> (Shelton 306)

In a footnote from "The Mark on the Spade," Allen Shelton provides this topography of Freud's intellectual landscape in late nineteenth-century Vienna: Freud "marking" and being "marked" by a climate of neo-classicism. As Shelton suggests, the "new Third World" appears only by association, while the true finds of Freud's study are his prized collection of Greek, Roman, Near-Eastern and Chinese antiquities. The unconscious that Freud "discovered" was not nestled among the primal war masks of Oceania, but in a statuette of Athene. Consequently, the archaeology Freud used to define and structure the mind was the excavation of Greek reason: remote but not foreign, not Pater's return of a rival religion, not Picasso's resuscitation of ancient energies, but a reclamation of origins through a return to "rationality."

The citation of the rational as a property of the past positions Freud in opposition to the other writers studied here. The forces Freud seeks to usher into the present are not the sensuous paganism of Gautier, the antinomian spirit of Pater, the mythological energies of Pound, or the disruptive intensities of the surrealists. If, for Freud, the substratum of the mind is the dwelling place of some irrational quality, it is a quality that he seeks to realign, cure, or expel. Perhaps this difference is what marks Freud as a scientist rather than an artist. Despite, or perhaps because of this difference, Freud is an interesting candidate for archaeological analysis. Like Gautier, the relationship between archaeology and dreams is important to Freud. Like Pater, Freud perceives archaeology to be an appropriate structural expression for creative production. Yet for Freud, archaeology is always a means to reason, an excavation of the unsettling that will return the patient to normalcy. Despite this difference in emphasis, Freud occupies a central position in the development of artistic archaeological modalities. In Chapter 5 we will explore how Ezra Pound rejects this interiorized archaeology in favor of a social template and how Adrian Stokes and H.D. operate between the two models. In Chapter 6, we will see how the surrealists accept Freud's archaeological formation of the mind, while rejecting anything resembling a return to the undisturbed surface. Despite these later modifications, Freud's identification of a subterranean realm dwelling within us all is one of the most powerful expressions of archaeological dynamics, an imaginative model that would create a new stratigraphic understanding of the interiorized realm.

Freud's archaeological moment offers us a context for one of the most pervasive metaphors in psychoanalysis. As Sandra Bowdler notes, Freud lived the archaeological epoch from its beginning to its fruition: "When he was born in 1856, Troy was a myth and looting ancient treasures was a profitable business; at the end of his life, in 1939, archaeology was a science, and national archaeological museums had been established in many ancient cities, including Cairo and Athens" (420). More than once Freud proclaimed that he had read more archaeology than psychology, and while this was an exaggeration his bookshelves were full of texts on ancient civilizations and recent finds including: "Heinrich Schliemann's *Ilios, Mykenai, and Tiryns*, Wilhem Dorpfeld's *Troja und Ilion*, Sir Arthur Evan's account of his work at Knossos, *The Palace of Minos*, and the world-famous discovery by Howard Carter, *The Tomb of Tut-Ankh-Amen*" (Botting and Davies 185). Freud never participated in an archaeological excavation. Like Gautier, his archaeology is fundamentally an imaginative one. However, like thousands of other members of the European bourgeoisie, Freud toured the sites of Greece and Rome, collected with passion, and imaginatively partook in the archaeological adventure through the gateway of the text.[1] Also like Gautier, we can speculate that it was this textual mediation which caused Freud to understand archaeology in particular ways and to ingrain textuality and literariness into the fabric of his archaeological imagination. Taken as a whole, Freud's archaeology emerges as the site of sustainable contradiction, a matrix of coalescing forces and spatio-temporal dynamics that are elaborated through a series of metaphorical and metonymic associations. Despite the fact that Freud's multi-faced use of the archaeological topos shifts in significant ways, it is consistently underwritten by an attention to composition itself, a text driven archaeology that would have distinctive resonance for modernist writers working from his excavational templates.

Freud was not the first to turn to archaeology to explain the mind's mechanisms. Pierre Janet, who first coined the term "subconscious," attempted to classify hysterical symptoms according to their depth (*profondeur*) and developed a five-tiered model of the stratified mind. A similar

---

1   Freud's archaeological tendencies have not gone unexamined in more contemporary criticism. Three volumes of essays have appeared in the last twenty years (*Sigmund Freud and Art* (Eds Lynn Gamwell and Richard Wells, 1989), *Le Sphinx de Vienne: Sigmund Freud, l'art et l'archaéologie* (Eric Guble, 1993), and *Excavations and their Objects* (Ed. Stephen Barker, 1996), though Suzanne Bernfeld published "Freud and Archaeology" in *American Imago* in 1951. Academic conferences have been devoted to the subject and the museum of Freud's London home at Maresfield Gardens prominently exhibits his antiquities. In short, the propagation and replication of Freud's archaeological *mentalité* has become a fundamental part of Freudian discourse – an archaeo-echo that continues to resound through contemporary psychoanalytic theory.

mapping has been attributed to Jean-Martin Charcot. And in 1901 Henri Bergson declared that: "to explore the unconscious, to work in the subterranean of the mind with especially adequate methods, this will be the main task of psychology in the opening century" (qtd. in Ellenberger 321). Furthermore, in illustrating that "dreams have at their command memories which are inaccessible to waking life" (13) in "The Scientific Literature Dealing with the Problems of Dreams," Freud draws from several academic studies which allude to an archaeo-structuring of the mind, including this 1877 quote from Strumpell:

> The position is even more remarkable when we observe how dreams sometimes bring to light, as it were, from beneath the deepest piles of debris, under which the earliest experiences of youth are buried in later times, pictures of particular localities, things or people, completely intact and with all their original freshness.
>
> (15)

There is an interesting parallel here between Strumpell's perception of a dream bringing an event back to life, with all of its "original freshness" and Pater's commentary on Browne's reputation for returning a dead object "to freshness ... out of its ashes, under genially fitted conditions of the chimeric art" (*Appreciations* 485). The wording suggests a similar pathway of thought, a passageway of ideas leading to the idea that culture, memory, or objects can be resurrected from psychic debris. Freud is also operating in this mode when he highlights Binz's view that dream images emerge from the "remote and almost extinct past" ("The Scientific Literature Dealing with the Problems of Dreams" 19).

If Freud was not the first to employ the archaeological metaphor he was the most appreciative of its imaginative appeal for his generation. Donald Kuspit writes: "Freud's appeal to archaeology can be regarded as an effort to ingratiate psychoanalysis with society – to win its approval and trust, to gain an influential place in it – and even to have some of the heroic quality associated with archaeology rub off on psychoanalysis" (134). As an intuitive reader of his own culture's narratives, Freud recognized that coding psychoanalysis in archaeological terms made analysis both familiar and palatable; in addition, archaeology lent the mind's indefinable mechanisms a visual equivalent. As Sabine Hake suggests: "The archaeological metaphor makes visible the invisible, structures the seemingly unstructured ... Its visual qualities increase his readers' ability to imagine and comprehend, and its historical significance validates (at least at the time of Freud) their cultural preferences as members of the educated middle class" (149–50). To elaborate on Hake's point, for Freud archaeology operated on the one hand as a kind of "visual aid" for psychoanalytic discussion, a popular imaginative template that enabled understanding through tangible representation. On the other, archaeology provided a veiled consolidation of middle class education, taste and values, an echo of the Homeric norm of the gentleman's education, a standardizing element which might buffer the shock waves his theories of sexuality would generate. This double-hook of clarifying and *class*ifying now strike us as a standard in advertising; in Freud's case, archaeology was very successful advertising for a relatively new and unknown science.

If scholars can agree on Freud's popular motivations for archaeological adoptions, however, it is nearly impossible to garner a consensus on what archaeology means in the Freudian text. Debates over the implications of surface and depth, the sexual dynamics of digging, and the metaphorical nature of the archaeological analogy itself have thrown into question the legitimacy of the archaeological paradigm for considerations of the mind. In terms of memory and meaning, a discussion which holds particular interest for literary considerations of Freud's archaeology, the debate revolves around Freud's apprehension of the interpretive nature of mnemonic "recovery." For some, the archaeological metaphor represents the nineteenth-century positivist view that memory can be recovered and interpreted according to its original structures. For others, it is precisely the subjective activity of *reconstruction* and an awareness of interpretation and language that make the pursuit of archaeological traces in Freud relevant to the post-modern condition.

In general, critics who believe the recovery of ancient objects is too pat a comparison for the complexities of recovering human memory refer to Freud's archaeologically influenced section in "Civilization and its Discontents." Here, Freud addresses the "problem of preservation in the sphere of the mind" (720). Contrary to popular belief, Freud states, forgetting is not synonymous with the destruction of the memory trace. Rather, Freud adopts "the opposite view, that in mental life nothing which has been formed can perish." Freud illustrates this assertion by asking the reader to engage in a rather unusual mental exercise – imagining that various stages of Roman history are not successive states of human habitation but "a psychical entity" and that all of these historical structures are present at the same time: the *Roma Quadrata*, the *Septimontium*, "the city bounded by the Servian wall," "all the transformations during the periods of the republic and the early Caesars," "the city which the Emperor Aurelian surrounded with his walls" (726). Through this example, Freud attempts to illustrate the intangible and demonstrate that in memory "nothing that once came into existence will have passed away and all the earlier phases of development continue to exist alongside the latest one."

It is this idea that "nothing ... will have passed away" which evokes contemporary skepticism. Donald Spence has written that archaeological-psychoanalysis promotes the false "idea that the pieces of the past remain intact and can be recovered unchanged" (146). Similarly, Hake notes that Freud's model fails to address issues of deterioration:

> In the unconscious, there exists no process comparable to natural decay. The childhood experience, whether it falls prey to forgetting or takes on different shapes in the memory, lives on unchanged, as if in a vacuum. Only its "excavation" (if one wanted to continue in the spirit of the archaeological metaphor), its bringing into the light of day, puts an end to this eternity of the past and can (but must not) lead to an irreversible process of decay.
>
> (154)

"Intact" – "unchanged" – the words that repeat in these critiques question Freud's apparent assumption of mnemonic stability, its lack of distortion, and probe the legitimacy of archaeological terrain for psychoanalytic structure.

By contrast, in "The Ruins of Memory: Archaeological Fragments and Textual Analysis," Eugenio Donato argues that Freud's archaeological analogy is precisely focused on the subjective act of reconstruction. According to Donato's interpretation of Freud's archaeology:

Dream, Delusion, and Dynamite 93

> Consciousness, then, is continuous with itself neither temporally nor spatially. The past of an individual does not allow itself to be apprehended as simple, immediate, transparent, or total presence. The past as memory remains buried and ruined, a well inhabited by fragments incapable of presenting themselves to the light of memory without the elaborate machinery of linguistic constructions and representations.
>
> (575)

Donato claims that Freud is fully aware of the elaborate mechanisms of reconstruction required to bring fragments to the surface of consciousness and interpretively piece them back together – the antithesis of the objections lodged by critics who believe Freud is presenting a changeless, entombed approach to the mnemonic fragment.

This difference in opinion rests partly on the inattention to Freud's own statements disclaiming the validity of archaeological modes of perception and partly on the choice of texts. To address the first issue, of the disclaimer, Freud's Roman history analogy ends with an unusual twist – a frustrated proclamation of the analogy's inadequacies:

> There is clearly no point in spinning our phantasy any further, for it leads to things that are unimaginable and even absurd. If we want to represent historical sequence in spatial terms we can only do it by juxtaposition in space: the same space cannot have two different contents. Our attempt seems an idle game. It has only one justification. It shows us how far we are from mastering the characteristics of mental life by representing them in pictorial terms.
>
> ("Civilization and Its Discontents" 727)

Here, Freud is much more critical than his critics. At its limit, the metaphor crumbles into the "unimaginable" or "absurd." Rather than providing an exact replica of the structure of the mind, the attempt to "represent historical sequence in spatial terms" highlights the very impossibility of concrete analogies, including those related to archaeology. At the end of the day, the archaeological metaphor does not provide flawless representation but rather underlines the opposite truth: it "shows us how far we are from mastering the characteristics of mental life by representing them in pictorial terms."

This keen awareness of the limits of pictographic representation and the reconstructive act of literary transcription are also central to "Constructions in Analysis," which is the text Donato chooses in order to elaborate his theory of Freud's reconstructive awareness. Thus, Donato is able to suggest that central to Freud's argument is the fact that memory fragments are "incapable of presenting themselves ... without the elaborate machinery of linguistic constructions" because this is the very facet of archaeology that Freud emphasizes in his writing on the "construction" side of psychoanalysis:

> The analyst has neither experienced nor repressed any of the material under consideration; his task cannot be to remember anything. What then *is* his task? His task is to make out what has been forgotten from the traces which it has left behind or, more correctly, to *construct* it.
>
> ("Constructions in Analysis" 258–9)

Rather than employ the archaeological metaphor in order to celebrate the successes of analytic recovery, Freud invokes the figure of the archaeologist to demonstrate the problematic position of the analyst. Neither professional uncovers the "whole story" with his finds but, rather, must create a narrative from fragmentary evidence. Both, according to Freud, "reconstruct by means of supplementing and combining the surviving remains" and "both ... moreover, are subject to many of the same difficulties and sources of error" (259). It is, therefore, the responsibility of both the archaeologist and the analyst not to "omit ... to mention in each case where the authentic parts end and ... constructions begin" ("Fragment of an Analysis of a Case of Hysteria ('Dora')" 41).

Despite the admission of the limits of the archaeological metaphor in "Civilization and its Discontents," Freud explicitly professes the indestructibility of the memory trace. Conversely, in "Constructions in Analysis," the recuperation of memory is likened to the process of the archaeologist searching for sense and logic in fragments irretrievably damaged and charred. The dialectical ideal that both includes and transcends these models is one that turns on the image of the archaic text. In "A Note Upon the 'Mystic Writing-Pad,'" Freud compares the perceptual systems of memory to the child's toy – more commonly referred to today as "The Magic Pad" – a writing device that consists of a piece of waxed paper laid over a transparent sheet and secured to a wax slab. The benefit of this device for children

Dream, Delusion, and Dynamite

is that it never runs out – lift the piece of celluloid and the image that has been inscribed on it with a pointed writing utensil disappears, ready for a new masterpiece. To this extent, the surface of the pad, for Freud, resembles consciousness – the "flickering-up and passing-away ... in the process of perception" (231). However, the mystic pad also possesses another layer, invisible to the eye on the object's surface:

> But it is easy to discover that the permanent trace of what was written is retained upon the wax slab itself and is legible in suitable lights. Thus the Pad provides not only a receptive surface that can be used over and over again, like a slate, but also permanent traces of what has been written, like an ordinary paper pad; it solves the problem of combining the two functions by *dividing them between two separate but interrelated component parts or systems.*
>
> (230)

The celluloid on top and the wax below provide the two "component" parts of consciousness and unconsciousness. For anyone who has examined a Magic Pad the complexity of Freud's analogy is illustrated by the condition of the wax which, while it retains the impressions of the stylus, often requires a good deal of scrutiny to decipher the characters that have been impressed on top of each other, each modifying the next. The analogy of the mystic pad synthesizes Freud's two archaeological perspectives on memory through the material act of writing, a particular kind of writing which Freud compares to the "ancient method of writing on tablets of clay or wax." The association between analogies is concretized through the image of the "ancient slab" as well as by the similarity of Freud's description of the mystic pad to its archaic equivalent, the palimpsest. The most interesting component of this associative chain for literary critics is the way it highlights writing as trace – memory not just as archaeological but dominated by the archaeo-*logos* –characters which must be interpreted or deciphered through the light of the present day, with all of the reconstructive nuance this entails. "A Note Upon the 'Mystic Writing-Pad,'" therefore, illustrates how the traces of writing underwrite the archaeological analogy.

It is in this vein of archaeology as text that Derrida presents "Freud and the Scene of Writing." Derrida's interpretation of Freud's stratigraphic analogies, particularly in "A Note Upon the 'Mystic Writing-Pad,'" highlights the complexly contradictory nature of Freud's invocation of archaeology and memory. For Derrida, the most intricate point in Freud's theory of the memory trace is the moment "trace starts to become writing." As an illustration, Derrida quotes a letter Freud wrote on December 6, 1896:

> As you know, I am working on the assumption that our psychic mechanism has come into being by a process of stratification ... the material present in the form of memory-traces ... being subjected from time to time to a *rearrangement* ... in accordance with fresh circumstances to a *retranscription* ... Thus, what is essentially new about my theory is the thesis that memory is present not once but several times over, that it is laid down ... in various species of indications ... I cannot say how many of these registrations ... there are: at least three, probably more ...
> (qtd. in Derrida, *Writing and Difference* 206)

Freud's presentation of the concept of re-transcription contradicts the critique of entombed memory. As Derrida elaborates:

> There is no present text in general, and there is not even a past present text, a text which is past as having been present. The text is not conceivable in an originary or modified form of presence. The unconscious text is already a weave of pure traces, differences in which meaning and force are united – a text nowhere present, consisting of archives which are *always already* transcriptions. Originary prints. Everything begins with reproduction. Always, already: repositories of a meaning which was never present, whose signified presence is always reconstituted by deferral ... belatedly ... *supplementarily*.
> (211)

This absence of "primariness" is for Derrida a virtue in that it complicates our sense of the memory process and refutes the myth of origins. Derrida is also careful to highlight Freud's distrust in the concept of "psychical locality" which Freud proclaims to "avoid ... in any anatomical fashion" (216). For Derrida, the Mystic Pad is an exceptional analogy because it is able to maintain the contradiction of the flickering conscious mind and the unconscious retention and re-transcription of traces. In drawing out the virtues of the analogy, moreover, Derrida maintains Freud's archaeological resonance and vocabulary:

Dream, Delusion, and Dynamite 97

> Let us note that the *depth* of the Mystic Pad is simultaneously a depth without bottom, an infinite allusion, and a perfectly superficial exteriority: a stratification of surfaces each of whose relation to itself, each of whose interior, is but the implication of another similarly exposed surface. It joins the two empirical certainties by which we are constituted: infinite depth in the implication of meaning, in the unlimited envelopment of the present, and, simultaneously, the pellicular essence of being, the absolute absence of any foundation.
>
> (224)

It is perhaps this "absolute absence of any foundation" which makes the archaeological metaphor so appealing to Freud. "A depth without bottom," constantly changing in relation to what is discovered underneath, the layers of psychoanalytic truth can only be interpreted in relation to other excavated layers and a solid analytic interpretation is at consistent risk of dislocation. This peripatetic sense of memory, combined with the idea of perpetual re-transcription, makes room for a sense of the present in relation to the past that permits multiple interpretations, a site that sustains contradiction in a manner very similar to the "archaic thought" that, according to Freud (in both "The Interpretation of Dreams" and "The Antithetical Meaning of Primal Words") characterizes the dream-realm:

> The way in which dreams treat the category of contraries and contradictions is highly remarkable. It is simply disregarded. "No" seems not to exist so far as dreams are concerned. They show a particular preference for combining contraries into a unity or for representing them as one and the same thing.
>
> ("The Antithetical Meaning of Primal Words" 94)

Dialectically superior to the dichotomy, dreams combine "contraries into a unity." Similarly, in "A Note Upon the 'Mystic Writing-Pad,'" the writing pad as archaeological site permits Freud an imaginary and discursive realm for the mind as paradoxically and legitimately an arena of sustainable opposites where memory's perpetuity is dependent on the processes of a mnemonic writing and re-writing.

If in "A Note Upon the 'Mystic Writing-Pad'" Freud offers readers his most complete and complex schema of memory traces and the individual mind, then it is in "Moses and Monotheism" that he attempts to do the same for group psychology. "Moses and Monotheism" is archaeological in several senses. Most directly is Freud's proposition, somewhat strange to us but not terribly odd in the wake of Schliemann, that the way to find the remains of lost civilizations is through more literal readings of epic poetry by Germans, Indians and Finns (though, as Bowdler points out, this particular kind of textual treasure hunting was only successful in India "with the recovery of the Indus civilizations at Mohenjo-daro" 25). More subtly, however, is the way in which Freud posits group memory traces residing in the depths of the collective mind, which can only be explicated through an inverted reading of cultural and religious progress. For Freud, these traces are the basis of tradition and, when very faint, the ghost-muse of creative production. This emphasis on collective recollection makes "Moses and Monotheism" unique in Freud's archaeo-repertoire and proffers a new vein of consideration the excavation of a communal history.

"Moses and Monotheism" is Freud's advancement of the thesis that Judaism is actually descended from a forgotten Egyptian religion, and that "Moses" was not the original prophet of monotheism but rather a disciple of a monotheistic pharaoh, who was killed for his religious doctrines. After the death of the pharaoh, Moses turned to "a group of foreigners" and "tried to realize his ideals in them" (60). However, one day these disciples, the original Jews, "killed him and threw off the religion ... which had been imposed on them, just as the Egyptians had thrown it off earlier" (60–1). This incident was collectively repressed only to remain a "memory trace" until eventually the "remorse for the murder of Moses provided the stimulus for the wishful phantasy of the Messiah, who was to return and lead his people to redemption and the promised world-domination" (89).

For Freud, the evolution of religion relies on the basic psychoanalytic principles of repression and return. Freud makes this comparison explicit through the phrase "in the history of religion, that is, as regards the return of the repressed" and the sense of latent underground theisms is highly reminiscent of the pagan paradigm of returning "stone gods." Freud's schema, of course, transforms this model into a series of psychic mechanisms – resentment – reprisal – repression – remorse – which are meant to account for the gaps in documented religious history. More importantly, it is the combined force of repression and retention – the consciously forgotten but unconsciously retained event that becomes the well-spring of future

Dream, Delusion, and Dynamite 99

action and events: that is to say, the period of "latency" common to both group and individual psychology.[2]

Freud's latency theory is in many ways similar to Pater's understanding of cultural return. However, rather than elaborate this through metaphors in art, as Pater does, Freud embroiders on the possibility of group memory by supplying examples of the psychological disorders of the individual patient. In order to make the group theory of latent memory clear, Freud begins with the example of an individual who experiences a railway accident and leaves the scene unharmed but consequently develops severe neurotic symptoms. For Freud, this lag time can be described as an incubation period – a dormant state whereby the trauma is repressed, only to reappear later in symptomatic form. This delay is key to the parallel between the psychological repressions of the individual and of the group. Despite "the fundamental difference between the two cases – the problem of traumatic neurosis and that of Jewish monotheism – there is, nevertheless, one point of agreement, namely, in the characteristic that might be described as 'latency'" (68). It is this cohesion, the fact that memory remains dormant in the brain only to be reactivated at a later date, that leads Freud to believe that "there is

---

2   It is interesting to note that Freud's fascination with the figure of Moses extended to other writing – the art critique "The Moses of Michelangelo," which also maintains the archaeological motif. In this piece, Freud self-deprecatingly underplays his ability as an art critic but maintains that there is some similarity between the process of art criticism and psychoanalysis in that both are "accustomed to divine secret and concealed things from disappeared or unnoticed features, from the rubbish-heap, as it were, of our observations" (265). This sense of "divining" the depths of the statue, of drawing out latent forces in the work of Michelangelo, in particular, is one that we also see in Pater. It is difficult to know if Freud is referring to Pater's piece on the latent forces in Michelangelo and was influenced by its archaeological resonance, though it is likely he read it given that it was published in the same edition of *The Renaissance* as the da Vinci study, which Freud refers to explicitly. Either way, in Freud's Michelangelo, the archaeological theme is repeatedly interpolated into a psychic landscape, from the search for "concealed things" to the figure's exhibition of "three distinct emotional strata" (273). Adding to the element of concealment is the fact that Freud did not disclose his authorship of the piece until 1933, though it was published anonymously in *Imago* before the outbreak of the First World War.

an almost complete conformity in this respect between the individual and the group: in the group too an impression of the past is retained in unconscious memory traces" (94).

While the literal belief that a whole religious group may have a repressed memory that reasserts itself at a later date may seem far fetched, Freud, in fact, goes much further. Rather than stopping at the idea of one generation, Freud posits a system of biologically inherited memory, the "archaic heritage," whereby offspring of the original generation of witnesses retain the impressions of their ancestors. For Freud, "an individual's psychical life may include not only what he has experienced himself but also things that were innately present in him at his birth, elements with a phylogenetic origin" (98). It is at this point that Freud again turns to the literary and linguistic realm, this time suggesting that it is not just instinct that can be attributed to these inherited memory systems; it is also a common appreciation for the meaning of symbolism:

> There is, in the first place, the universality of symbolism in language. The symbolic representation of one object by another ... is familiar to all our children and comes to them, as it were, as a matter of course. We cannot show in regard to them how they have learnt it and must admit that in many cases learning it is impossible. It is a question of an original knowledge which adults afterwards forget. It is true that an adult makes use of the same symbols in his dreams, but he does not understand them unless an analyst interprets them to him, and even then he is reluctant to believe the translation ... Moreover, symbolism disregards differences of language; investigations would probably show that it is ubiquitous – the same for all peoples. Here, then, we seem to have an assured instance of an archaic heritage dating from the period at which language developed.
>
> (98–9)

There are familiar overtones here in Freud's sense of symbolism – ultimately the core of the poetic – as the primal language of the earliest peoples, the "original knowledge" that we are born with but soon forget. While Freud's thesis that symbolism is the "same for all peoples" is arguable, the sense that the poetic is at the root of a universal and genetically transferable knowledge is resonant with an archaeological *mentalité* that perceives a densely imagistic primal vocabulary to be at the root of human communication and the core of the poetic tradition.

What is most interesting in terms of psychoanalysis' foray into the realm of symbolism is the way in which Freud posits the analyst as the authoritative literary critic of this original language: "It is true that an adult makes use of the same symbols in his dreams, but he does not understand them unless an analyst interprets them to him, and even then he is reluctant to believe the translation" (99). Dream-symbols, remnants of "an archaic heritage dating from the period at which language developed," are the indecipherable if omnipresent memory traces of an earlier age. Only the Champollion of the mind, the psychoanalytic "reader" fluent in archaic symbolism as well as contemporary scientific dialect, is able to complete the "translation" from archaic to modern.

For Freud, however, it is not only the analyst who is able to read into the symbolism of the archaic heritage. These "permanent traces" which form the basis of "tradition" are also the materials of the creative artist (129). Freud frequently used this archaeology of the artist with reference to the artist's own life: Leonardo da Vinci, for example, producing a woman's look on canvas in the long remembered image of his mother. In introducing the concept of the archaic heritage, Freud also posits "tradition" or the collective memory trace as the root of artistic inspiration. Contrary to expectation, it is not the artist's above normal ability to intuit the contours of the tradition that provides inspiration. Rather, it is the *gaps* in his understanding that make creation possible; indeed, "the vaguer the tradition has become the more serviceable it becomes for a poet":

> If all that is left of the past are the incomplete and blurred memories which we call tradition, this offers an artist a peculiar attraction, for in that case he is free to fill in the gaps in memory according to the desires of his imagination and to picture the period which he wishes to reproduce according to his intentions.
> (72)

Interestingly, Freud does not comment on whether incomplete information is also more serviceable for the psychoanalyst – most likely because the artist's ultimate goal is "fiction" while the psychoanalyst strives for "truth." Still, within this paradigm it becomes evident that Freud finds parallels between psychoanalysis and creative expression through the archaeological act of reconstruction from distant traces. This mode of imagining resonates distinctly with Pater's rationale for fleshing out archaeology's fragmented remains with illustrative detail in aesthetic criticism as well as Gautier's archaeological romances where the narrative emerges from an encounter with a hollow or incomplete relic.

If the image of the archaic text provides Freud with the most complete analogy for the processes of memory, and the creative act is expressed as the reanimation of incomplete remains, it is in Freud's archaeology of hysteria that we find the most explicit traces of popular archaeological narratives. In "The Aetiology of Hysteria," Freud's metaphorical mode of recovering a patient's memory of trauma is elaborated through a Schliemannesque account of archaeological method:

> Imagine that an explorer arrives in a little-known region where his interest is aroused by an expanse of ruins, with remains of walls, fragments of columns, and tablets with half-effaced and unreadable inscriptions. He may content himself with inspecting what lies exposed to view, with questioning the inhabitants – perhaps semi-barbaric people – who live in the vicinity, about what tradition tells them of the history and meaning of these archaeological remains, and with noting down what they tell him – and he may then proceed on his journey. But he may act differently. He may have brought picks, shovels and spades with him, and he may set the inhabitants to work with these implements. Together with them he may start upon the ruins, clear away the rubbish, and, beginning from the visible remains, uncover what is buried. If his work is crowned with success, the discoveries are self-explanatory, the ruined walls are part of the ramparts of a palace or a treasure-house, the fragments of columns can be filled out into a temple, the numerous inscriptions, which, by good luck, may be bilingual, reveal an alphabet and a language, and, when they have been deciphered and translated, yield undreamed-of information about the events of the remote past …
> ("The Aetiology of Hysteria" 252–3)

Here, Freud seems to be offering a comparison of the "good" and the "bad" analyst through the parable of the archaeologist. The less competent archaeologist interviews the natives; the thorough archaeologist sets the natives to work, clearing out the rubble to uncover the secrets of their own past. Suddenly, something like the Third World has appeared in the Freudian text – only it is not indigenous people who are the natives of the hysterical landscape; it is women.

For Hake, it is precisely the sexual dynamics of mastery that make the archaeological mode appealing to Freud. Woman, in all of these cases, is the riddle, the sphinx, the site of desire. The "unknowness" of hysteria is cause enough to reach for a conquering epistemology:

> ... the power of the analyst as archaeologist is reflected in the image of archaeology as an active, intrusive, and explicitly male activity, while the woman, who, as *terra incognita*, makes his quest for knowledge both necessary and possible, is regularly identified with images of the unknown: the buried city, the hidden treasure. Both sides of the metaphor, its eroticism and its sexism, are fully present in the treatment of Elisabeth von R., when Freud reports triumphantly that the sudden mention of a young man "had opened up a new vein of ideas ... the contents of which I now gradually extracted."
>
> (151)

Certainly the archaeological metaphor does coincide with tropes of exploration and colonization – the "African" landscape of a dark and unknown femininity. Probing into the depths of the mind through archaeological terminology also tends to lead to further historical associations of looting, exploitation or fraudulent finds. The claim that archaeology provided psychoanalysis with a mastering or colonizing discourse of the "hysterical" mind is legitimized by Freud's own sense of himself in "The Aetiology of Hysteria" as the intrepid analyst, the midnight marauder in a primitive wilderness searching the inner recesses of treacherous terrain. Freud, who in all of his hysteria writings identifies himself with the active role of the pocketbook archaeologist, is so caught up in this scenario that he gives little if any thought to the implications of dividing women into two alienated components – an unthinking, "semi-barbaric" people on the one hand, on the other, their minds rendered earthen, silent, and passive.

Springing from the aspirations of mastery invoked by Freud's archaeology of hysteria, critics have laid heavy gender-bias charges against Freud's most ambitious archaeological writing – "Delusions and Dreams in Jensen's 'Gradiva.'" Grounded in the short story, "Gradiva: a Pompeiian Phantasy," by Wilhelm Jensen, Freud's interpretation has been viewed as wrought – or fraught – with an uncompromising triple connotation of woman as archaeological site, woman as man-haunting phantom, and woman as the bottomless pit of domestic entrapment. Much of this division of the feminine is rooted in Jensen's story, which turns on the principle of mistaken identity and the division of a real woman versus *la fantasie féminine*. Briefly, Jensen's tale centers on the delusions of Norbert Hanold, a young archaeologist, who becomes obsessed with the stone relief of a young woman, whom he names "Gradiva." Norbert pursues the idea of the image to Pompeii, where he meets a woman whom he assumes is Gradiva incarnate. Gradually, through the woman's manipulations, Norbert comes to understand that the young woman he meets in Pompeii is in fact his childhood friend, Zoe Bertgang (in German, "she who steps lightly") and it is the recollection of her that originally spurred his desire for the Grecian image of the walking woman.

Jensen's story is among several turn of the century works that employed the archaeological motif as a metaphor for repression and consequent recognition of lost love or desire. Henri Ellenberger mentions several of these stories in *The Discovery of the Unconscious*, notably, *Journey to the Center of the Earth* where: "Jules Verne depicted an old German professor trying to decipher a cryptogram with the help of his nephew, who is secretly in love with the professor's daughter Grauben. The young man believes to have found the key, and to his amazement it gives him these words: 'I am in love with Grauben'" (Ellenberger 495). Even more similar to Jensen's work is the earlier text *The Disciples of Sais*: "Novalis [tells] the story of a young man who wanders from place to place, searching for the object of his vision, arriving finally at the temple of Isis, where this object is revealed to him and he recognizes in her his childhood sweetheart" (293). Henry James uses a similar if more complex psychological adaptation of this trope in "The Beast in the Jungle." For Freud, this thematic of "love" buried in the depths of the mind and consequently "excavated" or "deciphered," which was clearly pervasive in the literary landscape of the late nineteenth and early twentieth century, accords directly with his sense of a patient's repression of sexual feelings and the analyst's role as archaeologist who disinters these desires later in the patient's life.

Jensen's story enacts the primary patterns of the nineteenth-century adventure narrative, where the young protagonist becomes infatuated by the delirious erotic possibilities of a southern landscape only to, in the end,

Dream, Delusion, and Dynamite

find "home" in his familiar childhood friend. Certainly Freud approves of this ending, finding the return to Zoe and a future of bourgeois German domesticity the signal of restored emotional health and well-being. The feminine in both Jensen's story and Freud's analysis, however, plays not only the role of repressed desire but also that of its cure: Zoe is undoubtedly the psychoanalyst in Freud's mind and as such, the more stable of the two characters.

While Hake suggests that the sexual dynamics of "Delusions and Dreams" are identical to Freud's hysteria cases, that the young woman is the object of the archaeologist's scopophilic gaze and that her psychoanalytic power "only underscores Norbert's triumphant return to masculinity" (163), it is difficult to dispute Freud's admiration for Zoe, the "embodiment of cleverness and clarity" ("Delusions and Dreams in Jensen's 'Gradiva'" 58). Despite the suggestion that Freud's archaeological paradigm inevitably associates the woman-hysteric with the dark force of the undisclosed *femme fatale*, in "Delusions and Dreams" it is the male protagonist, Norbert, who suffers from delusions, paranoia, and hysterical behavior. Freud, depicting Norbert in the same mode as Jensen, does not construe any individual woman or feminine force to be the source of Norbert's delirium. Rather, it is Norbert himself who is to blame:

> If Norbert Hanold were someone in real life who had in this way banished love and his childhood friendship with the help of archaeology, it would have been logical and according to rule that what revived in him the forgotten memory of the girl he had loved in his childhood should be precisely an antique sculpture. It would have been his well-deserved fate to fall in love with the marble portrait of Gradiva, behind which, owing to an unexplained similarity, the living Zoe whom he had neglected made her influence felt.
>
> (62)

Here, Norbert's fate is "well deserved" due to his neglectful behavior toward Zoe. It is not the feminine that acts as the lost object of archaeological uncertainty, but rather *repression itself*, which performs the metaphor of the archaeological site. Or, as Freud articulates mid-text: "there is no better analogy for repression ... than burial of the sort to which Pompeii fell a victim and from which it could emerge once more through the work of spades" (65).

In *Still Crazy After All These Years,* Rachel Bowlby elaborates on this view of the Woman-as-Analyst and not as site in order to demonstrate the potential of an un-sexist Freudian gender division. Contrary to Freud's archaeology of hysteria, the archaeological machinations of Jensen's story provide Freud with an outlet to examine a strong, centered woman as *something other than* the "vestiges of something which might once have been a woman ... buried deep down, in the ancient world that has no communication from the present – lost from the past, impossible to recover, or uncover, in the future" (Bowlby 158). Rather than the lost relic of an idealized femininity, Zoe Bertgang is a perceptive and psychoanalytically intuitive woman of the present, who is as capable of assessing Norbert's situation as she is able to decipher her own. In the end, it is Zoe who is cognizant of her own feelings and able to excavate Norbert's, reconfiguring his mythic infatuations into the pattern of his own past. Bowlby writes, "[a]s though in mockery of the forms of masculine fantasy, the feminine ghost that Norbert thinks he sees turns out to be no ghost, but something more (or less): a down-to-earth living woman who wants to get away from the deathly monumentality of her identification by him as a timeless aesthetic ideal."

What we can gather from all of this is that just as Freud's use of archaeological imagery slips in discussions of memory, so it shifts in relation to the feminine. The division of discovery versus reconstruction in mnemonic recovery and the difference between woman as site versus woman as excavator and colleague both hinge on varying usages of the archaeological metaphor. These fluctuations cannot really be attributed to Freud's changing views of archaeology or, indeed, of women or memory over time since various views are represented in each stage of Freud's writing. Rather, it may well be symptomatic of the inconsistencies and contradictions within the *mentalité* itself. "Archaeology" and all that that meant for the nineteenth century embodied the predicament of a period searching for the past with the technologies of the future. It is not surprising that within this space the idea of "Woman" which was itself in tremendous flux would also sway

Dream, Delusion, and Dynamite

from the position of excavated to excavator, unfixed definitions in uneasy relationship with each other.

Rather than providing a lock on interpretation or too definite a metaphorical grid, then, archaeology proved to be a dynamic and consistently undulating source of interpretation in Freud's work. Moreover, Freud is ultimately not the unambiguous archaeological zealot most critics have described. Underlying Freud's sense of the usefulness of the archaeological paradigm is a competitive drive as well as a lurking modernist suspicion of antiquarianism. While there is no question that Freud made full use of archaeology's popularizing effects, he also ingrains the superiority of psychoanalysis into the fabric of the comparison. At times the agent of scientific reason, which Freud attempted to transfer to psychoanalysis, archaeology also serves as a model of the overly academic which Freud frequently pits psychoanalysis against.

This tendency appears throughout Freud's archaeological writings. In "Constructions in Analysis," for example, Freud alludes to the superiority of psychoanalysis to archaeology through the suggestion that the "working conditions" are much better, a comment which also seems to suggest that the quality of the product is far superior (258). Freud notes that compared to the archaeologist, the psychoanalyst has "more material at his command" meaning, in essence, that psychoanalysis has a constant source of information in the living patient while the archaeologist is the mortician of the long dead. At a certain point, Freud does grant archaeology a few points against the "extraordinary advantages ... enjoyed by the work of analysis: namely, that psychical objects are incomparably more complicated than the excavator's material ones [and that in analysis there is] so much that is still mysterious" (260) – a left-handed compliment which again positions the analyst in a more complex, intellectually challenging domain. It is in "Delusions and Dreams," however, that the impulse to deride archaeology is most obvious since Jensen's tale follows Norbert's transition from death to life, from the remote past to his own future, from the academic to the erotic – and all that this implies as he transfers his libidinous impulses from his vocation (archaeology) to the true site of desire (Zoe). Freud, who within this essay positions himself on the side of the "common people" and the "convictions of antiquity" ("Delusions and Dreams" 33) consistently identifies the process of analysis not with the science of archaeology (that metaphor is performed by repression here, not by the archaeologist/psychoanalyst) but rather with the creative writer. The writer, Jensen, in this case, repeatedly plays on the trope of the antiquarian interest robbing the individual of a creative, satisfying life in the moment. And Freud, in his summary of the story, repeats the theme of archaeology as life-denying twelve times in the course of his analysis.

The trope of archaeology at once as the site of eros as well as its antiquarian counterpart is one of the more pervasive themes in archaeological fiction. Thus, in "Gradiva," Norbert feels the first pangs of desire in front of the Grecian relief. However, once he meets the woman he believes to be the real "Gradiva" (Zoe, whom he mistakenly identifies as the form from the frieze), archaeology ceases to satisfy:

> When, later on, at the "hot and holy" mid-day hour, which the ancients regarded as the hour of ghosts, the other visitors had taken flight and the heaps of ruins lay before him desolate and bathed in sunlight, he found that he was able to carry himself back into the life that had been buried – but not by the help of science "what it taught was a lifeless, archaeological way of looking at things, and what came from its mouth was a dead, philological language. These were of no help to an understanding through the spirit, the feelings, the heart – put it as you please."
> ("Delusions and Dreams" 42)

Shortly after, Norbert develops "an uncanny horror of antique collections" (44) and this too is symbolic of his turn from the dead to the living. What is interesting within "Delusions and Dreams" is the way in which Freud positions the turn from archaeology to psychoanalysis as the *same* movement from a morbid fascination with the antiquarian to the living potential of contemporary erotic desire within the patient. Like Norbert, who abandons his critical archaeological tendencies to embrace human love, Freud ventures "in the face of the reproaches of strict science" (33) to take the side of antiquity and superstition – in other words, to abandon the overly academic tendencies of archaeology for a living science of the human heart.

This turn away from science and the invocation of what we might call "negative-archaeology" neatly places psychoanalysis and literature in the same camp, a parallel which Freud repeatedly emphasizes in his

Dream, Delusion, and Dynamite 109

astonishment over Jensen's psychoanalytic intuition. Freud asserts that from 1893, in his own investigations of delusional behavior, it had never occurred to him to refer to literature for case studies: "I was thus more than a little surprised to find that the author of *Gradiva*, which was published in 1903, had taken the basis of its creation the very thing that I believe myself to have freshly discovered from the sources of my medical experiences" (79). Here, it is not archaeology that is the privileged discipline of reference but literature. While archaeologists discover, creative writers interpret and find motivation in the same mode as the psychoanalyst. Indeed, in the effort to lessen the distance between literature and psychoanalysis (while at the same time widening the gap between analysis and "strict science"), Freud goes so far as to attack the discursive terms of his own field, suggesting that the psychiatrist's vocabulary, tends to "coarsen everything" in its use of terms like "fetishistic erotomania" and "all such systems of nomenclature and classification" have "something precarious and barren about them" (70). Zoe says to Norbert: "... when archaeology took hold of you I discovered ... you'd become an unbearable person" (qtd. in "Delusions and Dreams" 57). Freud, keenly aware of the alienating effect of a dry science, attempts to keep the forces of eros and creativity on board with the psychoanalytic enterprise by tightening psychoanalysis' connection to literary production: "... the creative writer cannot evade the psychiatrist nor the psychiatrist the creative writer" (69). "Strict" scientific archaeology is, therefore, ousted in "Delusions and Dreams" to be supplanted by the pairing of literature and psychoanalysis – and a more dynamic, erotically charged archaeology of the self.

However, there are times in "Delusions and Dreams" when this division between archaeology in one camp and psychoanalysis and literature in the other breaks down all together. The site of this breakdown is in the return of the archaeo-logos – in this case, lost words that prove to be the completing pieces of the puzzle. For Freud, language is the hinging point of consciousness and unconsciousness and it is the utterance that provides entrance into the realm of buried desires and associations. Thus, Norbert's christening of the woman in the frieze "Gradiva" is significant because "as we learn from our hero himself at the end of the story, after he has been cured of his delusion, it is a good translation of the surname 'Bertgang' which means something like 'someone who steps along brilliantly or splendidly'" (75). For Freud, Zoe, too, performs the dynamics of the archaeo-logos by comparing Norbert to an "archaeopteryx, the bird-like monstrosity which belongs to the archaeology of zoology" (59). According to Freud, this word applies to both Norbert, the archaeologist, and Zoe's neglectful father, the zoologist, thus exposing Zoe's association between the two men. In both these instances, words play the role of the double-signifier and are, therefore, like hieroglyphics that must be decoded or "double-read" in order to mean within the context of the speaker's comments as well as within the greater pattern of the psychiatrist's analysis.

The hieroglyph itself emerges in Freud's work as the most explicit signifier for the archaeo-literary gateway between dreaming and waking. Freud owned a statuette of Baboon of Thoth, the Egyptian deity credited with the invention of hieroglyphs, and often invoked Egyptian writing as the condensed language of dreams:

> If we reflect that the means of representation in dreams are principally visual images and not words, we shall see that it is even more appropriate to compare dreams with a system of writing than with a language. In fact the interpretation of dreams is completely analogous to the decipherment of an ancient pictographic script such as Egyptian hieroglyphs. In both cases, there are certain elements which are not intended to be interpreted (or read, as the case may be) but are only designed to serve as "determinatives," that is to establish the meaning of some other element. The ambiguity of various elements of dreams finds a parallel in these ancient systems of writing.
> ("The Claims of Psycho-analysis to Scientific Interest" 177)

This sense of it being more "appropriate to compare dreams with a system of writing than with a language," like the mystic writing pad, foregrounds the importance of writing processes in Freud's theories of the mind and his continuous linkage of writing to ancient or forgotten scripts, either in form (i.e. the hieroglyph) or in its materials (the tablet, the stylus). Freud's association of the dream-realm with a certain type of ambiguity attached to the image of the hieroglyph is an attractive stance from a poetic perspective. As H.D. wrote in her *Tribute to Freud*, "there are all these shapes ... the *hieroglyph of the unconscious*, and the Professor had first opened the field of study to the vast, unexplored region. He himself – at least to me

Dream, Delusion, and Dynamite

personally – deplored the tendency to *fix* ideas too firmly to set symbols, or to weld them inexorably" (93). Derrida also stresses relative meaning in Freud's adoption of the hieroglyph suggesting that: "The model of hieroglyphic writing assembles more strikingly – though we find it in every form of writing – the diversity of the modes and functions of signs in dreams. Every sign – verbal or otherwise – may be used at different levels, in configurations and functions which are never prescribed by its essence" (*Writing and Difference* 220). This sense of contingent meaning, of a mode of writing which makes sense out of the play of various signs, is resonant with the dynamics of modern poetry. In the next chapter, we will see how H.D., in particular, built on Freud's understanding of the hieroglyphic dream symbol as an archaic image with contemporary resonance.

Recent metaphors of excavation in psychoanalytic writing are indicative of the ways in which archaeological modalities have persisted in psychoanalysis as well as poetry. One of the most convincing contemporary examples is Maria Torok and Nicholas Abraham's adoption of the image of the "crypt." Like Freud, however, latter day critics both rely on these images and topographies and are suspicious of them. In "Psychoanalysis and Transphenomenology of the Symbol," for example, Abraham notes that:

> We are accustomed to approaching symbols as an archaeologist struggles to decipher documents in an unknown language. What is given is a thing that contains no meaning. We live with the handy prejudice that all one has to do is attach the meaning to the thing, its support, join the semantic significations to the hieroglyphics, in order to pride oneself on one's success in the act of deciphering. But all this process really accomplishes is to convert one system of symbols into another, which then in turn becomes accountable for its secret.
>
> (qtd. in Derrida's introduction to *The Wolfman's Magic Word* xxix)

Here, the process of translation is suspect because of the constant "repetition" of symbols in the name of meaning. The movement is circular and indefinite, leading nowhere. The archaeological allusion serves to underpin an exercise in the impossible. Nevertheless, this does not prevent the archaeo-vocabulary from forming the centre-piece of *The Wolf-Man's Magic Word*, where the crypt is multi-representational, containing both the secret desires we might expect from such a gothic invocation, as well as more phenomenological presences such as the un-mourned spirit of a dead loved one, the memory of the primal scene, or the kernel of undisclosed self-identity.

It is with an eye on the suspicions of critics who are sensitive to the violence of psychic disinterment that Derrida comments on the aesthetics of violation implicit in both "excavation" and "the opening of the crypt":

> To track down the path to the tomb, then to violate a sepulchre: that is what the analysis of a cryptic incorporation is like. The idea of violation [*viol*] might imply some kind of transgression of a right, the forced entry of a penetrating, digging force, but the violated sepulcher *itself* was never "legal." It is the very tombstone of the illicit, and marks the spot of an extreme pleasure [*jouissance*], a pleasure entirely *real* though walled up, buried alive in its own prohibition.
> (*The Wolfman's Magic Word*, Introduction xxxiv)

Whether the social legality of individual secrets (pleasurable or painful) really is an "invitation to the analyst to proceed with the exhumation" (xxxv) is up for debate since it does very much seem to follow in Freud's logic of "extrication" and all of the difficulties we might have with this kind of trespass. The notion that the crypt marks "the spot of extreme pleasure," is, of course, not unknown to us, for as we have seen it is the unwrapping of the mummy, the regression into Pompeiian phantasy, the opening of the sacred sepulcher that is often the site of the most heightened eroticism in archaeological narrative. Here, in figurative terms, Derrida is applying this truism to the psychical system: in the heart of the inner crypt lies not only the darkest secrets but also the root of *jouissance*.

In this figuration of the crypt, we see the persistence of a *mentalité*. In other works, Abraham and Torok postulate beyond the crypt of the individual to hypothesize the existence of a multi-generational "phantom." In a footnote the authors explain that:

> ... should a child have parents "with secrets" ... the child will receive from them a gap in the unconscious ... The buried speech of the parent will be (a) dead (gap) without a burial place in the child. This unknown phantom returns from the unconscious to haunt its host and may lead to phobias, madness, and obsessions. Its effect can persist through several generations and determine the fate of an entire family line.
> (*The Shell and the Kernel* 140)

Dream, Delusion, and Dynamite

This "gap" or "buried speech" is an inherited absence, which is filled by the specter of the unknown, the maddening or symptomatic "phantom." In contrast with the crypt, the phantom is not experienced by the individual but rather is an acquired void, the unspoken event in the life of an ancestor. According to the editor, Nicholas Rand: "The concept of the phantom moves the focus of psychoanalytic inquiry beyond the individual being analyzed because it postulates that some people unwittingly inherit the secret psychic substance of their ancestors' lives. The 'phantom' represents a radical reorientation of Freudian and post Freudian theories..." (Editor's Note, *The Shell and the Kernel* 166). But does it really? For in both the "buried" resonance of the crypt and phantom figures, in the inherited and perhaps latent contents of the primal scene, do we not detect echoes of Freud's archaeological formulation of the archaic heritage?

The consequences of this continuation of the archaeological mode of psychoanalytic examination take on increased meaning for our study when applied to literature. Therefore, Rand's *Le Cryptage et la Vie des Oeuvres* is of particular interest since it applies the cryptonomic theories of Abraham and Torok to works by Baudelaire, Flaubert, Benjamin, Heidegger and Ponge. For Torok, who wrote the preface to the 1989 volume, searching these works for crypts reveals "secret light," the text functioning "in another time" – "time and light that opens up unanticipated depths and unpredictable paths" (7). To decipher the inner life (or inner death) of the text, one must learn to listen to the silences of the work, though Torok admits that we are in the early stages of such a method, that the procedure is still imprecise: "How to listen to the silence of a work? What tool does the text present to make heard its intimate reversals?" (9). The idea of crypts hidden within the text is encouraging to archaeological reading, as it promotes the kinds of excavation embarked upon here – the hunt for hidden recesses, stratified meaning, and phantom presences operating within the literary work.

The research of Abraham, Torok and Rand is interesting not only because it proffers another example of an archaeological approach but also because it solidifies the idea of a persisting *mentalité* in psychoanalysis and literature. The work of Abraham and Torok clarifies a concept that is fundamental to Freud's oeuvre – that haunting occurs at the site of the individual secret or family silence as well as at the intersection of disciplines – the haunting of psychoanalysis by archaeology and the continuing usefulness of this phantasm for literary discovery.

CHAPTER 5

"Original in the right sense": Ezra Pound, Adrian Stokes, H.D., and the Archaeology of the New

In the inaugural issue of the short-lived avant-garde magazine *Blast!* (1914) Ezra Pound would publicly introduce the idea of the "vortex," which would set the stage for modernist appropriations of history. "The image," Pound later wrote, "is not an idea. It is a radiant node or cluster; ... a VORTEX, from which, and through which, and into which, ideas are constantly rushing" ("Vorticism" in *Gaudier-Brzeska* 92). The conceptual implications of the vortex, through which all times and places rush in an atemporal flux of energies, provides a distinctly modern flavor to the rehabilitation of the past. For while the vorticists with whom Pound was briefly affiliated learned much from the radical typography and rushing intensity of the Italian Futurists, they differentiated themselves through their lack of interest in the annihilation of the past which the Futurists propounded. Indeed, while the name *Blast!* implies the destruction of conservative models and staid artistic expression, it also has an archaeological resonance in the explosion of earth which reveals more dynamic layers below the surface.

It is T.S. Eliot, who in describing Pound as "archaeological," gives us the deepest insight into Pound's energized archaeological mode. Eliot's decisive invocation of archaeology in the introduction to Pound's selected poems situates Pound at the center of the vortex, dredging up the powers of the past in order to create the truly new: "Pound is often most 'original' in the right sense, when he is most 'archaeological'" (11). Here, "Original in the right sense" seems to mean the process of excavating ancient forces or materials matched by the application of new technique. This paradox of old and new is at the centre of our archaeological paradigm, wherein the processes of writing mirror or are informed by a discipline that at this time was literally excavating the old with the aid of new technologies and methods. In Pound, this dynamic tension manifests itself as a longing for origins that is matched by the desire for innovation, a dynamic archaeology of the future which supplants traditional notions of past-fetishizing antiquarianism. Therefore, the "return to origins" which for Pound "invigorates because it is a return to nature and reason" (*Literary Essays* 92), is in effect a hunt for the new – a retrieval or reactivation of an existential and social mode that can be projected forward. Like Pater, Pound subscribes to knowledge as a form of Platonic recollection. But Pound distinguishes his type of recollection by making mnemonic excavation a search for the traces of tomorrow – templates which can right the course of a drifting civilization, a social, utopian, and futuristic emphasis which differentiates Pound's archaeology not just from antiquarian models but also from Freud's excavations of the psychic self.

If Pound succeeded in creating an agenda for modernist composition which stressed the reclamation of ancient energies and fragmented shapes as well as a disordering of conventional time, there were also significant ways in which he could not control the forms these excavations would take in the work of other Anglo-American modernists. For Pound the reclamation of the past was a social project, a reactivation of forces and personalities that could right a history gone wrong. In Pound's digging there is an emphasis on an exteriorized discourse which resists psychic murkiness and privileges a virile, heterosexual masculinity in acts of war and artistry alike. In creating this paradigm, Pound borrows the "hardness" of Gautier's marbleized poetics and the release into other ages created by Pater's sedimented significances but refuses the dreamy quality of Gautier's archaeological imaginations and the homo-sensual drift of Pater's meditations on Greek statuary. By contrast, modernists like Adrian Stokes and H.D. would adopt elements of Pound's archaeo-modernism while subverting it with the "free radicals" of archaeological discourse abandoned by Pound's formulations, particularly the more sexually ambiguous aspects of Gautier and Pater as well as a thorough incorporation of Freud's subterranean reveries. As will become apparent, these combinations and reconfigurations would result in the inscription of a very different type of modernism, one which relies

"Original in the right sense"

on similar sites but different extractions and reformulations of the groundwork we have explored so far.

Pound's archaeology did not begin as an archaeology of the future. If we can speak of an archaeology of Pound, then the earliest layers of his writing are still enmeshed in a nineteenth-century nostalgia, which is to say that Pound is a transitional figure from nineteenth-century models to twentieth, a transition that was mirrored by the move toward systematic archaeological methods. In Pound's walking tour of Southern France, which he undertook in the spirit of experiencing a *rapprochement* with the medieval troubadours in 1912, we can detect clear connections between poetry and landscape, the desire to retrieve cultic energies and make contact with lingering ghosts. Pound's abandonment to the past, a type of self-hypnosis brought about by the rhythms of walking, results in an impressionistic account of his travels and it is through the notebook of his journeys that we achieve the clearest sense of Pound's "out of placedness" in his own time, a longing for the past which results in a kind of emotional, re-creationary archaeology – the archaeology of loss and desire that transforms landscape and romanticizes ruins. As Richard Sieburth writes in the introduction to the walking tour notes:

> Pound's account ... vacillates between a confidence that the mysteries of Provençal song might be philologically or imaginatively recovered and an elegiac awareness that the world he is seeking to resurrect is irrevocably lost, accessible only as trace or ruin.
>
> (xv)

The "elegiac" quality of Pound's passage through Provence roots this work in the archaeological tradition of homesickness for the distant past. Walking through a land "thick with ghosts" (*A Walking Tour in Southern France* 35) the phantasmic presence of the troubadours is at once an invitation and an unbridgeable gap.

In the fragments for *Gironde*, the abandoned manuscript for which he sought inspiration in the landscape of Provence, Pound suggests: "There are three ways of 'going back,' of feeling as well as knowing about the troubadours, first, by way of the music, the second, by way of the land, third, by way of the books themselves" (84). In the poem "Epilogue: (To my five books containing mediaeval studies, experiments, and translations)" Pound figures going back "by way of the books" as an exercise in tomb-labor:

> I bring you the spoils, my nation,
> I, who went out in exile,
>   Am returned to thee with gifts.
>
> I, who have laboured long in the tombs,
>   Am come back therefrom with riches.
>
> (*Personae* 209)

While there is a certain amount of irony present in Pound's poem, "labouring long" in textual-tombs is also emblematic of archaeological-archivists sieving through the textual remains of the past in search of "luminous detail" (qtd. in Kenner 152). On many counts, it is this descent into history, the steeping of oneself in the past to extract the riches of anterior thought that represents the first step of Pound's compositional method, here expressed in a semi-satirical play on the exploratory narratives of Elgin and Belzoni. Yet going back "by way of the land" was a mode that may equally have been conditioned by the archaeological climate of the previous forty years. Kenner speculates that the influence of Schliemann's discovery of Troy had immeasurable influence on emerging modernists: "Schliemann had been to Troy, and a cosmos had altered. There had been such a city" (42). The material reality of the *Iliad*, both the substantial treasure and the daily domestic objects discovered at Hissarlik, shifted the mythic from the domain of the imagination to the realm of the real.

Pound's perception of the increasingly material nature of the mythic was augmented by Victor Bérard's 1902 study, *The Phoenicians and the Odyssey*, which traced Odysseus' voyage through land and sea-scapes: the actual bays, islands, and rock formations observed by Phoenician sailors. According to Bérard, his two volume treatise on the material reality of Odysseus' journey is the development of two phrases from Strabon: "If Homer described exactly the regions, as well as the Interior sea and the Exterior sea, it is because he took his science from the Phoenicians ... The Phoenicians, conquerors of Libya and Iberia, were his masters" (Strabon qtd. in Bérard 3). Pound alludes to Bérard's theory in the *ABC of Reading*, asserting that: "Another French scholar has more or less shown that the *Odyssey* is correct geography; not as you would find it if you had a geography book and a map, but as it would be in 'periplum,' that is, as a coasting

"Original in the right sense"

sailor would find it" (43–4). Mythic connections were no longer solely the property of the text and of the imagination: they were now also indelibly associated with the land itself.

It is in Cahors that Pound seems to gesture toward the archaeological moment that propelled his journey: "Troy, with a horse outside of it, is possibly to be discovered, but these plains are of romance itself" (*Walking Tour* 41). In view of the wake of Schliemann and the controversy surrounding his discoveries, the "Troy" "to be discovered" is suggestive of Schliemann's excavations, an imaginative version of which Pound himself was about to perform on the landscape of Provence. In an inaction of the concepts of "periplum" and the material realities of Troy, Pound imagines the mythic landscape to be a product of close encounters with actual topographies. By "grounding" encounters with the unreal in real objects, the sublime in details of the land, Pound is also able to advance his poetic project of pairing away excessive abstraction. But the possibility of discovering Troy can also be read as referential of Pound's view that the troubadour tradition contained within it a latent polytheism inherited from the cultic atmosphere of ancient Greece, a feeling for cultural re-emergence which reminds us of Pater's views on the recurring "Greek conception" (*Appreciations* 437). For Pound, the plains of Provence, which are "of romance itself," literally at the heart of troubadour lyrics, are doubly resonant with the possibilities implicit in landscape (brought about by Schliemann and Bérard), as well a topos imbued with the Greek spirit, which in its surviving, vestiginous form had informed troubadour lyricism and might well, in some receptive state of mind, be yet apprehensible.

The concept that the land might provide the key to the mysteries of Provençal poetry – or, in a more heightened fantasy, that the earth itself encases the core of the poetic – figures prominently in Pound's roving meditations. In the Provençal notebooks, the poetic attaches itself to earth: landscape is the riddle to be deciphered, the root of a lost language to be drawn out. For Pound, Poitiers, in its maddening elusiveness, "is trobar clus" (*Walking Tour* 6) – according to Sieburth's definition, "an 'enclosed' or hermetic troubadour composition containing hidden or esoteric meanings" (111). The idea of place as concealed composition – a site of writing which contains its true poetic meaning or seed of memory within itself

– illustrates Pound's perception of landscape's ability to act as poetry, and, in turn, poetry's ability to become a multi-veiled *location* to and from which both the poet and readers may pass and return. Above all, the affinities between coded troubadour composition and the Provençal topos highlight the way in which Pound understood landscape to be a repository of forgotten knowledge, a smooth shell from which a multiplicity of meanings and memories could potentially be released.

Despite the sense of immediacy and possibility provided by landscape, the beginning of Pound's account, in particular, is filled with doubt. Newly arrived in Poitiers, for example, Pound admits:

> I was discouraged. The people wore the clothing of Milan and Paris, the cathedral is too newly whitewashed, the faint hopes aroused by the portal of St. Porchaire faded again, and I came upon a quiet street, empty of people. Poictiers, said I, has the charm of Germantown or Utica. There are here quiet gardens but this is not what I came for. All of which evils befell me for my natural sin, to wit, that of having come into Poictiers obviously & by steam contrivance.
>
> (*Walking Tour* 6)

Here it is modernity that is the concealing element – fashion, renovation, and newly planted gardens "whitewash" the authentic historical truth and impede any kind of authentic historical encounter. "Poictiers," in what Pound believed to be the archaic spelling of the town's name, had been replaced with "Poitiers," a modern town as mundane as the prosaic "Germantown or Utica." Pound's undesirable position as a representative of the modern is highlighted by his entry into Poitiers by "steam contrivance."

This chronic sense of having arrived too late or in too modern a condition ties Pound to the elegiac tradition of belatedness. The sense of loss that pervades Pound's account is resonant with Gautier's nostalgia for ancient Egypt and Pater's longing for classical Greece. In all of these cases the overriding feeling is of a paradise lost that can only be semi-re-ignited in a particularly poignant encounter with trace, ruin, or object. Yet, for Pound, in the spirit of the vortex "from which, and through which, and into which, ideas are constantly rushing," encountering the past is also a matter of recapturing persistent and moving energies:

> We appear to have lost the radiant world where one thought cuts through another with clean edge, a world of moving energies *"mezzo oscuro rade," "risplende in sè perpetuale effecto,"* magnetisms that take form, that are seen, on the border of the visible, the matter of Dante's *paradiso*, the glass under water, the form that seems a form seen in a mirror, these realities perceptible to the sense, interacting …
> (*Literary Essays* 154)

In Pound, this "lost" world is one to be reclaimed, and there is a consistent faith in the possibilities of reconnecting with archaic powers and harnessing these magnetisms for the purposes of modern artistic production. However de-centered they may be, these energies continue to exist peripherally, "on the border of the visible," and obscurely as a "glass under water" or a "form seen in a mirror." In spite of the sense of loss involved in the disappearance of the "radiant world" the past is still, for Pound, a matter of "realities" not just "perceptible to the sense" but consistently "interacting."

Unwilling to surrender to a fixed picture of historical sedimentation and to the loss that this would entail, Pound's identification of lingering energies renders the past peripatetic. The dynamism and persistence of these historical forces also make possible various modes of resurrection, the most Paterian of which are the historical possessions to which the poet succumbs. In the walking tour, Pound essentially sets out in search of this overtaking, a self-abandonment to the lost voices of the troubadours: "And finding these things so, seeing in a way how many persons may flow thru us or flow past us while we are alive" (*Walking Tour* 68). In an existence that is both "individual" and "continuous" the conversation among generations is maintained by this "cycle" of "reminiscence," which in some moments results in an utter sublimation of the ego and the full presence of historical forces and personalities, a sentiment that Pound would later crystallize in "Histrion": "No man hath dared to write this thing as yet, / And yet I know, how that the souls of all men great / At times pass athrough us" (*Personae* 71).

The notion of magnetisms in perpetual flux also brings forward the sensuous quality of Pound's engagement with the past. In the Provençal notebook, much of the journey is sustained by a desire that feeds on the very elusiveness of its object. Alone in Arles, Pound comments:

> You can not in any real sense *see* such places, you pass & return, & you know like fate in the weaving that some time you will come back for good there, for a time that is, for a liaison, for this is in the run what it comes to, a satiation, a flowing out from yourself into the passion & mood of the complex.
>
> (*Walking Tour* 64)

Here, actual geography gives way to the fantasy of place – the image of what had happened at this site overlapping with what could happen: the return, the liaison, an exteriorization of the self and abandonment to energies which results in "a satiation, a flowing out from yourself" as the limits of the individual are broken down and mind and body are given over to the infinite flux of the collective tradition. This amplified, at times ecstatic mode of recollection and historical participation is in stark contrast with and frequently followed by conservative and depressive self-questioning. In the most vivid moments of the text, however, Pound gives himself over to historical possibility, to free flowing expressionism, to an almost oracular rambling unhindered by self-censure, logic, or form. In these sections, the past appears to him as the composite woman of troubadour composition and desire itself becomes a desirable mode: "Be not cheap or mediocre in desiring. Almost, not quite, I was quoting Baudelaire's Be drunken" (61). The transformation of material realities into energies and this genuine abandonment to the forces of the past are perhaps what make past epochs nearer in Pound than in the writers we have encountered thus far. Rather than engage in a imaginative version of the self that would have been more spiritually in accord with a vanished era, Pound, as a modernized version of the poet intermediary, channels the voices of the past into a poetry of the new. In essence, Pound surmounts the difficulties of history that had plagued Gautier and Pater by breaking with chronology, making all eras retrievable through their persistence as energies. As Charles Olson would write, Pound "turned time into what we must now have, space & its live air" (*Mayan Letters* 26).

It is in the Provençal landscapes: half real, half reverie, part close scientific observation, part mystical invocation, stratified sites of disparate times and places where the memory of the poet intermixes with communal historical recollection that we can ascertain the topographical shape of *The Cantos*: the multi-layered, multi-spatial, multi-temporal landscapes that appeared to Pound during the walking tour and set the geographical and historical scope for his longest work. In the "Pisan Cantos," in particular, Pound, in the mounting tension of his imprisonment for treason against the allied forces, places maximum pressure on the poem so that the dramatically shifting topographies create a densely compacted historical site. Hence in "Canto LXXIV," Pound again references the "periplum" – landscapes at once real and mythic overlap in a richly sedimented topos of actual geography and mythical aura:

> But the caverns are less enchanting to the unskilled explorer
>   than the Urochs as shown on the postals,
> we will see those old roads again, question,
>   possibly
> but nothing appears much less likely,
>   Mme. Pujol,
> and there was a smell of mint under the tent flaps
> especially after the rain
>   and a white ox on the road toward Pisa
>   as if facing the tower,
> dark sheep in the drill field and on wet days were clouds
> in the mountain as if under the guard roosts.
>   A lizard upheld me
>   the wild birds wd not eat the white bread
>   from Mt Taishan to the sunset
> From Carrara stone to the tower
> (*The Cantos of Ezra Pound* 448)

The preliminary setting is the South of France, illustrated by the "Urochs" or European bison, which were frequently the subject of the cave-paintings of Paleolithic cave-dwellers and which Pound references in the Vorticism manifesto: "The PALEOLITHIC VORTEX resulted in the decoration of the / Dordogne caverns" (*Guide to Kulchur* 20). This archaic example is juxtaposed with Pound's nostalgia for his own wanderings in Provence, with the reference to Mme. Pujol "a landlady in Provence" (Terrell 367) and to the line "will we see these old roads again," which echoes the walking tour inspired "Provincia Deserta": "I have walked over these roads / I have thought of them living" (*Walking Tour* 102). This moment of reminiscence is made more poignant through the recollection of the "smell of mint." This impulse to firmly plant memory in the sensory details of landscape is also present in the pastoral references to ox and sheep as well as to the gradually more eastern landscapes characterized by mountains (particularly Mount Taishan) and the semi-fantastical lizard. Undulating between Provence and China, Italy also interfuses the mix through the Carrara marble which was used to build the leaning tower but which is also most famously linked to Michelangelo's half-formed statues, which must, at this point, have resonated with Pound's sense of a perpetually emerging poem that may never be completed. Inextricably tied to earthen landscapes, Pound's poetic topography is based on a Paleolithic foundation and moves through a series of personal, mystical, artistic, and historical plains which are fused and compacted by the danger and immediacy of the present situation. At once visionary and empirical, personal and historical, this interweaving of place and memory creates a condensed historical site of personal, historical, and poetic accumulation. Rather than simply an exercise in private meditation, however, Pound's landscapes are meant to serve a distinctly public function. As Peter Nicholls writes, the "splicing together of mythological and historical materials ... seeks to surmount the modern split between history as a public expression of the life of the nation, on the one hand, and memory as something purely private, on the other" (168). The creation of a collective space of mnemonic retrieval invites readers into a participatory form of digging which leads them deeply into the text and into a journey that is meant to awaken them to a sense of communal past as well as shared responsibility for a collective future.

It is in the poem "Hugh Selwyn Mauberley" that Pound begins to shape his Provençal meditations into a working theory of instructive historical immersion. Detailing the trajectory of a failed poet, Pound's alter-ego, from his arrival in London in the 1890s to his obscure death, the poem is also a biting critique of modern culture in its race to create an inferior level of art and civilization. "Hugh Selwyn Mauberley" is also noteworthy because of its connections with *Enamels and Cameos,* which, as we saw in the chapter on Gautier, is a vivid locus of archaeological encryptions. In his 1955 book, John Espey devotes a chapter to the influence of Gautier on

Pound's composition. Espey notes Pound's admiration for Gautier in his 1928 letter to René Taupin: "I studied Gautier and I revere him" (Pound qtd. in Espey 27). But Espey is still more concerned with Pound's formal inheritances from *Enamels and Cameos*, most notably: "Gautier's vocabulary, his method of flat statement and his general frame of reference" (28). Other critics have followed Espey's lead by positing further links between Gautier's collection and "Hugh Selwyn Mauberley." Ralph Baldner, for instance, suggests that *Enamels and Cameos* encouraged Pound to pursue: "The right word only, avoid the easy rhyme, and above all, keep the verse as clean as chiseled marble, free of sentimentality, non-rhetorical, non-metaphorical" (248).

Baldner's emphasis on the sculptural nature of Pound's borrowings from Gautier is supported by Pound's comments on French poetry in the essay "The Hard and the Soft":

> By "hardness" I mean a quality of which is in poetry nearly always a virtue – I can think of no case where it is not. By softness I mean an opposite quality which is not always a fault. Anyone who dislikes these textural terms may lay the blame on Théophile Gautier, who certainly suggests them in *Émaux et Camées*; it is his hardness that I had first in mind. He exhorts us to cut in hard substance, the shell and the Parian.
> (*Literary Essays* 285)

Pound's preference for the "hard" in poetry, a poetic obtained through a process of paring away the excess – we are reminded here of Pound's comment in Cavalcanti, "the rhyme pattern is, after all, a matter of chiseling" (169) – is indeed in tune with Gautier's "enamels and cameos" – classically inflected, highly wrought fragments achieved through an equally Paterian process of removing the surplus. Like Pater and Gautier, moreover, Pound consistently sculpts language in order to retrieve something pre-existing. Rather than improvising the truly new, achieving sculptural poetics is essentially a matter of arresting a pre-existing force – a process of unveiling that for Gautier, at least, is defined by the archaeological.

For Pound, however, burdened by a sense of social responsibility, the simple retrieval is never enough. Rather, excavations are performed on the past in order to harness anterior energies for future ambitions with the aid of new perspectives and techniques. The first body to be entombed in

"Hugh Selwyn Mauberley" is, therefore, not the Egyptian princess of Gautier's tales, but the poet himself: "E.P. ODE POUR L'ELECTION DE SON SEPULCHRE" (61). Here, the French gestures toward Gautier, but so does the internal resonance of the line. In "son sepulchre" we are reminded of Gautier's Egypt "Où sous le pied sonne la crypte" ("Nostalgie d'Obélisques," *Émaux et Camées* 74). Pound's play on "son" (at once "his" and "sound") echoes Gautier's resounding tomb. In addition to interring himself (if we assume E.P. to be self-referential), Pound has also literally encrypted Gautier into the epithet. In this sense, Gautier is at once acknowledged and subsumed, a stratum of Pound's modernism, an encoded influence that, nonetheless, continues to act on the rest of the poem.

The poet, Mauberley, is also entombed – his epitaph engraved into the poem: "*Vacuos exercet in aera morsus*" (71) – a repetition of the line that Pound quotes in "Cavalcanti" within the sentence "the god is inside the stone" (*Literary Essays* 152). This consistent process of interment and exhumation causes Daniel Tiffany to comment that for Pound "the successful poem is one in which the poet digs up a corpse and sets it out for the reader's curiosity or pleasure" (176) – though not always for pleasure and certainly not in section IV where the soldiers of the First World War are interred:

> Daring as never before, wastage as never before.
> Young blood and high blood,
> fair cheeks, and fine bodies;
>
> fortitude as never before
>
> frankness as never before,
> disillusions as never told in the old days,
> hysterias, trench confessions,
> laughter out of dead bellies.
> ("Mauberley" 64)

Within the context of a poem written in 1920 that is filled with death and haunting, it seems inevitable that the war would surface, and in such a manner that would change conceptions of earth. The catastrophic, degenerative trauma of losing so many, including Pound's friend and fellow vorticist

Gaudier-Brzeska, would result in the identification of earth with graves, a projection of ferocity and loss onto the material trenches. For Pound, in particular, the landscapes of France, once paradisal, would have been irreparably altered by the horrific carnage lying just beneath the earth's surface. If we consider the poem itself to be a semantic field, then it is the war section where meaning lies closest to the surface, the most recently interred. The rest of the poem's references, more deeply embedded in history, require an archival digging or tracing backward through the strata of successive epochs to a limitless original source. Readers are led from the story that is most familiar to them, the immediate history of friends and loved ones buried in France, to a broader underground history which Pound insists they must also claim – the mythic "Samothrace" (62) where the statue of winged victory had been discovered in 1863 and the "Minoan undulation" (75), suggestive of the landscape where King Minos' palace had been discovered by Arthur Evans on the eve of 1900.

It is toward the end of the poem that Pound elaborates on the importance of the archaeological to modernity's necessary reinvention. While the "Medallion" poem is perhaps the most heatedly debated as to whether Mauberley or Pound is speaking, the Gauterian mode of poetic chiseling is clearly in evidence:

> Luini in porcelain!
> The grand piano
> Utters a profane
> Protest with her clear soprano.
> (77)

Here, the short lines, the regular rhyme, and the images of hard materials – porcelain, the keys of the piano, clearly echo *Enamels and Cameos*. It is in the third stanza, however, that Pound also seems to invite Gautier's archaeological obsessions:

> Honey-red, closing the face-oval,
> A basket-work of braids which seem as if they were
> Spun in King Minos' hall
> From metal, or intractable amber;

The references to hair and King Minos re-invoke Arthur Evans' discovery of the Minoan civilization at Knossos.[1] One of the most striking and celebrated of Evans' finds was a series of portraits of women whose hairstyles were practically identical to those sported by Parisian society women in the cafés of the 1890s. As Evans wrote in an early article on his preliminary discoveries:

> To the north of the palace, in some rooms that seem to have belonged to the women's quarter, frescoes were found in an entirely novel miniature style. Here were ladies with white complexions – due, we may fancy, to the seclusion of harem life *décolletées*, but with fashionable puffed sleeves and flounced gowns, and their hair was elaborately curled and *frisé* as if they were fresh from a *coiffeur's* hands. "*Mais*," exclaimed a French savant who honoured me with a visit, "*ce sont des Parisennes!*"
>
> (193)

The vividness of the Minoan example demonstrates the ways in which Pound perceives certain energies to be timeless, consistently recurring, or as Kenner suggests: "they exist now, with the strange extra-temporal persistence of objects in space" (31). The invocation of Minoan archaeology illustrates the persistence of the past in the present and demonstrates again how Pound perceives history to be a space laden with harbingers of the new.

This feeling, that the future is somehow encased in the past, is also fundamental to Pound's political archaeology. The most prescient example is the reactivation of the figure of Sigismundo Malatesta, the fifteenth-century war-lord, in *The Cantos*. If in "Hugh Selwyn Mauberley" Pound employs the text as a burial ground, the Malatesta Cantos are tantamount to a resurrection. This reanimation takes place in several ways: the assumption of Malatesta's voice in the narration of battle, the animated recounting of historical detail, and the privileged presentation of the Tempio Malatestiano, a church renovated by Malatesta in the height of Renaissance craftsmanship, as a location where cultic energies of the past reassert themselves through

---

1   Stan Smith comes to a similar conclusion in his 1994 volume, *The Origins of Modernism* (79). While I came to the same conclusion independently, original credit must go to Professor Smith.

the stone reliefs of mythical scenes. The general mood of the Malatesta Cantos is that of resurgence – Malatesta pressing against his enemies in battle, the sensuous love for his mistress and then third wife Isotta stressing the strictures of the Vatican, and the reemergence of the ancient gods through the hardness of the Tempio's stone reliefs. The archaeological "veracity" of these scenes is anchored through the mechanisms of "text-aided" archaeology: the turn to documents and written sources which verify or give greater clarity to the material sites. This method emerges most clearly in the post-bag section, where a wide variety of letters "captured" by Sigismundo's enemies provide a sense of the whole man: father, lover, patron, and war-lord. Here, similar to when eighteenth-century visitors began exploring Pompeii, the past acts forcefully on the viewer because of a privileged, voyeuristic vantage point on domestic affairs. The daily reality of the past is vividly present in the accumulation of documentary evidence: the letter Pound improvises from the tutor of Sigismundo's son: "Messire Malatesta is well and asks for you every day. He / is so much pleased with his pony, It wd. take me a month / to write you all the fun he gets out of that pony" (*The Cantos* 38); the updates on the progress of the Tempio: "This to advise your / Mgt Ldshp how the second load of Veronese marble has / finally got here, after being held up at Ferrara …" (40); and the final letter, a testament of Sigismundo's love for Isotta:

>"*et amava perdutamente Ixotta degli Atti*
>e "*ne fu degna*"
>   "*constans in proposito*
>"*Placuit oculis principis*
>"*pulchra aspectu*"
>"*populo grata (Italiaeque decus)*
>"and built a temple so full of pagan works"
>   i.e. Sigusmund
>and in the style "Past ruin'd Latium"
>The filigree hiding the gothic,
>   with a touch of rhetoric in the whole
>And the old sarcophagi,
>   such as lie, smothered in grass, by San Vitale.
>(41)

The composite Italian and Latin testimonial: "And he loved Isotta degli Atti to distraction / and she was worthy of it / constant in purpose / She delighted the eye of the prince / lovely to look at / pleasing to the people (and the ornament of Italy)" (Terrell 48) testifies to the dignity of Sigismundo's love as well as for Isotta as a deserving recipient, guaranteed, for Pound, by the transposition of emotion into the building of the Tempio. From the letters in the post-bag, Pound invites us to create a picture of the man, to imaginatively exceed the evidence presented and to participate in the process of archaeological fantasizing which creates living, moving, historical realities from documentary and material evidence. This invitation to reverie, to become a part of a collective fantasy which would define the mythos of a new order, is, for Pound, at the basis of creating a social system connected by its common sense of origins.

Pound's archaeology, which encases Gautier's sculptural elements and Pater's release into other ages, yet insists on an exteriorized, social mandate for literature, can be contrasted with other modernist writers who also borrow from the nineteenth-century substrata, though with distinctly divergent intents. In terms of Pound's Malatestan interests, the most pertinent example is Adrian Stokes, who shared Pound's fascination with the Tempio and wrote *Stones of Rimini* as an aesthetic tribute to its Renaissance artistry parallel to Ruskin's appreciation of Gothic form in *The Stones of Venice*. While Stokes and Pound shared a common conceptual sense of the processes of exteriorization as they relate to the Tempio, the nature of that exteriorization was vastly different. For Pound, the church was a repository where a social force could be unleashed. For Stokes, on the other hand, working from much more Paterian and Freudian perspectives on artistry and the unconscious, the release achieved by the Tempio was above all a working through of sublimated desire. In *Stones of Rimini*, for example, Stokes comments: "I do not myself consider it a matter of any importance for interpretation, to decide what were the exact *conscious* aims of Tempio sculpture" (233).

In a passage on the ornamental putti we can sense the ways in which Stokes's fantasying is related to the elemental human impulses that are at play in the Tempio reliefs:

"Original in the right sense"

> The putto makes the air move. Indeed he is associated with all the elements. He bursts stone like earth, at Rimini he rides the dolphin, his tempestuous energy kindles a flame that withers tasteful ornamental foliage poor in sap, and heats the luscious growth to a vibrant, tropical bulbosity. The putto is elemental force under the symbol of the infant's animal nature. He is the emblem of Europe ... we of the West have symbolized fecundity by the infant, by the play of infants in whom the primary desires that make the adult world limitless, subterranean, dark, are seen bright and immediate and in their least unsettled state.
>
> (*The Quattro Cento* 133)

Here, in the cumulative cadences, we can sense the influence of Pater's aesthetic historicism, where within one frozen moment the entire history of the West is captured in a symbol or an icon. For Stokes, this emblem is the putto, who not only encapsulates a collective history, but also a history of collective desiring. Within the Tempio friezes the inner recesses of the communal subconscious are made manifest, a move from the "limitless, subterranean dark" of repressed desire to a vital, disinterred state of brightness and immediacy. Like Freud moving from mnemonic latency in the individual to collective latency in "Moses and Monotheism," Stokes essentially perceives cultural re-emergence to mirror the forces of the individual unconscious. In Florentine art, Stokes, therefore, discerns the presence of cultural "substrat[a]" which over time "transmut[e] into humanism" (50). Within the emergent stone of the Tempio reliefs, Pound and Stokes both discern a recurrent polytheism and an exteriorization of desire – for Pound, the collective desire for a society and a mythology in tune with nature; for Stokes, the pluralistic desires of the individual made manifest through stone. For Pound, the Tempio is the embodiment of the magnetisms he searched for in the landscape of Provence. For Stokes, the Tempio is a rich ground which emulates, through the forces of stone and water, sculptor and sculpted, the return of the psychically repressed.

While Pound encouraged Stokes' interest in the Tempio and admired his early writing on the subject, it is quite possible that, as Richard Read has noted: "[Pound] might not have admired them so readily if he had realized that they were also 'phantasies' in the Freudian sense of bearing a profound relation to the unconscious" (132). Pound's hostility to Freud and to psychoanalytic theory generally is part of his profound aversion to the interiorized experience, which detracts from fully released expression as well as from outwardly directed social concerns. But Pound's later distancing of himself from Stokes may also have been the result of the recognition of Stokes' reading of bisexual possibilities in the art of the Tempio. In one of the reliefs, for example, Stokes makes explicit connections between Isotta and Ganymede:

> None the less, Ganymede has the Isotta features ... he is young and beautiful ... Again one is aware of a heightened erotic symbolism that reinforces the direct and primary sexual symbolism of the old astrological myths ... Isotta, young and serene, presides throughout the skies' hemispheres and interminable alternations ... She is Ganymede, she is Mercury ... she is the Moon, Diana who confounds the heights with the depths, goddess of waters, of pools and stones.
>
> (*Stones of Rimini* 246)

Stokes' portrayal of the sexual ambiguity of Renaissance sculpture is reminiscent of Gautier's "Contralto," where the erotic figure encodes both male and female characteristics: "Est-ce un jeune homme? est-ce une femme? / Une déesse, ou bien un dieu?" (*Émaux et Camées* 60). In the tradition of Winckelmann and Pater, Stokes foregrounds the traces of sexual pluralism in ancient art. Like the elemental fantasy of the putto, the sculptures, for Stokes, exteriorize modes of desire repressed in contemporary culture.

Stokes, of course, was not the only modernist and Pound protégé to borrow from more occluded aspects of nineteenth-century archaeological models. H.D., who used this fragmented form of her own name, Hilda Doolittle, as a *nom-de-plume*, was also a contemporary of Pound's who operated within the tradition of sculptural encoding. The statue of the *Hermaphrodite Sleeping*, which we last encountered in Gautier's Palazzo Massimo resurges in H.D.'s novel *Paint it Today*, where the narrator, Midget, stands transfixed before the "gentle breathing image, modeled in strange, soft, honey colored stone" (65). Like Winckelmann and Pater, H.D. attaches appreciations of same-sex figures to Greek statuary, as in Midget's appraisal of the Venus de Milo:

> Here in the flow of visitors, Midget hardly dared let go realities. She dared not follow the curve of the white belly and short space before the breasts brought the curve to a sudden shadow.
>
> (60)

Moreover, when H.D. opts to usher these intensities into the present, in the figure of a living person, it is, like Gautier in sections of *Mademoiselle de Maupin*, through an elaborate system of classical allusion and interpolation of the human body into masonry:

> It was her eyes, set in the unwholesome face; it was the shoulders, a marble splendor, unspoiled by the severe draping of straight cut rainproof; it was her hand, small, unbending, stiff with archaic grandeur; it was her eyes, an unholy splendor.
>
> (*Paint it Today* 9)

In essence, these modernist appropriations of nineteenth-century modes of expression continue a semi-veiled discussion of desire for the same. It also illustrates how modernists like Stokes and H.D. would extract elements of nineteenth-century models that Pound would leave untapped.

H.D.'s work, generally, provides an illustrative contrast to Pound's archaeology. Imagists for a brief time in London, both Pound and H.D. valued the role of the object as an expression of perfect clarity. Moreover, working together in the library of the British Museum as young poets, they were exposed to the archaeological finds of Egypt, the Middle East, and Greece, as well as the Sapphic fragments on display. Inspired by a torn parchment, Pound would write the poem "Papyrus": "Spring ... / Too long ... / Gongula ..." (*Personae* 165) while H.D. would use Sapphic fragments as epithets of some of her best known poems: "I know not what to do: / my mind is divided" ("Fragment Thirty-six," *Collected Poems* 165), "Neither honey nor bee for me," ("Fragment 113" 131), "Love ... bitter-sweet" ("Fragment Forty" 173) and "... thou flittlest to Andromeda" ("Fragment Forty-one" 181). While H.D.'s poetry is much more responsive to the overtones of same-sex desire in Sapphic lyrics, there would remain in both modern poets a pleasure in the shard, the absent, the unspoken, a preference that would endure in the work of Pound and H.D., modulating into a fragmented poesis that would come to define the modernist aesthetic.

Yet despite a shared preference for fragmented modes of expression and the beauty of the object, a fundamental difference can be found in Pound and H.D.'s poetic presentations of time and space. While Pound regularly fused the mythical and the mundane and channeled the voices of the past there was, nonetheless, in *The Cantos* an insistence on maintaining a separation between historical periods. As Donald Davie describes:

> ... several commentators have followed Hugh Kenner in seeing ... what is to be a common procedure in many of the cantos, a procedure that they call "cultural overlaying." ... But the important point was made by Williams:
>
>> Only superficially do the Cantos fuse the various temporal phases of the material Pound has chosen, into a synthesis ...
>
> One culture may "overlayer" another; but the layers remain, and are meant to remain, distinct. What is intended is a sort of lamination, by no means a compounding or fusing of distinct historical phases into an undifferentiated amalgam.
>
> (123)

In H.D., by contrast, we find a temporality that is, in fact, synthesis. As a more inward-oriented writer than Pound, H.D.'s modernist impulse toward the layering of epochs was mitigated by a profoundly Freudian feeling for dream condensation. Like Freud's analysis of dreams, H.D.'s poems: "show a particular preference for combining contraries into a unity or for representing them as one and the same thing" (Freud, "The Antithetical Meaning of Primal Words" 94). This is particularly true of disparate historical periods, which often emerge in H.D.'s work as imaginatively fused.

The immersive dimensions of H.D.'s temporality are elucidated in the novel *Asphodel*, where the narrator notes that life is a series of transparent layers which interpenetrate "like water":

> Sometimes for a moment we realize a layer out of ourselves, in another sphere of consciousness, sometimes one layer falls and life itself, the very reality of tables and chairs becomes imbued with a quality of long-past, an epic quality so that the chair you sit in maybe the very chair you drew forward when as Cambyses you consulted over the execution of your faithless servitors.
>
> (152)

This historical synchronicity – where you are at once yourself in a daily domestic situation and also a punitive Persian King encountered in Herodotus – is elaborated by H.D. as a function of realizing "a layer out of ourselves" which is simultaneously "another sphere of consciousness." In this sense, H.D. perceives history to be something that is internalized, with various historical moments as retrievable as our own memories, and as prone to melding and overlap.

For H.D. the image of the palimpsest, a parchment that has been written over many times with traces of the past underwriting the current text and at times interfering with its legibility, is an apt description of the psychic dimensions of time.[2] In H.D.'s palimpsest we sense echoes of Freud's Mystic Writing Pad and the traces of memory that underwrite conscious perception, and it is in these similarities that we can detect H.D.'s admiration for Freud as well as the traces of her 1933–4 sessions with him in Vienna. In contrast with Freud's formulation, however, H.D.'s palimpsests are at once individual in their reflections of one person's experience of time and space, and an experience that exceeds the self in that the other realms that can be accessed may include other epochs, other people, and other material realities. While this belief has overtones of Pound's view in "Histirion" that "things pass through us while we are alive," H.D.'s method is more immersive in its dream-like condensation of disparate times and places.

This palimpsestic approach to history is realized in the long poem "Trilogy," which opens with the dedication: "To Bryher / for Karnak 1923 / from London 1942." The locations in the poem's opening section are, therefore, identified for readers as the Egyptian complex near Luxor – which H.D. and her long-time companion Bryher Ellerman visited at the same time that Howard Carter was opening King Tutankhamun's tomb

---

2   In her study of the palimpsest, Sarah Dillon documents the ways various critics have interpreted the concept in H.D.'s oeuvre. Interestingly the palimpsest is most typically read as a gender strategy rather than a historical strategy – a means of counteracting dominant male/female dichotomies rather than past/present ones. It could be argued that H.D. is challenging a "patriarchal" sense of time, but this seems a reductive reading of what H.D. presents as a complex dissolution of the self into historical "otherness."

– and London, where Bryher and H.D. lived throughout the second war. The poem begins by alternating locations, first the war-torn city, then the hieroglyph-inscribed temples and obelisks of Karnak:

> An incident here and there,
> and rails gone (for guns)
> from your (and my) old town square:
>
> mist and mist-grey, no colour,
> still the Luxor bee, chick and hare
> pursue unalterable purpose
>
> in green, rose-red, lapis;
> they continue to prophesy
> from the stone papyrus:
> (*Collected Poems* 509)

The alternation between locations, a modern metropolis and an antique temple, is reminiscent of Gautier's "Nostalgia of the Obelisks," one obelisk in Paris, the other in Luxor. Rather than retain the sense of distance between the two arenas as Gautier does, H.D. opts to create a strong sense of cohesion between the two moments, the two monuments:

> there, as here, ruin opens
> the tomb, the temple; enter,
> there as here, there are no doors:
>
> the shrine lies open to the sky,
> the rain falls, here, there
> sand drifts; eternity endures:
>
> ruin everywhere, yet as the fallen roof
> leaves the sealed room
> open to the air,

The feeling that a church in the old town-square has been bombed to the point that the "shrine lies open to the sky" makes it, in H.D.'s mind, a parallel point to the Egyptian tomb which "ruin opens" – a pointed remark on modernity's destructive imposition of itself on both past and present.

"Original in the right sense" 137

The repetition of the line "there, as here" closes the gap between these two locations, creating a visual montage of a bombed out square which is also an Egyptian tomb; "sand drifts; eternity endures" while the hubristic leadership of each civilization brings about its end.

Within this visual overlap, H.D. summons another archaeological image:

> to another cellar, to another sliced wall
> where poor utensils show
> like rare objects in a museum;
>
> Pompeii has nothing to teach us,
> we know crack of volcanic fissure,
> slow flow of terrible lava,
> (510)

Here, the invocation of Pompeii creates a sense of London as a city that has also been "struck." The description in the first stanza takes on the voice of the archaeologist or archaeological tourist: "another cellar ... another sliced wall" but the static scene of "poor utensils" displayed like "rare objects" quickly gives way to the human dimension that is edited from archaeological sites and museums, narrated by the first-person witness:

> pressure on heart, lungs, the brain
> about to burst its brittle case
> (what the skull can endure!):
>
> over us, Apocryphal fire,
> under us, the earth sways, dip of a floor,
> slope of a pavement
>
> where men roll, drunk
> with a new bewilderment,
> sorcery, bedevilment
>
> the bone-frame was made for
> no such shock knit within terror,
> yet the skeleton stood up to it:

> the flesh? It was melted away,
> the heart burnt out, dead ember,
> tendons, muscles shattered, outer husk dismembered
>
> yet the frame held:
>
> we passed the flame: we wonder
> what saved us? what for?
> (510–11)

If the movement between East and West via the monument is an echo of Gautier, then the biting critique of a civilization gone mad shares common ground with Pound. Rather than inter the dead in the shallow surface of the poem, H.D. creates a unity of pain as the flesh is "melted away, / the heart burnt out, dead ember," and the "slow flow of terrible lava" overtakes both past and present in a synchronic moment of destruction. There are similarities with Pound in that H.D. finds mythic parallels with these material realities – the next section of the poem creates an exhaustive set of correspondences among Egyptian, Judaic, and Christian religions – yet in the first section, where the archaeological is most present, there is a harkening back to the English romantic poetry of ruins in that the deadened specter of great civilizations predicts our own demise. Rather than a nostalgic, hypothetical invocation of ruin, however, H.D.'s own position at the centre of the London blitz creates a sense of trauma and immediacy. The spectacle of the dead and dying summons not the image of a faded Italian landscape but of the massive human suffering inflicted by the eruption of Mount Vesuvius in the moment the lava began to overtake a fleeing population, echoing Bulwer-Lytton's description of "the half-hid limbs of some crushed and mangled fugitive" in *The Last Days of Pompeii* (397).

This sense, that the remote past intrudes on the present in the moment of devastation, is evident throughout "Trilogy" and highlighted by the formal fusion of present and past, stark, halting lines, and the fragmented perceptions of the traumatized subject. This war-time archaeology, in which the blasting of the earth would seem to summon the past to the surface, would have a significant influence on later poets. Charles Olson, who was profoundly affected by events at Buchenwald and Hiroshima, would begin

"Original in the right sense" 139

to collapse the "distances" between historical epochs in his own poetry and would, like H.D., come to see that the disasters of war had reduced us to a primitive condition: "yet the ancient rubrics reveal that / we are back at the beginning" ("Trilogy," *Collected Poems* 517).

In archaeology, Anglo-American modernists would, paradoxically, find the means to newness: in Pound, the recapturing of the historical moments that pointed out the path to the future, in Stokes an expressive mode of ushering the suppressed into the present, in H.D. alternate visions of an internalized history and dream-disordered commentary on the modern condition. If Pound succeeded in creating an agenda for modernism, it was partly through a mining of the strata that had come before: selective extractions and imaginative additions to a field that Gautier and Pater had already plumbed. The "modernism" of Pound's modernism was in many ways his rebellious sense of time and space, a reconfiguration that H.D. and Stokes would be attentive to even as they set about combining it with other aspects of the archaeological inheritance. The modulation of Freudian archaeologies that we saw here would endure still more significant modification in French surrealism, while Pound's alternate chronology surfaces again in the work of Charles Olson.

CHAPTER 6

Urban Archaeologies of the French Surrealists

If we consider the modernist branches of archaeological thought discussed in the previous two chapters – the Freudian/H.D. interiorized archaeology on the one hand and the Poundian exteriorized archaeology on the other, then French surrealism must be considered primarily part of the Freudian line, though it is a branch that consistently intersects with its social counter-part. Despite its goals of social transformation, surrealism was essentially a revolution of individual consciousness inspired by immersion in psychoanalytic possibilities. We know that the surrealists read Freud and proclaimed: "Freudian criticism to be the first and only one with a really solid basis" (André Breton, *Manifestoes of Surrealism* 160). Moreover, the surrealist interest in the unconscious, automatism, dreams, and the general emphasis on interiority were largely developed through contact with early Freudian texts. Added to this, the surrealist preoccupation with artistic renderings of densely layered subjective world-views marks the movement as a prime inheritor of Freud's topography of the mind.

Yet, as many have pointed out, the surrealist relationship with their psychoanalytic mentor was ambiguous and it is unlikely that Breton would have adopted any Freudian paradigm without considerable modification. As S. Dresden notes: "When in 1924 the French Surrealists gathered around the first manifesto, they based themselves among other things on Freud's writings of twenty-five years before. But Freud happened to have changed his ideas radically in his metapsychology of the 1920s ... [a]s far as can be ascertained, the Surrealists took no notice of this evolution" (128). This seeming lack of interest in psychoanalytic development along with the surrealists' repeatedly stated distrust of the psychoanalytic profession were compounded by luke-warm communications with Freud himself. While Freud apparently revised his opinion of surrealism in 1938 after a successful encounter with Dali, Breton was deeply disappointed by an uncomfortable 1921 meeting with Freud and published a disapproving report of Freud's seeming incomprehension of the movement's motivations.

For those who have read both Freudian and Bretonian works, an uneasy personal relationship between the two men and Freud's difficulty in comprehending surrealist ambitions seems only to be expected. While Freud acted as a departure point for the surrealists, their artistic and theoretical contributions stretched psychoanalytic concepts to their very limit. But the disparity between Freud and the surrealists is not so much one of divergent theoretical constructs as of vastly different intents. After all, the overwhelming thrust of the Freudian method is to return patients to rationality. The surrealists, on the other hand, perceive bourgeois rationalism to be the disease. Freud believed in free association as long as the initial concept was kept within reach; the surrealists frequently extolled the wild bounds of imagination that came from unregulated automatism. Freud privileges conscious reality and charges the intellect with the task of deciphering the unconscious through traditional prose. The surrealists consistently work toward accessing the unconscious directly and allowing it to speak unrestricted by structure, tradition, or aesthetic taste. Freud studies dreams in order to determine their relationship to reality; the surrealists view them as autonomous fragments of a richer state of perception. This divergence in values is well summed up by the surrealist critic Clifford Browder who writes:

> ... the analyst is on the side of reason and common sense: whatever reservations he may have about society's moral conventions, he may adjust to normal existence. But Surrealism spurns such a compromise, envies the neurotic his exuberant imagination, and itself seeks revelations that discredit reality. It does not abandon the rational, but by confronting it with its opposite enriches and transforms it.
>
> (67)

The "discredit[ing of] reality" through a process of Hegelian dialecticism is perhaps the central focus of the surrealist campaign. Indeed, the desire to "amalgamate apparent contradictions into a higher unity" (Dresden 119) is at the base of surrealism itself, where the overriding goal is to blur the line between reality and dream in order to create a new field of consciousness: "I believe in the future resolution of these two states, dream and reality, which are seemingly so contradictory, into a kind of absolute reality, a *surreality*, if one may so speak" (Breton, *Manifestoes of Surrealism* 14). The blurring of the dream/real distinction, which characterizes the surrealist enterprise also extends to other "outmoded" oppositions. For the surrealists, the utopian beyond consists of a perceptual plane that obliterates contradiction of all kinds: "the real and the imaginary, the past and the future ... cease to be perceived as contradictory" (165), thereby ushering Freud's contradictory dream-state into the living, waking world.

The most striking description of this erasure of contradiction appears in *Communicating Vessels*, where Breton describes dream as "capillary" tissue, through which the real and the unreal, consciousness and unconsciousness are in constant communication and exchange. The incorporation of opposites is also implicit in a 1941 portrait of Breton by André Masson. In the sketch, Breton appears Janus-like, one face staring determinedly into the future, the other looking back with eyes closed. Between the two faces, an opening into the recesses of Breton's brain reveals phantom-like tissue. The portrayal clearly gestures toward Breton's theory of dream-reality interchange in *Communicating Vessels*. Yet the Janus overtones also speak to the temporal tensions in surrealism, the desire to transcend contradiction, and Breton's double-bound interest in the utopian future as well as the obscure mythological past.

Therefore, while Freud and the surrealists differ on the ideal state of being (rationality versus a rationality confronted and modified by its opposite), they do share a common interest in maintaining the legitimate integration of apparent opposites. In the chapter on psychoanalysis, we saw how Freud accomplished this accommodation through varying uses of the archaeological metaphor: dream, time, space, and desire subject to logical irreconcilability achieve recognition in Freud's archaeological topography. As we will find, the surrealists appropriated this Freudian paradigm but used it in a variety of ways that far exceed Freud's original intent. Rather than a space reserved exclusively for dialectical redemption, the dynamics of the archaeological mode permit the surrealists to break down the past/present distinction and to integrate mythic content into the quotidian context. Moreover, archaeological overtones unveil not only the "sur"reality of suspended contradiction but also the "sous"reality – a hidden realm buried beneath the surface of the city and the dwelling place of the "*merveilleux*." Finally, the adoption of archaeological optics gave the surrealists the analytic distance required to become "readers" of their own civilization: to address and interpret the signs of city life as though they were hieroglyphic codes gesturing toward a deeper understanding of the modern metropolis.

While measuring influence can often prove a challenging task, it, therefore, seems useful to see how the surrealists "borrowed" archaeological imagery from Freud and how they then went about refining its metaphoric possibilities to suit their own revolutionary purposes. In pursuing this line of inquiry, Freud's Gradiva is a helpful model. "Delusions and Dreams" was the surrealists' introduction to Jensen's story and to the archaeological figure who would become central to their avant-garde iconography. The themes of the analysis: dreams, desire, repression and return, all illustrated through the archaeological landscape, were of particular interest to the surrealist movement. Not surprisingly, the level-headed figure of Zoe, beloved by Freud and the textual representative of cool analytic recovery and bourgeois family values, was not especially intriguing to the surrealists. Rather, it was the figure of Gradiva, the frieze transformed to life and the embodiment of Pompeii's pagan traditions that proffered an aesthetic model of artistic/erotic enchantment.

Gradiva became a central symbol in surrealist art and literature, an emblem that more often than not stood for the erasure of contradiction. One of the classic examples of surrealist painting, for example, is Masson's ghoulish 1939 rendition "Metamorphosis of Gradiva" which features an ambiguously gendered figure, half sculpture, half human body. Two years earlier, Breton had opened an art gallery called "Gradiva" and commissioned Marcel Duchamp to create entrance doors that spoke of androgynous impulses. "Gradiva" was the name of the avant-garde surrealist journal of the 1930s with a copy of the ancient Greco-Roman frieze on its cover. The women of the surrealist circle were even nicknamed "Gradiva" when cast in the role of artistic muse. As Whitney Chadwick comments, Gradiva became "the most concentrated expression of the Surrealist cult of love" (77). But more than "love" – or perhaps *because* of love's supreme transcendental significance in surrealist art – we can also detect the ways in which Gradiva became the symbol of the reconciliation of opposites, as art/life, man/woman, new/old were ideologically and artistically fused in her name. Rather than just a recurring image, Gradiva became a figure of the absolute, an ideal archaeologically inspired amalgamation: the past combined with the present, dream phantom with concrete reality, and aesthetic creation with living flesh ... a figure far exceeding Freud's estimation as simply an embodied return of the repressed.

While Gradiva's pervasiveness in surrealist work could provide a suggestive lead as to the preponderance of archaeological themes in the surrealist oeuvre, there is, contrary to the vast proliferation of work on archaeology and Freud, very little criticism on surrealism and archaeology.[1] There are several reasons for this. To begin, by modulating the Gradavian figure and other archaeological motifs to suit a wide range of theoretical parameters, the surrealists tended to obscure the archaeological nature of their work. Like Pound, the surrealists avoid an earth-and-spades type archaeology in favor of the optics or dynamics of the archaeological enterprise. In surrealist work, this translates into an interest in the perpetuity of past forces, hieroglyphics, and multi-layered realities rather than the literal unearthing we encountered in Gautier or the extended metaphors of Pater and Freud. In this sense, surrealist archaeology relies more on the echoes of excavation than on the types of direct comparisons that are characteristic of Freud's archaeological mode.

Despite the surrealists' refracted approach to archaeological concepts, an approach that extends to other types of scientific borrowings, critics have seen fit to continually look for scientific themes in surrealist work. To a significant extent, this has to do with surrealist theory, which frequently proclaims surrealism's ambitions as "scientific" rather than "literary," as within the surrealist lexicon, "science" signifies bold experimentation while

---

[1] See Johanna Malt's "Archaeology, myth and the commodity: Walter Benjamin and *Le Paysan de Paris*" and her consequent book, *Obscure objects of desire: surrealism, fetishism, and politics*. Michael Shanks also mentions archaeology as an aesthetic strategy of surrealism in *Experiencing the Past*.

"literature" is reserved for a contrived tradition of rote narrative texts. Whether or not the products of surrealism could genuinely be called scientific, this penchant for science compounded by the surrealist interest in reclaiming "primitive" powers has led to many comparisons between surrealism and anthropology. As both anthropology and archaeology are scientific disciplines that lend themselves to ideas of reclaiming the "primitive," we might speculate that the reason for this critical privileging of anthropology over archaeology has partly to do with a series of connotations that surround the two disciplines. It would not be too much to say that archaeology is still enmeshed in connotations of death, antiquarianism, and classical culture, a compounded "negative" archaeology we have encountered in previous chapters. Anthropology, on the other hand, is largely considered a wilder, more contemporary cousin interested in the rituals of often still living exotic civilizations. To suggest the surrealists are "archaeological" is to create a complex paradox where "avant-garde" must be reconciled with a "regarde-arrière." The avant-garde attraction to primitive energies can be reconciled within the anthropological paradigm, but how can surrealism, an avant-garde phenomenon, be said to dwell in the ancient past?

Part of the difficulty in naming archaeological traces in avant-garde art has to do with the way in which the avant-garde has traditionally been portrayed as intent on overcoming history. We might consider the Italian futurists, for example, who flamboyantly promised to "blow-up" the past and ranted against the "necrophilia" of the archaeologist.[2] Despite the fact that the futurists perceived themselves as motivated by primal impulses, their most memorable rhetoric concerns the destruction of history. There

---

2   See F.T. Marinetti's "The Founding and Manifesto of Futurism" (1909) which establishes the movement's futuristic aims on the abolishment of archaeology and antiquarianism: "It is from Italy that we launch through the world this violently upsetting incendiary manifesto of ours. With it, today, we establish *Futurism*, because we want to free this land from its smelly gangrene of professors, archaeologists, *ciceroni* and antiquarians. For too long has Italy been a dealer in second-hand clothes. We mean to free her from the numberless museums that cover her like so many graveyards" (12).

is a clear demarcation here between the surrealists, who lauded interiority and ancestral connections and the futurists who wanted to explode introspection and saw themselves as largely self-generated. At the same time, both of these movements have utopian aims that depend on the modification of the past – in the case of the futurists, the destruction thereof, for the surrealists, the reconciliation of past and present. In other words, both movements, in their double-bound preoccupation with past and future, are implicated in the dynamics of the modernist archaeological modality. Therefore, while the avant-garde, even in its most extreme forward-looking manifestation is not generally considered to be "archaeological" in intent, we can perceive the ways in which the temporal dynamics of avant-gardism coincide with the past-future tensions of modern archaeology – a cohesion which, though paradoxical, legitimizes the search for archaeological traces in avant-garde production.

In order to deduce the shape and scope of archaeological motifs in surrealism, it is useful to return to the anthropological paradigm and observe the kinds of connections critics have made between surrealism and anthropology. The first event to which critics tend to refer is the 1941 meeting between André Breton and Claude Lévi-Strauss on the ship that carried both passengers toward New York and away from Nazi occupied France. This meeting led to a prolonged friendship and intellectual exchange, which, for Lieve Spaas, was underpinned by "the common search which underlies these major twentieth century intellectual movements: the search for the primitive" (163). For Spaas, the difference between surrealism and structural anthropology is that while anthropology searches for lost civilizations, surrealism seeks to discover lost dimensions of the hidden self (166). Michel Beaujour and Louis Tremaine go one step further by linking the anthropological paradigm to surrealist novels. Beaujour compares *Nadja* to the anthropologist Michel Leiris' journal *L'Afrique fantôme* (*Phantom Africa*) and suggests Breton's novel is "the tale of an ethnological expedition into the interior of a singularly unnerving city, a haunted Paris" (23). Tremaine echoes this set of associations in his in-depth comparison of *Nadja* to Carlos Castaneda's trilogy of anthropological works on mysticism and the Yaqui aboriginals of the American Southwest. For Tremaine, the similarity between *Nadja* and Castenada's works lies not so much in direct anthropological references, as in common thematic preoccupations: "the search for self-understanding, the consideration of non-rational modes of perception, the close relationship between the narrator and an individual who seems to live a different order of reality" (92). Rarely, if ever, do the surrealists mention anthropology per se. Rather, the links critics have established are a matter of interests, perspectives, or dynamics common to both surrealist and anthropologist.

I would agree with Spaas, Beaujour and Tremaine that the search for the "primitive," coincidental themes in anthropological and surrealist oeuvres, and the bond between Breton and Lévi-Strauss do create a suggestive arena for comparison. Breton's visits to American Indian reservations and his participation in Haitian voodoo ceremonies provide further evidence of anthropological intent – though perhaps Breton's interest was not so much that of the impartial scientist as of someone who desired to *replicate* a mode of being in the world that was in-tune with the philosophical aims of surrealism. What few of the anthropological arguments on surrealism take into account, however, is the way in which the surrealists equally often viewed the coveted "primitive force" as a property of the ancient past – a paradise once extant and now lost that in some sense must be excavated to be reclaimed.

As we have seen, surrealism, unlike most of the avant-gardes, admits to a long and complex genealogy. Like Pater, Gautier, Heine, Pound, and Stokes, Breton subscribed to the idea that at the advent of Christianity, the forces of paganism and magic did not disappear, but rather went "underground." For Breton, this subversive current was the well-spring of surrealism which could regularly be tapped into. As Browder notes: "Breton's movement, revolutionary as it is, recognized innumerable antecedents dating back to the remotest time and consciously renews contact with them" (144). This renewal involves an immersion in the power of the past and, consequently, immersion in the power of memory in order to connect with latent forces. As Breton himself suggests: "Surrealism will usher you into death, which is a secret society. It will glove your hand, burying therein the profound M with which the word Memory begins" (*Manifestoes of Surrealism* 32). For J.D. Hubert, this emphasis on memory is part of an overwhelming "nostalgia" for the past: "a past as much imaginary as *merveilleux*" but, nonetheless, a "paradise lost" Breton sought "to recover and recreate" (200). The idea that the contemporary *merveilleux* is in fact pieces of a "paradise lost" is coherent with the message of the first manifesto, which clearly states that the marvelous is not something to be created, but rather to be retrieved: "the fragments ... come down to us"; "they are the romantic *ruins*" (16). These "fragments" are just that – bits and pieces of a mythic age, pagan sentiment and indigenous freedoms now essentially lost, except for the remnants buried in the gritty corners of the modern metropolis. This emphasis on a lost civilization, memory, and recovery, compounded by an affinity for the archaic and underground forces, suggests a closer relationship between surrealism and archaeology than has generally been acknowledged.

What has been established *vis-à-vis* surrealism and the archaic is a pervasive surrealist interest in the obscure and the occult. In "André Breton et l'Héritage Méditerranéen," Anna Balakian notes that before Breton boarded the ship on route to New York that would provide the fateful meeting with Lévi-Strauss, Breton became immersed in the culture of Langue D'oc and the Provençal courts, finding (as did Pound) correspondences between his own poetry and cult of love and that of the troubadours. This led to lively exchanges with other refugees on the subject of ancient cultures and myths. Balakian's study of letters and documents of the time suggest that Breton began studying the Cabala and reading, "the history of hermetic rites and hieroglyphic linguistic codes with Eliphas Levi and Fulcanelli" (562). In the myths of the French Meridian, Breton discerned traces of Egyptian paganism and the mythos of Melusine that had interested him for years and which emerge in the pages of *Arcane 17*. Far from diverging from typical surrealist interests, I would suggest that this Marseilles period, characterized by an attraction to hieroglyphic codes, ancient energies and the perpetuity of the mythic, is prototypically surrealist in its archaic and archaeological preoccupations.

But how does the profound "M" of surrealist memory translate into archaeological dynamics in the ultimate surrealist milieu: the streets of Paris? The surrealists make the connection between these two modern impulses by adopting an archaeological optic that is both a way of seeing and a way of being in the modern metropolis. Archaeological seeing refers to the way in which the surrealists understand the everyday city to be made up of hieroglyphic signs which can be read and interpreted to decipher the mysterious nature of the seemingly mundane. Hence Breton's comment in *Nadja*: "Perhaps life needs to be deciphered like a cryptogram" (112). The gray and quotidian machinations of metropolitan life must be "deciphered" in order to discover another reality lurking just beneath the surface, the "sous-reality" of the historical marvelous. In surrealist wanderings through old neighborhoods, parks, cafés and restaurants, the city itself is text – the deceptively mundane scrawl which must be read and interpreted to reveal hidden mysteries like the markings on the Rosetta Stone. This mode of archaeological "reading" is linked to a phenomenological position which Jean Pierre Cauvin has identified as "dépaysement": "the sense of being out of one's element, of being disoriented in the presence of the uncanny, or disconcerted by the unfamiliarity of a situation experienced for the first time" (17). Literally, we might interpret "dépaysement" as "out of country", or "displaced from one's homeland." Within the surrealist context, it refers to a cool disassociation from the mores of twentieth-century Parisian culture so that everyday material objects are freed from their ideological trappings and all of Paris opens itself up as a strange civilization to be "read" for the first time.

One of the clearest examples of "dépaysement," an example that also highlights the hunt for the "ruins" of the *merveilleux*, is the surrealist hyper-sensitivity to the forces of the past that dwell beneath the surface of modern metropolitan culture. In the surrealist topography of the city, certain sites emerge as densely layered in uncanny historical resonance. Most often, these are the locales of old Paris: The Porte Saint-Denis, the Tour Saint-Jacques, the Place Dauphine, and the Passage de l'Opéra, the "sacred" landmarks that give shape and meaning to the urban landscape. Like Pound's wanderings in Provence, the attraction to these locations is rarely rational, but rather an instinctive response to underground echoes. As Breton writes in *Nadja*:

> I don't know why it should be precisely here that my feet take me, here that I almost invariably go without specific purpose, without anything to induce me but this obscure clue: namely that it (?) will happen here. I cannot see, as I hurry along, what could

constitute for me, even without my knowing it, a magnetic pole in either space or time. No: not even the extremely handsome, extremely useless Porte Saint-Denis.

(32)

The "magnetic" pull of these historical locations, even the apparently "useless" Porte Saint-Denis, is consistently linked with the full-presence of the past. These locations are surreally charged because they are areas where the past and present can contradictorily co-exist; one can at once *be* in twentieth-century Paris and *feel* the force of history, just as Pound could sense the force of the troubadours acting on the twentieth-century French landscape. For Margaret Cohen, the importance of the surrealist locations is political: they are the sites of Parisian revolution and revolt, hence magnetized poles of surrealist sympathies, the repositories of an "unstated social past" (101). In this sense, the surrealists, even while their project was essentially geared toward a revolution of individual consciousness, can be seen to share some of Pound's social-archaeological concerns in their hunt for revolutionary energies. For Browder, the surrealist attraction to public sites is more coincidental with a psychoanalytic archaeological mode, a topography of surface and depth where the traumatic past is stored in the inner recesses of the earth: "Breton did not doubt that what emanated from [these locations] were the dark forces of the city's unconscious" (26). We can, therefore, perceive surrealist archaeology to be a kind of amalgam of psychoanalytic and social concerns, a stratum of archaeological thought that absorbs the energies and preoccupations of both branches of its archaeological lineage.

While surrealist Paris is geographically limited – Jean Gaulmier, for example, comments that Breton's "essential" Paris is organized around a north–south axis running from the Porte Saint-Denis to the Porte Saint-Jacques – it is, nonetheless, both psychologically and historically layered, plunging "instead into the depths of time immemorial" (163). The frisson of Breton's night prowls arises from a Paris "still charged today with hallucinatory force, heavy with the past or with history and legend that are directly intermixed" (186). For Gaulmier, the draw of the historical pulse also accounts for Breton's sense of architecture in *Poésie et Autre* as an active source of both stabilizing and destabilizing powers:

> In a city like Paris, it seems impossible to me to view structures as uniquely physical. Their interest is that to a large extent they are made up of what *did happen* here or there, and that, if we look clearly, they would make us conscious of that which makes us wobble as well as that which gives us balance.
>
> (Breton qtd. in Gaulmier 186)

Breton's emphasis on the pervasiveness of the past, obvious if one can "look clearly," suggests a layered optical approach to the semiotic structures of urban centres. By reading the buildings, or looking beyond their everyday contemporary use, Breton perceives that these structures are the repositories of past events. Not only is this history in some sense "visible," it also acts on the sensitive observer, creating a sense of well-being or imbalance depending on the location. This receptivity to both the historical layers and the lingering presence of "what *did happen*" suggests a surrealist *mentalité* deeply in tune with both the acting forces and material remnants of the near and ancient past.

While the electric history of the city and the inherent magnetism of ancient monuments are central to the surrealists' urban topography, it would be wrong to assign the movement an awed historical sensibility. Though Breton and his circle were drawn to various well-known sites, the civic pride and historical pomp often associated with these monuments also made them a source of ridicule. Haim Finkelstein's research has brought to light a surrealist survey whereby participants were asked whether the Arc de Triomphe, the Obelisk, and countless other monuments around Paris should be moved, modified, transformed or suppressed. The responses include Breton's suggestion that the Obelisk be transported to a washroom entrance, where a giant gloved woman's hand would hold it while Eluard suggests that the Colonne Vendôme be replaced by a factory chimney climbed by a naked woman (113). Rather than diminishing the importance of historical monuments in surrealist thought, this humorous take on the city's topographical markers highlights the surrealist interest in these locations. In typical surrealist fashion, the "sacred" sites are equally the locations of the profane.

Not surprisingly, it is in the emphasis on the return of the repressed rather than in zany topographical humor that the surrealists once again coincide with Freud. After all, the sense of disorientation or "dépaysement" the surrealists experience in the presence of the past can be defined as little other than "uncanny," Freud's term for the strange but familiar. However, the surrealist understanding of the uncanny again pushes a Freudian concept to its very limit. As Cohen articulates, while "the uncanny effect of the Parisian past on the present observer [in surrealism] ... is consonant with the Freudian ... uncanny ... [the surrealists' extreme sense of the presence of the past does] not so much contradict Freud as dwell in the outer margins of Freud's theory, from which Freud prefers to retreat" (102). The outer margins of the Freudian uncanny include the idea of a still living/acting social past, an intractable belief in ghosts rather than treatable "psychological demons" and the desire for a direct and explosive encounter with history – all of which the surrealists believed or sought out. In this sense, Freudian margins are the surrealist center; where Freud desists, the surrealists continue to move beneath the surface as each stab into the depths of the historical unconscious reveals another layer which could potentially serve to destabilize the monolithic foundations of the present and discredit the smooth flowing narrative of bourgeois reality.

In addition to the desire to destabilize and discredit, the surrealist penchant for the energies of the past can be regarded as a two-prong theoretical maneuver. On one level, espousing the importance of the "unstated social past" in a collective sense mirrors the surrealists' aims for the individual; just as the surrealists seek to discover the hidden recesses of the individual unconscious, to live fluidly between dreaming and waking, to tap into a primal and authentic nature, so on a social level, the earth itself must have secrets – an unconscious made up of collective desires, a primal history and a history of revolution. Combined with this notion is the temporal interest in the past – the sense that these undetected energies may be extracted to bring about the utopian future. It is this conjunction, the "lost marvelous" buried in the geographical equivalent of unconscious recesses, that makes the obscure locales of the city repositories of hidden wonder. Where Pound sees potential cultural resurrections springing from the template provided by the Tempio Malatestiano, the surrealists are much more inclined to seize on the underbelly of quotidian city life: trash heaps, flea markets, and decrepit movie theatres, which are the sites of forgotten knowledge.

As the social version of the individual unconscious, these public locations have the potential to encase hidden treasures which can be recovered from their depths.

Of all of these "underground" locales, the flea-markets are the most fruitful ground to pursue the "ruins" of the *merveilleux*. Among the odd assortment of objects, the surrealists search for those items that activate their own unconscious desires. For Finkelstein, these objects become "an extension of our subjective self and serve as a point of departure for a new *connaissance* of reality" (1). In this archaeology of objects, the old and the abandoned mysteriously fit with the archaeology of the unconscious. Like the sacred sites, the surrealists recognize these objects "demodés, fragmentés, inutilisables" by the physical sensations they incur in the observer: "a feeling of disorientation, a *vertige* or any other reaction which proves indefinable as the object itself" (Finkelstein 20). In the wasteland of the Saint-Ouen flea market the "out of fashion, fragmented, and unusable" can be the "indefinable" key that fits into the lock of unconscious desire. It is this emphasis on the un-useful which also separates surrealist thought from Pound's urgency of function. Rather than perceiving these objects as the gateway to a time of clear social rules, the strangeness of these objects mark them as belonging to an original topos of mystery.

Often, these found artifacts are so old-fashioned their function is indiscernible, like Breton's "irregular, white, shellacked half-cylinder covered with reliefs and depressions that are meaningless to me, streaked with horizontal and vertical reds and greens, preciously nestled in a case under a legend in Italian" (*Nadja* 54). After prolonged examination, Breton concludes that this lost relic is "some kind of statistical device, operating three-dimensionally and recording the population of a city in such and such a year," though he adds, "all this makes it no more comprehensible to me." Here, Breton is playing urban archaeologist, searching the ruins of the present for meaningful discoveries. Unlike the conventional archaeologist, however, Breton is not so much attempting to uncover the secrets of a forgotten civilization, as see what secrets of his own unconscious the object might unlock.

The flea market passage in *Nadja* is crucial because it sets up a series of incidents which outline the surrealist theory of the object in which seemingly mundane items are at once retrieved fragments of the *merveilleux* and physical manifestations of an interiorized archaeology of desire. The trip to the flea-market shows how outside objects fit the unknown crevices of the unconscious causing Breton to reflect on how these objects correlate with some subterranean lack. This connection is vividly illustrated in the passage following the flea-market section, a series of reminiscences concerning a glove and the woman who once owned it:

> I also remember the apparently jocular proposition once made in my presence to a lady, asking that she present to the "Centrale Surréaliste" one of the remarkable sky-blue gloves she was carrying on a visit to us at this "Centrale," my sudden fear when I saw she was about to consent, and my supplications that she do nothing of the kind. I don't know what there can have been, at that moment, so terribly, so marvelously decisive for me in the thought of that glove leaving that hand forever.
>
> (55–6)

Breton confesses that this matter assumed bizarre proportions in his psyche until the woman "proposed coming back to lay on the table, on the very spot where I had so hoped she would not leave the blue glove," a remarkable bronze glove which even now, he can "never resist picking up, always astonished at its weight and interest." Clearly, the glove is not as intrinsically interesting in itself as in its relationship to the woman in question, a superseding libidinous interest.

The glove, as charged a symbol to the surrealists as shoes were to Freud, itself becomes a concentrated object of desire, a remnant or fragment of exceeding erotic potential. We can sense Gautierian outlines here, the glove acting in the same capacity as the charred cast of Arria Marcella or the foot of the princess Hermonthis, a metonymic object that inspires fantasies of connection and return. The glove is also resonant with the decree from the first manifesto: "Surrealism will usher you into death, which is a secret society. It will glove your hand, burying therein the profound M with which the word Memory begins" (32). The glove, here, is also a state of consciousness, an empty relic that evokes an anterior state of mind, in this case a time when the woman herself was in full presence, the moment which is the glove's original context.

Modulations of Gautier's theme of the desirability of the abandoned object are common in surrealist work such as Breton's *Poisson Soluble* where he mentions a "wonderful hollow cast, more beautiful than a breast" (45). Like the glove, the cast is the remnant, a calcified and hollow memory of the original which, nonetheless, retains magnetic power. Referring to *Poisson Soluble* Michael Riffaterre identifies this power of the remnant as belonging "to an erotic tradition" beginning with Bulwer-Lytton's *Last Days of Pompeii* where "the shapely woman perishes in the catastrophe, but her beauty is preserved in imprint form in the lava" (62–3). By the time we reach surrealism, the lava itself is rarely in evidence (except, perhaps, in its most eroded form, the black sand beaches of *Mad Love*). But the electric power of the object persists.

The talismanic, fetishistic quality of the object is perhaps the most pervasive theme in archaeologically influenced literature. In Gautier, it is the charred cast or abandoned foot, in Pater the work of art, in Freud the dream-symbol that must be deciphered, in Pound the objects of the walking tour, or like Stokes, the figures of the Tempio reliefs, in H.D. the concrete symbols of the dream-realm, and in the surrealists the mundane objects of the modern metropolis. Always there is a sense of an object exceeded by an auratic mystique, a feeling of hollowness or absence that these writers attempt to fill with imaginative contexts. In this sense, archaeo-logic is very much in line with Derrida's logic of the supplement and also contains within it the same contradictory qualities: "The supplement adds itself[;] it is ... a plenitude enriching another plenitude, the *fullest measure* of presence ... But the supplement supplements. It adds only to replace ... if it fills, it is as if one fills a void" (*Of Grammatology* 144–5). In a similar manner, the archaeological reconstruction fills the void of the object's lost milieu. It attempts to repair the absence of the past. Language, like the ghost of Arria Marcella, is the phantom presence that takes off from the reality of the material remain. In explicating the logic of the supplement, Derrida makes this connection explicitly: "... if supplementarity is a necessarily indefinite process, writing is the supplement par excellence" (281). Writing, in all of the work studied thus far, supplements the fragments of a dissolving history.

Urban Archaeologies of the French Surrealists 157

But to return to the surrealists specifically, the section that follows the paragraphs on the Saint Ouen flea market and the lady of the glove continues to perpetuate the archaeo-resonance of surrealist thought by dwelling on the latent meanings implicit in everyday objects:

> Only a few days ago, Louis Aragon pointed out to me that the sign of a Pourville hotel showing in red letters the words: MAISON ROUGE consisted of certain letters arranged in such a way that when seen from a certain angle in the street, the word MAISON disappeared and Rouge read POLICE. This optical illusion would have no importance if on the same day, one or two hours later, the lady we shall call the *lady of the glove* had not taken me to see a *tableau changeant* ... This object was an old engraving which, seen straight on, represents a tiger, but which, regarded perpendicularly to its surface of tiny vertical bands when you stand several feet to the left, represents a vase, and, from several feet to the right, an angel. I offer, in closing, these two facts because for me, under such conditions, their connection cannot be avoided ...
>
> (*Nadja* 59)

The connection between the double meaning inscribed in the "Maison Rouge" sign and the *tableau changeant* would seem to have to do with hidden messages inscribed in everyday objects. In the case of Aragon's sign, this duality is a matter of chance and perspective, in the *tableau changeant*, a deliberate effort on the part of the artist to include the images of the tiger, vase and angel in a single *objet d'art*.

Breton's interest in this phenomenon signals the way in which the surrealists are consistently receptive to concealed meanings within the text of the city. It is not until the end of the novel that Breton makes the archaeological optic explicit, in his musings about Nadja:

> Who is the real Nadja – the one who told me she had wandered all night long in the Forest of Fontainebleau with an archaeologist who was looking for some stone remains which, certainly, there was plenty of time to find by day-light – but suppose it was this man's passion! – I mean is the real Nadja this always inspired and inspiring creature who enjoyed being nowhere but in the streets, the only region of valid experience for her, in the street ...
>
> (112–13)

In search of the "real" Nadja, Breton attempts to distance himself from her, to become an observer of her interaction with another man, the "archaeologist." Yet the passage belies this attempt at objectivity. The archaeologist "was looking for some stone remains" throughout the night, which as we know is the surrealists' time for wandering the city. Breton first presents the "logical" idea that these remains might also be found in the day, yet his identification with Nadja's companion leads him to interject "but suppose it was this man's passion!" Breton does not know if Nadja was indeed an "inspiring creature" to the archaeologist but assumes this is the case since Nadja is an inspiration to him. We can, therefore, recognize the archaeologist as Breton's alter-ego. But where the companion-archaeologist wanders the Forest of Fontainebleau, Breton the archaeologist, like Nadja, understands the street to be the "only region of valid experience," and it is there that they conduct their search for the "stone remains" of the *merveilleux*.

As the preoccupation with the MAISON ROUGE sign and the *tableau changeant* demonstrate, the surrealist archaeology of the urban is not only about collecting objects and traces; it is also about deciphering them. To this extent, the surrealist approach to the world is both hieroglyphic and semiotic. If the meaningful life needs to be "deciphered like a cryptogram" (112) then life itself is made up of hieroglyphic traces to be read and interpreted. In Nadja's case, she not only accumulates these traces, she also creates them:

> Nadja has invented a marvelous flower for me: "the Lovers' Flower." It is during a lunch in the country that this flower appeared to her and that I saw her trying – quite clumsily – to reproduce it. She comes back to it several times, afterwards, to improve the drawing and give each of the two pairs of eyes a different expression. It is essentially under this sign that the time we spent together should be placed, and it remains the graphic symbol which has given Nadja the key to all the rest.
>
> (116)

Nadja's ability to identify meaningful signs – in this case, "the Lovers' Flower" and reproduce them so that they act as symbols or syntheses of events – here, "the time" Breton and Nadja spent together, represents a significant part of her allure. More attuned to signs and alternate readings of the world than Breton, Nadja's ability to produce hieroglyphic notations separates her from those who see only an object as it is, without translation. Breton's attention to this point suggests the ways in which he views her

Urban Archaeologies of the French Surrealists 159

as in some sense mystically inspired since it is this talent for the "graphic symbol" which gives Nadja the "key" to "all the rest."

In *The Hieroglyph of Tradition*, Angelika Rauch advances the thesis that the hieroglyph has throughout the modern period been a symbol of lost authenticity, a connection to a more poetically rich mode of being. Rauch suggests that Novalis, for example, understood the hieroglyph as a "pre-representational notion of language" which "takes the side of the corporeal and the sensuous" (133). Rauch further notes that for both Novalis and Schlegel the loss of the hieroglyph "represented the loss of a mythology that spiritually connected the generations of past and present." She also suggests that the hieroglyphic tradition to which Novalis and Schlegel belonged "envisioned a new mythology, which needs to be understood not as a new inventory of myths but as a new form of meaning and of knowledge, created from the self's desire." Certainly this understanding of the hieroglyph is consistent with the surrealist hunt for "pre-representational language," the "corporeal and the sensuous" as well as the dawn of a new mythology. Interestingly, for Rauch, the hieroglyphic tradition resonates with surrealism in another way, in that she believes the hieroglyphic tradition is a precursor to Freud's theories of fantasy:

> Such fantasies are metonyms, experiential parts of the subject's unconscious past that in the dream work are assembled into rebus images. The specter of the past is visible in creations that stem from the unconscious mind. In bypassing the power of reason, which rules during the day, the "nightly mind" offers another world in which the things are miraculously transformed into imaginary signs and lose their referential character. They no longer point to a rational world of conscious perception and sensation but become pre-representational hieroglyphs whose meaning needs first to be created in a hermeneutic situation ...

In the previous chapter, we observed that Freud's theory of symbolism suggests that symbols are part of a genetically transferred "archaic heritage." Here, Rauch's analysis highlights the ways in which the metonymic nature of dream imagery also makes the elements of fantasy a kind of hieroglyphic code. For the surrealists, who obfuscate the line between dreaming and waking, all elements of dream and reality are subject to this kind of hieroglyphic analysis; the "nightly mind" is in constant effect, objects and symbols consistently displaced from their referential circumstances and transposed into art.

As *Nadja* demonstrates, however, too much immersion in a hieroglyphic mode of consciousness leads to an excessive interpretive distance which results in a complete detachment from reality. Breton notes that Nadja fails to hang on to the necessary grasp of the "real" that keeps the surrealists from losing touch with the actual world. And yet, Nadja's excesses are also the source of her power over Breton, at least to a point, until she begins to frighten even him. Eventually, Nadja becomes a case study for Breton, an enigma to be read and deciphered, as we ourselves read *Nadja* and try to unveil its strangeness.

To read the secret life of the city, to interpret the hieroglyphics of contemporary culture and to feel the draw of historical places are themes that are also central to Louis Aragon's *Paris Peasant*. In the novel, Aragon presents a kind of archaeological narrative of Paris on the cusp, the old city close to extinction, threatened by modernizing renovations. As the cataloguer of a civilization that will soon cease to exist, Aragon compiles *Paris Peasant* like a time-capsule for the future, with peculiar inclusions that are meant to illustrate Paris as it was: newspaper clippings, restaurant signs, theatre posters, street signs and advertisements. The attention to non-literary material creates a mass of what Peter Collier calls "documentary residue" (219) – endless descriptions of streets, cafés, abandoned paraphernalia and shop windows – an archaeological account of the soon dead in the barely living arcades of Paris. While *Paris Peasant* is striking in its originality, it is important to note that the archaeological thematic was also a pervasive one in literature dealing with Baron Haussmann's campaign of metropolitan renewal. In *The Arcades Project*, Walter Benjamin dedicates a section to the excavation of Paris as archaeological exercise, including quotations from H. De Pène and the Pompeiian fanatic, Alexandre Dumas:

> The dust exceeded all expectations. The elegant folk back from the races are virtually encrusted; they remind you of Pompeii. They have had to be exhumed with the help of a brush, if not a pickaxe.
>
> H. de Pène, *Paris intime* (Paris, 1859, 108–9)

Urban Archaeologies of the French Surrealists 161

> The whole of the *rive gauche*, all the way from the Tour de Nesle to the Tombe Issoire ... is nothing but a hatchway leading from the surface to the depths. And if the modern demolitions reveal the mysteries of the upper world of Paris, perhaps one day the inhabitants of the Left Bank will awaken startled to discover the mysteries below.
> Alexandre Dumas, *Les Mohicans de Paris*, vol. 3 (Paris, 1863, 98)

Like Aragon, these writers seem especially taken with the paradox that while constructing the new, Haussmann mirrored the archaeological conditions generally associated with the pursuit of the archaic.

This archaeological optic suffuses *Paris Peasant*. At times elegiac, the archaeological romance is also mockingly used to describe the surrealists' wanderings through the Parc Buttes-Chaumont. Expressing pity for the unfortunates who "are in love with Egyptian mummies" (171), Aragon proceeds with his own archaeology of the modern. Much like Pound, who searches for the "new" through archaeological modalities, Aragon, Breton and Moll explore the recesses of the park under the transformational guise of night, gaining greater receptivity to hidden energies through the rhythm of their walking. As the three friends wander through the park, Aragon intimates that the Buttes-Chaumont had become more than a place; it had "stirred a mirage in us ... a shared mirage over which we all felt we had the same hold" (147). Transformed from a mundane locale into an exotic landscape, the random walking around the Buttes-Chaumont becomes "a miraculous hunt," "a field of experiment" for "great revelation" and most significantly, a "Mesopotamia for one half-hour" (148) as the three explore the ground "in which nestles the town's collective unconscious" (151). As Johanna Malt writes, while all of *Paris Peasant* "... is an archaeological exercise in that it involves reading the material culture of the past ... in the Buttes-Chaumont the analogy becomes explicit" (23). After a detailed geographical analysis of the park, which sets the parameters of the surrealist hunt, Aragon's imagination runs wild and the avenue teems with phantasmic workers, "my first slaves, their gleaming backs rippling above their straw loincloths, cleared a way for me and made the trees and the stones accomplices of my steps" (160) – a description which resonates with the colonial style of early archaeological narratives.

After several paragraphs of wandering around the park and literary digressions, Aragon returns to the theme of the surrealist as archaeological marauder. Enacting the movements of Arthur Evans, exploring tombs by torch-light, the friends come upon a pillar and "decipher one by one, with the aid of a whole succession of the lighted matches that are their firebrands, the inscriptions on the four-angled column" (172). Aragon proceeds to record with a ridiculous meticulousness every piece of writing on the column: the day nurseries, kindergartens, elementary, and municipal schools of the nineteenth arrondissement, as well as the cementers, metal-founder and clockmakers who worked on the "indicator-obelisk," the constructing engineer, meteorological information, the *quartiers*, the length of the streets, a map of the arrondissement with geographical points and a list of buildings assigned to religious institutions.

At the end of this lengthy exercise, Aragon compares the "work" he and his friends are doing to the deciphering of the Rosetta stone:

> Let us pause for a breather, modern Champollions that we are. Do you not think that the mysterious purpose which guided the hand of the engraver, which guided the spirit of the author of this inscription must have corresponded to some equivalent of the incomprehensibility and indecipherability of the cuneiform darkness, through which, nevertheless, one of your fellow creatures finally succeed in making his way towards daylight?
>
> (177)

The comment, which requires its own kind of deciphering, suggests an archaeological connection between artist and observer, as though through the act of reading the observer creates a tunnel through the "cuneiform darkness" to uncover the artist's voice and intent. To the extent that this voice from the past reaches the present through engraving, a labor intensive form of writing, Aragon seems to be suggesting that *Paris Peasant*, too, will some day be an archaeological artifact, excavated by the reader as a record of a forgotten age.

As Aragon is speculating on the nature of reading the past, the friends catch sight of another one of the surrealists' sacred places – the suicide bridge. The sight is sufficiently impressive for Aragon to launch into an extensive analysis of the nature of the sacred sites, their primal appeal and their status as repositories of the past. The bridge is described as one of the "nodal points of human thought" which even contemporary man is able to respond to with the force of "pagan" superstition (180). "Most often," Aragon continues, the sacred places are "legendary settings: some greatness of soul clings to these walls, these heights" (182). The clinging force of superstition, the resonance of the past within the "black ground" of "Violent Death" (180) makes the suicide bridge a place of literal death and despair, but also a magnetized location for creative inspiration and a repository for cultural memory. Within the bridge's force field, life and creation achieve new vividness: "At last each particle of space is meaningful, like a syllable of some dismantled word" (182). Here, within the text of the city, words have gaps. New meanings appear through the surface of the text at the site of the dismantled word because the import of the location causes the reader, the wanderer, to slow down and consider the primal draw of this gateway between life and death, the "threshold of all the mysteries."

In the Buttes-Chaumont passage, Aragon employs the tensions implicit in archaeology to highlight surrealist preoccupations with the realm between the living and the dead, the modern and the archaic, the visible and the hidden. But in the arcades, we are exposed to Aragon's archaeology of the future, a cataloguing of a way of life before its eclipse, the imminent destruction that threatens this microcosmic, underworldly civilization. From the beginning, the arcades are presented as a separate world, sealed off from the rest of Paris, desolate "human aquariums" which, nonetheless, contain a secret connection to a mythic existence:

> Although the life that originally quickened them has drained away, they deserve, nevertheless, to be regarded as the secret repositories of several modern myths: it is only today, when the pickaxe menaces them, that they have at last become the true sanctuaries of a cult of the ephemeral, the ghostly landscape of damnable pleasures and professions. Places that were incomprehensible yesterday, and that tomorrow will never know.
>
> (29)

The sense of the arcades as the land of the dead is compounded by descriptions of ghoulish prostitutes and abandoned storefronts, "a separate existence in a world apart" (49) which will gradually cease to be. This gothic mood is heightened by Aragon's descriptions of himself as a "sailor aboard a ruined castle. Everything signifies havoc. Everything is crumbling under my gaze" (61). In this no-man's land where only Aragon and a few other characters seem to travel, the former glory of the steel constructions and bright commodities in the store windows fade to a pathetic picture, a failed utopia filled with odd relics in which Aragon acts as a kind of site-assessor, come to take stock of the damage and relative value of the surviving items.

Above all, the descriptions of the arcades are a striking commentary on a capitalism that turns new commodities into abandoned objects from the very moment of their production. Within the arcades, the "new" becomes the quaint and forgotten at a startling speed. Revolutionary medical technology is transformed into arcane witchcraft within years, as Aragon's description of an orthopedist's shop window, the "... display of beautiful wooden hands, some articulated, others in one piece. And walking sticks, crutches, cupping glasses, headache pencils ... trusses for all kinds of hernias, simple or double, with their pads attached to springy metal belts, trusses for adults, trusses for children" (113). In these descriptions, the archaeologies Aragon seems to be alluding to are the "instant" archaeologies of capitalism, where commodities quickly become outmoded in the face of mass and rapid production. For Aragon, however, these devalued commodities can also be the source of revolutionary energy. Amid the peculiarly archaic contraptions of the orthopedists' window, for example, there are odd glimpses of "modern myth." Aragon makes this connection metaphorically, noting that among the trusses and crutches are two "painted statuettes":

> And how the gods of antiquity on either side of him have been modernized for our benefit! Two little painted statuettes, with rosy flesh and black hair and beard, represent Apollo and Vulcan: but each has an arm or a leg, a head or a belly supplemented by a truss or by articulated joints all achieving the classic gestures of the Belvedere and Etna.
>
> (114)

The picture of two mythological statues "supplemented by a truss or by articulated joints" is self-consciously kitsch. The "broken" mythology of the ancients can be found in obscure corners of the city, even in the most tragically comic of circumstances, an orthopedists' fading store-front: two outmoded icons among a host of outmoded commodities. Yet in the outmoded is power, for in these objects freed from the ideological spotlight are dormant energies that can be harnessed to bring about an authentic mythic return.

In Aragon's view, it is the bourgeoisie's inability to see through the ideology of capitalism, their lack of desire to even catch sight of the "sous-reality" of the historical *merveilleux* that makes them contemptuous: "It is enough to make one shudder to see a bourgeois family taking its morning coffee without ever noticing the unknowable that shows through the tablecloth's red and white checkered pattern" (190). This willed blindness, moreover, refuses to acknowledge the uncanny existence of historical forces, the phantoms that subsist alongside the living, the "obscure evocative words mistaken for telephone calls." The tablecloth here acts as a kind of grid for the rigid reality of the "bourgeois family," the "obscure evocative words" the murmuring forces of the primitive past.

It is the ideological act of digging through the surface reality in order to connect with a deeper, more poetic, more meaningful mythic reality that finally makes the surrealist enterprise both revolutionary and "archaeological." In the final pages Aragon taunts the reader by writing: "Doubtless you had been expecting archaeological and enraptured allusions, and the first pages of the manuscript must have disappointed you" (197). Rather than sustained specific archaeological "allusion," Aragon chooses to make *Paris Peasant* an archaeological enterprise, a semi-transparent optic which becomes a sustained way of being in the world.

Seeking out the locales of modern myth is, therefore, central to the surrealist *becoming*. Sometimes the mythic takes the form of the suicide bridge, an iconic emotional locus. Other times it is in the eerie cast of a dying *quartier* – the arcades, for example, wherein can be found the ruins of the *merveilleux*. More often, however, modern myth is hidden within the momentary blurring of past and present, an H.D. type approach to synthesis which borrows from the Freudian dream-realm: Nadja, for example, uninhibited by the barrier between then and now frequently fashions herself after the mythic: "Nadja has also represented herself many times with the features of Melusina who of all mythological personalities is the one she seems to have felt closest to herself" (*Nadja* 29). Or in the poem "Sans

Connaissance" (a play on the double-entendre of "Without Knowing" and "Without Consciousness") Breton places a newspaper article written about the abduction of a young girl within the mythological context of the kidnapping of Persephone:

> One has not forgotten
> The odd attempted abduction
> Hey a star and yet it's still broad daylight
> Of that fourteen-year-old girl
> Four more years than fingers
> Who was returning in an elevator
> ...
> To her parents' apartment
> The father a post firmly set in the shadows the mother a
>   pretty lampshade pyramid
> An apartment located on the fourth floor of a building in the
>   Rue Saint-Martin
> Not far from the Porte guarded by two giant salamanders
> Under which I stand several hours a day
> Whether I am in Paris or not
> The lovely Euphorbe let us call the girl Euphorbe
> Is concerned about the elevator stopping between the [second] and [third] floors.
> (*Poems of André Breton* 81)

The girl, "let us call the girl Euphorbe," is at once an average fourteen year old prosaically concerned with the mechanical soundness of the elevator and a mythic symbol of desire and pathos, as a man attempts to kidnap her in the elevator but kills her instead. At this point, the poem turns to newspaper prose: the man's "description is 1.65 meters tall," and "the concierge didn't dare stop / this unusual but polite visitor" (85). Here, the mythic is imbedded in the ordinary space of city life, imitating the ordinary text of a newspaper report. Within twentieth-century Paris, the girl's mother is bourgeois-average "pretty lampshade" yet still has ancient magna-mater resonance in her association with "pyramid." The Porte Saint-Martin is both a real landmark erected in 1674, and an imaginary locale, as Breton's speaker indicates in his admission that he stands under the Porte several hours a day, even when he is "in Paris or not." In essence, Breton succeeds in conquering the contradictions of past-present, reality-imagination, thereby succeeding in the surrealist goal of sur-reality through the unifying power of myth.

For Gaulmier, Breton's evocation of modern myth and his ceaseless "vagabondage" around Paris "is an unending Joycean Odyssey" (166). For Aragon, too, myth emerges as the key to the successful surrealist oeuvre:

> Having observed that all the mythologies of the past become transformed into romances [*romans*] as soon as people no longer believed in them, I formulated the idea of reversing the process and elaborating a novel [*roman*] that would present itself as a mythology. Naturally, a mythology of the modern.
> (qtd. in Simon Taylor's introduction to *Paris Peasant* 14)

The process that Aragon elaborates here in describing his method for *Paris Peasant* is essentially one of reversal: as myths had turned into novels (which the surrealists generally degraded at length), so the great novel must present itself as a new mythology. Again, this is essentially a strategy of recuperation, of redeeming ancient powers to form a new ideal. This recuperative process is one of the last ways in which we can say the surrealists are "archaeological" in their intent to make contact with a pervasive force of the past and reform it in their own image. As artists, however, the surrealists were not just concerned with the past but also with how the future would remember them. It is to this end that they accumulated the traces of their lives and art in distinct and memorable ways, and their novels, too, have become an archaeological record of their ambitions. As Nadja says to Breton when it becomes clear their love affair has ended: "André? André? ... You will write a novel about me. I'm sure you will. Don't say you won't. Be careful: everything fades, everything vanishes. Something must remain of us..." (*Nadja* 100).

CHAPTER 7

The Rhetoric of Resurrection: Charles Olson in Meso-America

The modernities we have encountered so far have been disparate instances of a similar impulse: the ushering of the past into the present through various doorways, the improvement of the present through a transformative encounter with desirable extractions from the past. These alchemic attempts have been thoroughly modern in their paradoxical use of contradictory forces and temporalities. Yet at the core of this modernist impulse is the consistent drive to exceed the modern: to escape or transform it, to change its direction or discredit it with other models. Of the writers studied so far, perhaps only Freud believed in modernity's rationalism, though at the end of his life, an exile in England, even he must have come to question the assumption. Generally speaking, the archaeological impulse is a subversive one, an "underground" or alternative version of vision or event. It is, therefore, not surprising that when modernity's limits were perceived to have been exceeded by the terming of the "post-modern,"[1] it was by a poet who considered himself to be profoundly archaeological and who equated this new era with a return: "any POST-MODERN is born with the ancient confidence that he *does* belong" (*Olson–Creeley Correspondence* 115).[2]

---

1   See George Butterick, "Charles Olson and the postmodern advance" (5) and Ralph Maud, "Charles Olson's archaic postmodern" (1). Maud writes: "The clarity of the chapter devoted to Charles Olson at the beginning of Perry Anderson's *The Origins of Postmodernity* (1998) means that the primacy of Olson is established and we do not have to labor the fact that he was the first literary figure to use the term 'postmodern' (preceded only by the historian Arnold Toynbee)."
2   This line appears in a letter to Robert Creeley dated August 20, 1951.

American poet Charles Olson's reputation as an "archaeologist" has been well noted and largely accepted, primarily through the poet's own insistence that archaeological processes are the best way of understanding his poetic role. Uncomfortable with the label of "writer," Olson coined himself an "archaeologist of morning" (*Collected Prose* 206), finding within the aesthetics of excavation the most direct expression of an archaic imperative: Man needs to "'get back' in order to 'get on'" (*A Charles Olson Reader* 80). Certainly the archaeological provides a vivid illustration for many of Olson's projects: the retrieval of an original language, a return to a familiarization with nature, and the recuperation of archaic vision, the "Beautiful Thing" (*Collected Prose* 207). So an archaeological understanding, too, provides the possibility of viewing Olson's poetics as part of a visceral praxis, and within this light his months excavating on the Yucatan peninsula in Mexico in the early 1950s become less of an eccentric whim and more broadly part of a thoughtful existential campaign. Yet the pervasiveness of the archaeological in Olson's work and work about him has naturalized the metaphor to the point that it seems an unavoidable part of Olson's poesis. It is easy to forget that Olson deliberately pursued the role of archaeologist or that the presence of archaeology within his work can itself be excavated. Yet this excavation is worthwhile, for Olson's archaeological practice encodes a driving existential and social desire. While Olson's poetry is sometimes perceived as obtuse and hermetic, his archaeology is often radical, resistant and political. It exists as a form of active protest and as a distinct call for social revisionism. From its ideological underpinnings to its formal presence on the page, as well as its departure from what we have established as the archaeological tradition, we can begin to understand how Olson's archaeological enterprise represents a "digging in" as much as a digging down, a trenchant appeal for a return to a humanized ethic that opposes the machinery of a dehumanized and dehumanizing modernity.

Perhaps archaeology's greatest attraction, for Olson, is its relationship to objects and their human contexts. As many have observed, Olson's philosophical stance very much resembles Heidegger's in that a return to a connection with objects restores a balanced sense of being in the world.[3] This position takes on special meaning within an archaeological paradigm, where contact with ancient objects (artifacts) facilitates a reconnection with the past itself – a rehabilitation that Olson perceives as essential to moving forward. Archaeology is, therefore, the vehicle for imagination as the objects it unearths reveal a potential future as well as a human past. This leap is occasioned by the material specificity of archaeological finds, the very presence of which summon up the phantasmagoric specter of an archaic past that might yet be projected forward. It is in these senses – the particular, the concrete, and the localized – that archaeology operates in opposition to Olson's understanding of history. Where archaeology relies on the material and provides the possibility for a paradoxical chronology, history supplies abstract knowledge of the past and an inevitable teleology. It is on these grounds, the abstractions of historical discourse as well as the egotism of constant progress, that Olson negates history. As Olson wrote to Robert Creeley while excavating Mayan fragments in Mexico: "... there is no 'history.' (I still keep going back to, the notion, this is (we are) merely, the *second time* (that's as much history as I'll permit in, which ain't history at all" (*Mayan Letters* 69).

For Olson, etymological change, like time, has perverted an original meaning, making "history," at once less specific and more socially corrosive:

> Obviously the word "history" is a word – unless you take it to root – which doesn't have any use at all. And the root is the original first use of it, in the first chapter if not the first paragraph of Herodotus, in which he says, "I'm using this as a verb 'istorin, which means *to find out for yourself*; and this is why I've been all over the goddamn Middle East and down into Egypt, been taught by the great Fathers of Egypt the ancient learning, and have learned everything I possibly could about the Persian War, and now I'm going to tell you about it."
>
> (*Muthologos* 3)

---

3   See Paul Bové, *Destructive Poetics: Heidegger and Modern American Poetry* and Judith Halden-Sullivan, *The Topology of Being: The Poetics of Charles Olson*.

"*[T]o find out for yourself*" is very much at odds with conventional history, which for the general population is the reception of received ideas about the past. By contrast, in archaeology Olson found a mode of inquiry more in line with Herodotus' "'istorin." The past is something to be touched and experienced not, like historical discourse, invisible but "objectification, the literal seeking and finding of *the objects* of the past of man which took down all generalization with it, made the specific pin or gold piece" (qtd. in Butterick 10). Similarly, in "Definitions by Undoings" Olson states that it was "due to archaeology ... one can go back to the history of the species and get another gauge on the individual man. One can be specific as to what civilization and culture are" (8). In these references we can sense that what appeals to Olson about archaeological modes of knowing is tangibility, object-knowledge, and direct particularity, "the specific pin or gold piece." On this point very much like a conventional archaeologist, Olson seeks to understand the world-views of ancient cultures, notably the Maya and the Sumerians, through the relics that remain. For Olson, this "new knowledge" dates from the 1880s, when Wilhelm Dörpfeld, a German archaeologist, excavated at Olympia using precise dating and context methods (which Olson privileges over Schliemann's less methodical, less context oriented tactics at Troy in the 1870s) (*Additional Prose* 83). For Olson, Dörpfeld's archaeology, the archaeology that matters, is a return to Herodotus' exploratory methods honed by an awareness of human contexts. It is the antithesis of the abstract and the second-hand, a working back by way of the object in its environment.

In *The Grounding of American Poetry*, Stephen Fredman has described this working backward as central to the American tradition, as poets have consistently interested themselves in "grounding," which "seeks to reinvent context, to dig down into the site of rupture in the hope of finding, not the old tradition or a new tradition, but the basis of tradition" (vii). Fredman's emphasis on the "dig" into the "site" of rupture illustrates an American archaeological *mentalité* which Olson's work makes manifest. In terms of the social responsibilities of poetry, however, and the emphasis on a fragmented, overlaying poetic, it is clear that Olson inherits directly from Pound. Like Pound, Olson also interested himself in hieroglyphs, motivated by the desire to reincorporate the object into the centre of human thought

The Rhetoric of Resurrection 173

and expression: "Logos, or discourse ... has ... so worked its abstractions into our concept and use of language that language's other function, speech, seems so in need of restoration that several of us go back to hieroglyphs or to ideograms to right the balance" (*Human Universe* 3–4). In "right[ing] the balance," Olson attempted to draw on the spatial, representational aspects of Mayan hieroglyphs, which for him represent poetry's ideal condition. As he wrote from the Yucatan: "Here is the most abstract and formal deal of all the things this people dealt out – and yet, to my taste, it is precisely as intimate as verse is. Is, in fact, verse. Is their verse" (*Mayan Letters* 43). The hieroglyphic quality of objects brought into space – the representation of birds or animals, for example, as modes of understanding the universe – also compelled Olson to think of Mayan writing as visual art. In a funding proposal to the Viking Fund & Wenner-Gren Foundation which he wrote while in Mexico, Olson proposed to study the hieroglyphs as a "graphic discipline of the highest order" ("Project [1951]" 95). Quoting Milton's "A Tractate on Education," Olson suggests that Mayan writing relies on the "solid things" in speech (96); in the "glyph world," objects have "tremendous levy" (*Mayan Letters* 66) and "unfold directly from content" (68). It is this original, representational language which Olson seeks to retrieve in order to proceed: a visual cosmology of man among objects which, as we will see, becomes so central to his own poetic method.

Yet there are also significant differences between Pound's archaeology and Olson's. Where Pound perceives that a turn to earlier models "invigorates because it is a return to nature and reason" (*Literary Essays* 92), Olson believes that the return should in fact take us much further: beyond reason, to an authentic, pre-rationalist condition, a tunneling propelled by the catastrophes "reason" itself had caused in the first half of the twentieth century. Olson's post-modern archeology, therefore, differentiates itself in part from its modernist precursors by the length of the leap: the "POST-MODERN," born with "ancient confidence" belongs not to fourteenth-century Italy or Hellenic Greece, but at the very beginning, again. In addition, as Christopher Beach notes (in an example of how critics, too, have come to see these poets as part of an excavational mode): "Pound's method is fundamentally that of the nineteenth-century cultural archaeologist: he studies the cultural archive for comparisons with, and supplements to, an unfavorable present. Olson's method, exemplified by his work on Mayan remains in the Yucatàn, is in a more rigorous sense that of the on-site archaeological researcher" (87).

In Pound's archaeology, intellectual as it was, Olson and the other Black Mountain poets found the beginning of something, a way around the "history" that hindered them. As Olson wrote Creeley from the Yucatan:

> 1: why I still beat up against this biz of, getting rid of nomination, so that historical material is free for forms now, is
> Ez's epic solves problem by his ego: his single emotion breaks all down to his equals or inferiors (so far as I can see only two, possibly, are admitted, by him, to be his betters – Confucius, & Dante. Which assumption, that there are intelligent men whom he can outtalk, is beautiful because it destroys historical time, and
> thus creates the methodology of the Cantos, viz, a space-field where, by inversion, though the material is all time material, he has driven through it so sharply by the beak of his ego, that, he has turned time into what we must now have, space & its live air.
>
> (*Mayan Letters* 26–7)

Pound's method of breaking through the ground of historical time using "the beak of his ego" conditioned a method of drawing upon all epochs without the chains of continuity. Pound's "space-field" where time is turned into "space & its live air" provided a model where time is unpacked and material references are distributed (not necessarily and, in fact, very rarely chronologically) on the visible surface of the page. By contrast, in Olson's view, William Carlos Williams: "completely licks himself, lets time roll him under as Ez does not, and thus, so far as what is the more important, methodology, contributes nothing, in fact, delays, deters, and hampers, by not having busted through the very problem which Ez has so brilliantly faced, & beat ..." (28). Similarly, Robert Duncan comments: "This is what we're trying to get around. 'Chronology' I guess they were in. Williams gets mixed up between the *history*, which he gets, but he also thinks he's responsible to *chronology*. In other words, he gets his story false because he is tied to: 'this happened after this happened after this happened is a story'" (*Muthologos* 9). Within these oppositions we find an implicit archaeological impulse, the desire to break down the historical site into

The Rhetoric of Resurrection

artifacts that may be lifted from the strata of various epochs and laid side by side on the page. If history belongs to narrative, with its chronological insistence on "and then," then archaeology is modern poetry's as it smashes the linear and recuperates the object.

As Beach suggests, Olson was also the much more visceral archaeologist, more interested in dredging shards of Mayan pottery from the earth than in studying manuscripts in the reading room of the British Museum. During his time in Mexico he literally dug in, enduring respiratory disorders, heat stroke, dysentery and blisters. While on the Yucatan he wrote archaeological funding proposals, liaised with local experts and officials, and was genuinely enchanted by his own excavations:

> christamiexcited. getting that load off my heart, to you, thursday, did a trick. for i pulled out, that afternoon, down the road AND BROKE THRU –
>
> > hit a real spot, which had spotted fr bus,
> > and which same, apparently, untouched:
> > Con & I came back with bags of sherds [sic]
> > & little heads & feet – all lovely things
> >
> > then, yesterday, alone, hit further south,
> > and smash, dug out my Ist hieroglyphic
> > stone! ...
>
> Had started to reply... But my nerves are so bunched toward these ruins, I better go and get back to these things later, if you will understand, please. For I am wild for it.
> (*Mayan Letters* 37–8)

Olson's exhilaration in this letter to Creeley is an intensely physical one, brought about by his concrete connection with ancient Mayan relics. More than just the excitement of unearthing artifacts, though, we can sense that the aesthetics of disinterment are crucial to Olson's poetic work. Most immediately, the archaeological site, like "post-historic" poetry, eliminates time. The Mayan fragments may be buried but, nonetheless, exist contemporaneously with the present and chronology is overcome by the will to dig and the ready existence of the past. This schema is coherent with the poetic method outlined in "Projective Verse," where Olson promulgates

"COMPOSITION BY FIELD" (*A Charles Olson Reader* 40) and emphasizes "OBJECTS, what they are, what they are inside a poem" (44). The parallels between field-composition and field-excavation are compounded when we consider Olson's desire to channel the energies of the past. As Paul Bové notes: "Olson's sense of origins means an attempt to regain an awareness of man's temporal and geographical nature in a world where poetry should only be written out of the complex, deep historical relationship between a man and the other objects within his world, his environment, his 'field'" (228). This "deep historical relationship" mediated by objects in the field situates Olson's intentions but also describes a working method: The poem itself as site.

This technique is particularly well illustrated in the poem "The Distances," which is actually intent on collapsing space – the distances that are created by chronology. Operating in a mode between Pound and H.D., Olson attempts to compress the space between various epochs without actually entering into H.D.'s model of synthesis. Instead event, linked thematically and by human impulse, is presented spatially in order to highlight what Baudelaire might have called the "*correspondances*" among ages:

> So the distances are Galatea
>   and one does fall in love and desires
> mastery
>   old Zeus – young Augustus
>
> Love knows no distance, no place
>   is that far away or heat changes
>
> into signals, and control
>   old Zeus – young Augustus
>
> Death is a loving matter, then, a horror
>   we cannot bide, and avoid
> by greedy life
>
>   we think all living things are precious

The Rhetoric of Resurrection 177

                – Pygmalions

                        a German inventor in Key West
who had a Cuban girl, and kept her, after her death
in his bed
                        after her family retrieved her
he stole the body again from the vault

Torso on torso in either direction,
        young Augustus
                        out via nothing where messages
are
        or in, down La Cluny's steps to the old man sitting
a god throned on torsoes,

        old Zeus
        (*Collected Poems* 491)

    Adhering to the idea that repetition knits human experience, Olson demonstrates history does not progress but repeats; hence his comment to Creeley, we are the "second time." The emphasis here is not on progress but what remains constant: "one does fall in love and desires"; one does fall in love and "desires / mastery": Old Zeus, the young Roman emperor Augustus, Pygmalion sculpting the statue that becomes his wife, a German inventor in Key West. By creating spatial proximity among these examples, Olson in fact breaks down the perceived "distances" among these traditionally historically disparate instances. They are, instead, mythically linked by the unacknowledged ritualistic processes of repetition; they are overlaying strata which highlight the similarities among epochs. Capturing the energy of ancient experience and placing it side by side with the contemporaneous illustrates a desire to replace historical and social alienation with a new form of coherence and connection. This patterning among ages is prototypical of Olson's poetic project, later demonstrated by the tightly bound connection between himself and the Greek philosopher Maximus in *The Maximus Poems*.

Another striking feature of "The Distances" is the way in which it utilizes space on the page. The poem is not a vertical progression of historical accumulation but a space field of fragmented lines which must be interpreted according to their context. Because the line: "Torso on torso in either direction" follows the story about the German inventor, for example, we assume that this action or memory applies to him; but as it is closely followed by the words "young Augustus" we are forced to recognize that the line also operates in "either direction" – that, in addition to bilateral desire within each gender, our desires are also torso on torso with those of past desirers. This connectedness is further illustrated when the reader taps into the chain of associations attached to the reference "throned on torsoes," a line which digs deeply into an artistic and human past. Most recently, the allusion is to Melville's *Moby Dick*, the passage where Ishmael comments on Ahab's darker motivations:

> This is much; yet Ahab's larger, darker, deeper part remains unhinted. But vain to popularize profundities, and all truth is profound. Winding far down from within the very heart of this spiked Hotel de Cluny where we here stand- however grand and wonderful, now quit it;- and take your way, ye nobler, sadder souls, to those vast Roman halls of Thermes; where far beneath the fantastic towers of man's upper earth, his root of grandeur, his whole awful essence sits in bearded state; an antique buried beneath antiquities, and throned on torsoes! So with a broken throne, the great gods mock that captive king; so like a Caryatid, he patient sits, upholding on his frozen brow the piled entablatures of ages.
>
> (185)

The Hotel de Cluny that drives the image here is the Musée de Cluny or the Musée National du Moyen Âge in the fifth arrondissement in Paris, built on top of the Gallo-Roman city of Lutetia. Melville visited the Hotel de Cluny in 1849, and undoubtedly visited the tapestries famously housed there as well as the Roman baths of Thermes still extant below the museum. The room on display is the "frigidarium" or cool water area in the baths of the Emperor Julian. Abandoned or neglected for several centuries, the area served at one point in the twelfth century as a storage room for a barrel

The Rhetoric of Resurrection

maker. By the time Melville saw it, it had been basically restored with what was believed to be an excavated statue of Julian residing within it.[4]

For Melville, the image of the Hotel de Cluny serves as a Jungian symbol for the human psyche, which contains within it an upper stratum and lower, more driving desires. For Olson, the statue of what was thought to be the last pagan emperor, "an antique buried beneath antiquities" is resonant with an archaeological paradigm where mythic energies dwell beneath the surface of contemporary life. When Olson writes "down La Cluny's steps to the old man sitting / a god throned on torsoes" he encourages us to dig into the ancient past, to embrace the mentality it houses, to relish the labors of the dig, and, by extension, to complete the incomplete trace left for us to find, much as an archaeologist would on discovering an ancient remain. While Olson's use of the Hotel de Cluny differs from Melville's, he, nonetheless, proceeds with similar intent, believing that the "recovery" of ancient forces (both subconscious and object-driven) will enrich the fabric of the now. As Olson notes in an unpublished essay, Melville: "recovered processes of the imagination and tapped reservoirs of image and feeling which are essentially primordial. It is his revolution in the sense of recovery rather than advance that leads me to call him mythographer rather than writer" (qtd. in Merrill 67).

For Olson, replacing narrative history with an archaeological poetic has everything to do with returning humanity to its primordial "senses," the particular task of the archaeologist/mythographer. In *The Special View of History*, Olson appeals to Einstein's physics to make the point:

> "[O]nly to space-time coincidence and immediate space-time proximity can we assign an intuitively evident meaning." In other words, touch as sensation (the meaning of feeling), not sensation as generalized as of the other senses as well (the false totality of the five senses without head – without the head of touch) [prehension, to seize, as with the hand or other member] produces actuality.
>
> (49)

---

4   More recent research has suggested that the statue in question is not of Julian.

The production of actuality through the senses is a much more humanized mode of being, for Olson, than abstract discourse, logic and classification. This view is encoded in the La Cluny reference, as in addition to the baths of Thermes, the museum's most well-known artifacts are the tapestries in "La Dame à la Licorne" series, which according to accepted interpretation signify the five senses and desire denied. In digging down through the recesses of the poem's meaning, we too are put "in touch" with the "senses," led by Olson's site-specific references. We are made to follow Herodotus' method by finding out for ourselves. In this sense, Olson is acting against an epistemological system in place since the Greeks: "What Socrates did was to isolate the value and thus raise and isolate the man-time from space-time. What he performed, however, was a removal from the particular" (27). For Olson, the type of concrete historical immersion he himself introduces is a mode of re-familiarizing readers with that with which we have become estranged (29).

However artful it may seem, Olson's re-gathering of ancient energies through the linguistic creation of a Cluny-like staircase into the living past is not just an aesthetic project. Rather, it is an intensely social one. A humanized poetic, a restored human sensibility, for Olson, is the only way to proceed in the face of the historically inhumane. Olson's digging is not French romantic exoticism nor Pater's Grecian reverie. It is the excavation of a poet who participated in the Roosevelt administration, who left politics but never left politics out of his poetry, a keen, at times angry observer of the Second World War. When Olson names himself an archaeologist, it is within this context: "I find it awkward to call myself a writer ... This is the morning, after the dispersion, and the work of the mornings is methodology: how to use oneself, and on what. That is my profession. I am an archaeologist of morning" (*Collected Prose* 206–7). To realize that Olson's archaeology is an archaeology of "morning" is to understand his digging in a very particular way. The night of the "dispersion" is at once a movement away from mythic modes of being, an at-homeness in nature, and a movement into the night of abstraction, individualism, capital, and war. The morning after the dispersion is the morning after the atom bomb: an archaeology of morning and of mourning, of hope but also of sobered recognition.

The Rhetoric of Resurrection

It is in an early poem, "La Préface," that Olson first brings together archaeological discovery and the newly unearthed horrors of the Nazi death camps. The poem begins:

> The dead in via
>   in vita nuova
>   in the way
> You shall lament who know they are as tender as the horse is.
> You, do not speak who know not.
>
> 'I will die about April 1st...' going off
> 'I weigh, I think, 80 lbs...'scratch
> 'My name is NO RACE' address
>
> Buchenwald new Altamira cave
> With a nail they drew the object of the hunt.
>
> Put war away with time, come into space.
> It was May, precise date 1940. I had air my lungs could breathe.
> He talked, via stones a stick sea rock a hand of earth.
> It is now, precise, repeat. I talk of Bigmans organs
> he, look, the lines! are polytopes.
> And among the DPs – deathhead
>   at the apex
>   of the pyramid.
>   (*A Charles Olson Reader* 2–3)

This poem was written in response to the drawings of Olson's friend, Corrado Cagli, whose allied company, according to Ralph Maud, was the first to enter Buchenwald (*A Charles Olson Reader* 1–2). Cagli produced a series of fine line drawings illustrating what he saw in the death camps, and Olson wrote the poem on seeing the exhibition in Chicago. The link is important as it emphasizes Olson's need to either see things for himself or hear from those who have witnessed events directly. From the evidence of the drawings, Olson creates a philosophical statement at the beginning of the poem: in this case, harshly devoid of sentiment: the dead are "in the way," necessitating but also blocking the road to a new beginning. Rather than attempt to evade this blockade, however, Olson crafts the first lines as a series of typographical steps into the hell of the historical reality, as though genuinely experiencing this descent is the only way to achieve transformation. Those who have seen and who know the extent of the atrocities are urged to "lament" and be heard. Those who have only second-hand knowledge are silenced.

In the second stanza, the concentration camp victims, seemingly in dialogue with the officials who are taking down their stories, assume the speaking voice. The victims speak of their death date, weight, and protectively, out of habit, deny both name and race. In response, the officials, less authoritatively out of quotation marks as those who don't "know," record actions, scratch the questions off their lists, or demand information. It is in this context of horror being recorded into history that Olson introduces one of the most startling juxtapositions of the poem: "Buchenwald new Altamira cave." Buchenwald, the Nazi concentration camp, operated from 1937 to 1945, housing 250,000 prisoners with an estimated 56,545 killed by execution, starvation, or medical experiment. Upper Paleolithic cave drawings were discovered in the Altamira cave in Spain in the early nineteenth century and were popularized by modernist artistic interest in the paintings of wild animals. Henry Moore, Picasso, and Miró were deeply influenced by the cave drawings, and Picasso famously commented "after Altamira, all is decadence." The combined image compels one to consider the concentration camp victims, reduced to primitive conditions, known to scratch out drawings with sticks in the dust or on walls with rusty nails. For Olson the intolerability of the death camps marks an end in the road of Western civilization. Yet the base-line of bodily resistance and the human will to express also signals a new beginning, a primitivism reclaimed as the starting point for a "new" art and society.

It is from this statement that Olson urges readers to put away both war and time – the chronological, teleological history that, for Olson, leads to dispersion and aggression – and to step into the new reality: space. In space, all ages are genuinely contemporaneous, including gentler, more authentic times that can be drawn upon as model. As demonstration, Olson suddenly retreats into his own past, his initial meeting with Cagli, when it was possible to "breathe." Without a common language – Cagli spoke Italian – they communicated as primal people meeting for the first time

The Rhetoric of Resurrection

with objects – "stones   a stick   sea rock   a hand of earth." They talk of Olson's biological poetry "Bigmans organs" and Cagli comments on the lines. Moving beyond personal history, Olson insinuates that these movements backward are possible for social history also: that civilization can leap back from the "deathhead" of the DP camps to the height of Mayan or Aztec achievement – the "apex / of the pyramid."

Here, we are somewhat reminded of Pound, who, on confronting the horrors of the First World War, and particularly the death of Gaudier-Brzeska, raided the past for a template that might right a "botched" civilization. The impulse in Olson is similar, though Olson's Brzeska was Jean Riboud, a friend who spent two years at Buchenwald and emerged tubercular and weighing ninety-six pounds (Maud 2). The difference is that while Brzeska died in the war, Riboud survived and inspired Olson to think in terms of what we can endure and what we must return to. In "The Resistance (for Jean Riboud)" Olson writes:

> Man came here by an intolerable way. When man is reduced to so much fat for soap, superphosphate for soil, fillings and shoes for sale, he has, to begin again, one answer, one point of resistance only to such fragmentation, one organized ground, a ground he comes to by a way the precise contrary of the cross, of spirit in the old sense, in old mouths. It is his own physiology he is forced to arrive at. And the way – the way of the beast, of man and the Beast.
>
> (*A Charles Olson Reader* 3)

Faced with the inhuman and the impossible, humans are left with nothing but their basest of resistances, and this resistance is housed in the body. In this state of desperation and survival, a primal mode, "the old sense" emerges, which for Olson is the first step toward a new recognition. The poet, whose physicality is insisted upon in "Projective Verse," must use his own breath in the service of resistance if poetry is to be of "essential use" (40) and this stylistic resistance and disruptive practice must form the very base of a new poetic: "... I do it gravely, as part of, my method, believing that, resistance must be part of style if, it is a part of the feeling" (*Letters for Origin* 40).

Resistance, the arrangement of artifacts/objects, and the backward road into the future are all crucial to "The Kingfishers." Indeed this poem, above all Olson's work, represents an archaeology of resistance, his *pièce de resistance*, as it were, propelled by the desire to "br[ea]k thru." Unsurprisingly, etymological digging yields the way into the poem and on probing we learn that kingfishers are related to Greek "halcyons" and that the expression "halcyon days," in contemporary speech referring to the lost days of youth, finds its origin in Greek and Roman mythology: Alcyone, daughter of Aeolus, ruler of the winds, lost her husband Ceyx to the sea. Overcome by grief she threw herself into the ocean. Intervening in the tragedy, Aeolus turned both Alcyone and Ceyx into birds and calmed the winds while they built a nest on the sea. These days of tranquil weather around the solstice are still called the "halcyon days" in parts of Europe.

In turn, the poem is at once a lament for these lost days of mythical richness, where natural events sparked the human imagination, and a manifesto for a new social order that takes the shape of a return. The desire for this reactivation is not passive but expressed through Mao's revolutionary statement:

> nous devons
> > nous lever
> > > et agir!
> > > (*A Charles Olson Reader* 34)

Rather than a particular political system, Olson seems to be praising the call to action: "We must rise up (raise ourselves up) and act." This cry is in accord with the unwavering human will toward change, a rejection of stasis, and the possibility of altering our course with a shift in attention: "when the attentions change / the jungle / leaps in / even the stones are split / they rive." In this context, Olson urges the contemporary reader to approach ancient knowledge not as the Spanish conquistadors did (though "we more naturally recognize / he so resembles ourselves" [34]), but by reclaiming an ancient reverence: to appreciate the Delphic "E / cut so rudely on that oldest stone," to see the kingfishers as they were once seen: "of green feathers feet, beaks and eyes / of gold," to understand time spatially as did the Aztecs or Mayans with their great calendars: "a large wheel, gold, with figures of unknown four-foots, / and worked with tufts of leaves, weight

The Rhetoric of Resurrection

/ 3800 ounces" (36). Through this tracing back of concrete objects – the E – the kingfishers – the calendars – the speaker is drawn into a visionary scene of the Mayan priests as the conquistadors descended:

> In this instance, the priests
> (in dark cotton robes, and dirty,
> their disheveled hair matted with blood, and flowing wildly
> over their shoulders)
> rush in among the people, calling on them
> to protect their gods
>
> And all now is war
> where so lately there was peace,
> and the sweet brotherhood, the use
> of tilled fields.
> (35)

Surrounded not only by these deaths: "Not one death but many" – we must maintain the desire to move forward, to change. The change that is possible at an individual level is illustrated by a crescendo of change and possible change: "how is it, / if we remain the same, / we take pleasure now / in what we did not take pleasure before?". Change, the way forward, (for Olson the will back) is natural and fundamental to being. Resistance is not resisting its pull.

The result, as George Butterick has persuasively argued, is that the archaic and the post-modern are, for Olson, one and the same (6). Unlike the moderns who are alienated from themselves and others by the catastrophic unfolding of history, the post-modern has at his disposal the confidence of his own belonging. Somewhat controversially, Olson eludes the violence of ancient peoples in this equation, suggesting that the "perjorocracy" of modern life is far worse than the Mayan walls "black from human gore" (37):

> with what violence benevolence is brought
> what cost in gesture justice brings
> what wrongs domestic rights involve
> what stalks
> this silence
> what pudor perjorocracy affronts
> how awe, night-rest and neighborhood can rot
> what breeds where dirtiness is law
> what crawls
> below
> (37–8)

In opposition to the ritualistic bloodshed of the ancient Maya, in Western "civil" society man is alienated from himself by law, bureaucracy, regulation, speech cleansed of authenticity, corruption and quotidian regulation. Overcoming requires a reclaiming. As Butterick observes: "The formula seems inescapable: the deeper man returns to his archaic, primordial, pre-rationalist condition, the further beyond modernism he advances" (12).

In advancing into the post-modern via the archaic, Olson may move beyond modernism, but it is through tunnels that had been operating at a subterranean level throughout modernism's development. If Olson chooses an earlier, more primal time in human history, he, nonetheless, achieves it through a transformative sensibility in operation since modernism's inception. In his fascination with the past and the desire for its rupturing of the present, there are overtones of Gautier, Pater, and Pound's dredging of ancient intensities, the French surrealists' existential journey into past mythologies, and Freud and H.D.'s interest in the subterranean pre-rational. The writers and poets of the stratified tradition were consistently, in this sense, paving the way for the post-modern via their imaginative journeying into the past and back again. In this sense, the modern and the post-modern are consistently underwritten by the presence of the pre-modern, the archaic text through which the traces of the future are divined.

In the final section of "The Kingfishers," Olson proposes the road into "ancient confidence," leading from the "intolerable way." This road is created by archaeological tunneling, propelled by a taste for earth and stones:

The Rhetoric of Resurrection

> It works out this way, despite the disadvantage.
> I offer, in explanation, a quote:
> si j'ai du goût, ce n'est guères
> que pour la terre et les pierres.
>
> Despite the discrepancy (an ocean courage age)
> this is also true: if I have any taste
> it is only because I have interested myself
> in what was slain in the sun
>
> I pose you your question:
>
> shall you uncover honey / where maggots are?
>
> I hunt among stones
> (38)

In interesting himself in "what was slain in the sun," Olson proposes a cultural regression into an object-oriented mythology driven by experiential reliance on the senses. Olson's question to readers compels them to ask themselves if the digging of earth will yield the treasure they seek. Affirmatively, Olson ends the poem by stating that this is the path that he will follow. Like a primal person, he will engage in the "hunt" – in this case, a hunter of the ritualized past.

As a final note, it is startling to observe how in concerning himself with the Maya as they lived and understood the world (though for the unusual purpose of replication or reactivation) Olson somewhat predated the movement toward "processual" archaeology in the late 1950s. The processual method, precursor to the New Archaeology of the 1960s, stressed an interpretive approach to archaeological finds with an emphasis on explaining the lived conditions behind the archaeological record. While Olson would never adopt the strict science of the New Archaeologists, he immersed himself in the "why" behind Mayan existence and demise. Despite this commonality with future archaeologists, Olson saw himself as distinctly unlike the institutional excavators and scholars working on the Yucatan at the same moment. For Olson, this "Peabody-Carnegie gang" were just "catching on" to "total life of a people" as expressed in art:

> The joker, is, they are "advanced" enough to justify the Mayapan operation as a step to discover more about the economic & political life of the ancient Maya! Which, of course, kills me. Here I am an aestheticist (which I have yet to be convinced *any* one of them, from Stephens on down, is). And now, when they, these professionals, are catching on (EP's 35 yr. lag, surely), to the validity of the total life of a people as what cargo art discharges, I am the one who is arguing that the correct way to come to an estimate of that dense & total thing is not, again, to measure the walls of a huge city but to get down, before it is too late, on a flat thing called a map, as complete a survey as possible of all, all present ruins, small as most of them are.
>
> (*Mayan Letters* 14)

As an "aestheticist," Olson's concern was with art as it revealed a complete picture of Mayan life and, more pragmatically, with site-preservation – interests that would eventually constitute two priorities of Meso-American archaeology. It is with a certain amount of glee, however, that Olson prefaces his bibliography of further reading for Creeley with a statement from Edward Hyams:

> "The scientific bias taken by our civilization has ... given to History and Archaeology a role, valuable and respectable, of course, but not inspired."
>
> (85)

Inspiration, Olson seems to suggest, is the work of the writer/mythographer. It is the labor, the dig of the morning.

Conclusion: Archaeologies Past and Future

> Modern memory is first of all archival. It relies entirely on the specificity of the trace, the materiality of the vestige, the concreteness of the recording, the visibility of the image. The process that began with writing has reached its culmination in high-fidelity recording. The less memory is experienced from within, the greater its need for external props and tangible reminders of that which no longer exists except *qua* memory – hence the obsession with the archive that marks an age and in which we attempt to preserve not only all of the past but all of the present as well. The fear that everything is on the verge of disappearing, coupled with anxiety about the precise significance of the present and uncertainty about the future, invests even the humblest testimony, the most modest vestige, with the dignity of being potentially memorable.
>
> (Nora 8)

In this passage from *The Realms of Memory*, Pierre Nora reminds us that the archaeological age is far from over. Rather than abandoning archaeological modes of remembrance, we are increasingly attached to the objects and documentary evidence of our own existence. Home movies, personal web pages, and the renewed vogue for the scrap-book all testify to our need to collect the traces of our own lives, to prove the materiality of our being to ourselves and to the future.

An archaeology with its eye fixed on the viewers of tomorrow is the most recent manifestation of a long-standing impulse. Placing archaeological modes in chronological order is in many respects a matter of recognizing the temporal object of each: Winckelmann, Pater, and Gautier, the substrata of our literary paradigm, pursue the excavation of the ancient past. Freud, in his own way, emulates this pattern though the psyche of the individual, dredging the patient's past for the historical key that will unlock the door to wellness. Pound, the modernist turning point, changes the dynamics of the archaeological mode by rendering the pursuit of ancient energies a matter of exhuming past templates for future use. The French surrealists bring archaeology one step closer to their own time by rendering contemporary life the site of their excavations. Olson, in some ways, circumvents this pattern by making the pre-rational past his object; but if archaeological modalities teach us anything, it is the delusiveness of the linear, and Olson's rhythmic, circular time brings the archaic in contact with the millennium. In other words, it is not surprising that we, in our current condition, are now intent on archaeologizing our existence for the benefit of tomorrow's inheritors. We are the recipients of a set of tools which we apply to a consistently accelerating temporality.

In many ways, the dissolution of memory is at the heart of the archaeological enterprise. Loosed from the traditions that incorporate memory into the fabric of everyday life, we reach for other modes of anchoring our experience. The loss of both personal and cultural memory, resulting from the sense that modernity is in some sense amnesiac, propelled most of the archaeologies studied here. Gautier asks us to remember a time of plenitude and sensory pleasure, which he sensed was evaporating in the hardening contours of industrial Paris. For Pater, remembering is the truest form of acquiring knowledge; imagining contexts from forgotten remains is a means of blocking the continuous process of cultural forgetting. For Freud, excavations are undertaken in search of the memory trace, in essence, that which we have already forgotten but might yet remember. For Pound, who thought the new poetic ought to replace the British Museum, poetry itself becomes a repository of cultural memory, a vision which H.D. internalizes and Stokes sees appearing in this history of art. For the French surrealists, the "profound M of memory" is the first step toward remembering a time before the barrier between waking and dreaming, and Olson's post-modern question asks if we might yet awaken to ancient knowledge.

More than passive remembering, a matter of fixing the past in a set moment in time, archaeological dynamics enabled all of these writers to imagine the past as retrievable. This took place in two distinct ways: the presence of the archaeological object inspired writers to imagine contexts which, in so far as they could be recreated in the present imagination, continued to exist, and from the earliest archaeological writing to the most recent, the past, through the archaeological lens, is imbued with the power

Conclusion: Archaeologies Past and Future

of return. Hence, paganism, the most persistent object of archaeological desire, is consistently perceived as capable of reemergence. Through the art of the Renaissance, the Tempio reliefs, the cultural repositories of contemporary Paris, myth may yet rise again. Perhaps the most attractive feature of archaeological imagining is its optimism; despite bouts of belatedness, cultural retrieval consistently implies the possibility of cultural return.

Yet with Pater's comment on throwing past ages in relief came the recognition that the past, ultimately, can never be retrieved unadulterated. This elusiveness motivated various types of fantasy. Archaeology presents itself as desirous ground. It encourages a kind of persistent seeking, embodies the tension between hidden and revealed. In so far as its object is a time most often removed from the present, it also creates a canvas for projection and the citation of the ideal. Hence, ancient Egypt and Pompeii are for Gautier embodied by the unobtainable woman, whose face we can dimly perceive as the composite woman of Pound's Provençal adventures. For Winckelmann, Pater, Stokes, and H.D., ancient art presents the possibility for pursuing modes of desiring that were censored in their own times. For Freud, the relationship between excavation and desire is much more direct. In essence, the analyst excavates in search of the desires of the patient, names them and brings them to the surface of the conscious mind.

The search for the pre-existing also summons the connection between writing and text. The archaeo-logic of poetic unveiling is particularly persistent in the work of Gautier, Pater, and Pound. Not surprisingly, it is also these writers who offer us the most profound archaeologies of the text: Gautier visualizing writing and reading as a process of encrypting and deciphering, Pater creating densely compacted accumulative moments. In Pound, the modernist topos absorbs this nineteenth-century archaeological inheritance yet also exceeds it by imbedding the ancient past more deeply into the site of the poem while more recent events inhabit its surface. It is this site that Olson modifies by collapsing the "distances" between eras in order to facilitate mythic return. Additionally, the personal and collective past become the spaces of mythic and material compression to create dense topographical sites of memory and history.

In Gautier, Freud, H.D. and the surrealists, it was the connection between writing, archaeology, and dream that was made explicit. For

Gautier, the dream acts as a kind of regression into a past that is also emblematic of the forgotten desires of the individual. For Freud, the dream itself is hieroglyphic, presenting an archaic symbolic language, which is deciphered by both analyst and creative writer. In H.D., the dream parallel acts as the condensed space in which past and present exist simultaneously. As for the surrealists, the mysterious object acts as a translocationary talisman and can evoke a reality that erases the barrier between dreaming and waking. The site of collective memory, archaeology also presents itself as the site of the individual unconscious. In essence, all of these writers are excavators in the sense that they attempt to dredge hidden depths through the processes of writing.

The fact that we can "trace" the archaeologies of modernism to nineteenth-century literary excavations demonstrates how that which is often considered pre-modernism acts as the substratum of modernism. In turn, the archaeologies of modernism are entombed in the vaults of the postmodern. Both lines of archaeological thought that we identified: the archaeology of the psychic self and the archaeology of the social body persist. In the work of Abraham, Torok, and Rand, we can see how the crypt and the phantom continue to operate as psychoanalytic modes of analysis. Olson's social topography illustrates how the post-modern is conceptualized as a return that is also a beginning. Where this beginning leads onto in the second half of the twentieth century and in the twenty-first is the site of another set of excavations. The tradition would suggest that we look to one of Olson's inheritors, perhaps Susan Howe and her overlapping sites of histories under erasure. But the archaeology of afternoon is global and unpredictable. In *Meditation on Ruins*, contemporary Portuguese poet Nuno Júdice bids us to accept the archaeological existence of today, defined by its fragmented form:

1
Accept the transitory; nothing
definitive, and enduring, can touch you.

2
Something visible crosses
the boundaries of being.

3
The wind broke, at night,
one of the back windows.

4
Only the sound of night survives
in the morning light and furor

5
(If those clouds, on the horizon,
would only come to me ...)

6
But the fragment expresses
the shattering intensity

7
In the final fragment, fix
on the ephemeral and rest.
(102)

Works Cited

Abraham, Nicholas and Maria Torok. *The Shell and the Kernel*. Trans. Nicholas Rand. Chicago, IL and London: U of Chicago P, 1994.
——. *The Wolf-Man's Magic Word: A Cryptonomy*. Trans. Nicholas Rand. Preface Jacques Derrida. Minneapolis, MN: U of Minneapolis P, 1986.
Appleman, Philip. "Darwin, Pater, and a Crisis in Criticism." *1859: Entering an Age of Crisis*. Bloomington, IN: Indiana UP, 1959. 81–96.
Aragon, Louis. *Paris Peasant*. Introduction and trans. Simon Watson Taylor. London: Jonathan Cape, 1971.
Austin, Linda. "The Art of Absence in the Stones of Venice." *The Journal of Pre-Raphaelite Studies* 6.2 (1986): 1–14.
Bachelard, Gaston. *The Poetics of Space*. Trans. Maria Jolas. Boston, MA: Beacon P, 1994.
Baines, John. "Literacy, social organization, and the archaeological record." *State and Society: The Emergence and Development of Social Hierarchy and Political Centralization*. Eds J. Gledhill et al. London: Unwin Hyman, 1988. 192–209.
Balakian, Anna. "André Breton et l'Héritage Méditerranéen." *Actes du VIe Congrès de l'Association Internationale de Littérature Comparée*. Eds Michel Cadot et al. Stuttgart: Kunst Und Wissen, Erich Bieber, 1975. 561–4.
Baldner, Ralph. "Ezra Pound: Image of Gautier." *Arizona Quarterly* 14 (1958): 246–56.
Barker, Stephen, ed. *Excavations and Their Objects*. Albany, NY: State U of New York P, 1996.
Baudelaire, Charles. *Le Jeune Enchanteur*. Paris: Bibliothèque Larousse, 1927.
Beach, Christopher. *The ABC of Influence: Ezra Pound and the Remaking of American Poetic Tradition*. Berkeley, CA: U of California P, 1992.

Beaujour, Michel. "Qu'est-ce que *Nadja*?" *Nouvelle Revue Française* 15 (April 1967): 7–97.

Belzoni, Gioavanni. *Narrative of the Operations and Recent Discoveries in Egypt and Nubia*. London: John Murray, 1820.

Benjamin, Walter. *The Arcades Project*. Trans. Howard Eiland and Kevin McLaughlin. Cambridge, MA and London: The Belknap Press of Harvard UP, 1999.

———. "Surrealism: The Last Snapshot of the European Intelligentsia." *Selected Writings*. Volume 2. Trans. Rodney Livingstone. Eds. Michael W. Jennings et al. Cambridge, MA and London: The Belknap Press of Harvard UP, 1999. 207–21.

———. "The Work of Art in the Age of Mechanical Reproduction." *The Critical Tradition*. Ed. David Richter. Boston MA: Bedford Books, 1998. 1106–21.

Bérard, Victor. *Les Phéniciens et L'Odyssée*. Paris: Librairie Armand Colin, 1902.

Bernal, Martin. *Black Athena*. New Brunswick, NJ: Rutgers UP, 1987.

Bernfeld, Suzanne. "Freud and Archaeology." *American Imago* 8 (1951): 197–228.

Botting, Wendy and Keith Davies. "Freud's Library and an appendix of texts related to antiquities." *Sigmund Freud and Art: His Personal Collection of Antiquities*. Eds Lynn Gamwell and Richard Wells. London: Freud Museum, 1989. 184–92.

Bové, Paul. *Destructive Poetics: Heidegger and Modern American Poetry*. New York, NY: Columbia UP, 1980.

Bowdler, Sandra. "Freud and Archaeology." *Anthropological Form* 7 (1996): 419–38.

Bowlby, Rachel. *Still Crazy After All These Years*. London and New York, NY: Routledge, 1992.

Breton, André. *Communicating Vessels*. Trans. Mary Ann Caws and Geoffrey T. Harris. Lincoln, NE and London: U of Nebraska P, 1990.

———. *Mad Love*. Trans. Mary Ann Caws. Lincoln, NE and London: U of Nebraska P, 1987.

———. *Manifestoes of Surrealism*. Trans. Richard Seaver and Helen Lane. Ann Arbor, MI: U of Michigan P, 1969.

———. *Nadja*. Trans. Richard Howard. New York, NY: Grove Press, 1960.
———. *Poems of André Breton: A Bilingual Anthology*. Ed. and Trans. Jean Pierre Cauvin and Mary Ann Caws. Austin, TX: U of Texas P, 1982.
———. *Poisson Soluble*. Paris: Gallimard, 1996.
Browder, Clifford. *André Breton: Arbiter of Surrealism*. Geneva: Librarie Droz, 1967.
Bulwer-Lytton, Edward. *The Last Days of Pompeii*. Glasgow and London: Collins, 1963.
Butterick, George. "Charles Olson and the Postmodern Advance." *Iowa Review* 11.4 (1980): 4–27.
Calder, William Musgrave and David Traill. *Myth Scandal and History: The Heinrich Schliemann Controversy*. Detroit, MI: Wayne State UP, 1986.
Carré, Jean Marie. *Voyageurs et Écrivains Français en Égypte*. Cairo: Imprimerie de L'Institut Français D'Archéologie Orientale, 1956.
Carter, Howard. *The Tomb of Tut-ankh-amen*. Vol. 1. New York, NY: Cooper Square Publishers, Inc.: 1963.
Cauvin, Jean Pierre. "The Poethics of André Breton." *Poems of André Breton: A Bilingual Anthology*. Ed. and Trans. Jean Pierre Cauvin and Mary Ann Caws. Austin, TX: U of Texas P, 1982. xvi–xxxviii.
Chadwick, Whitney. *Myth in Surrealist Paintings 1929–1939*. Ann Arbor, MI: UMI Research P, 1980.
Champollion, Jean François. *Lettres écrites d'Égypte et de Nubie en 1828–1829*. (1833). Geneva: Slatkine Reprints, 1973.
———. *Monuments de l'Égypte et de la Nubie*. (1835). Geneva: Éditions de Belles Lettres, 1970.
Chateaubriand, François-René, vicomte de. *Itinéraire de Paris à Jérusalem et de Jérusalem à Paris*. Paris: Le Normant, 1811.
Christie, Agatha. *Murder in Mesopotamia*. Boston, MA: G.K. Hall, 1991.
Cohen, Margaret. "Mysteries of Paris: The Collective Uncanny in André Breton's *L'Amour Fou*." *André Breton Today*. Eds Anna Balakian and Rudolf Kuenzli. New York, NY: Willis Locker & Owens, 1989. 101–10.

Collier, Peter. "Surrealist city narrative: Breton and Aragon." *Unreal City*. Eds Edward Timms and David Kelley. Manchester: Manchester UP, 1985. 214–29.

Conlon, John. *Walter Pater and the French Tradition*. London and Toronto: Associated UP, 1982.

Connelly, Frances. "Ruskin's True Griffin: The Relationship of Medievalism to Primitivism and the Formation of an Alternate Aesthetic." *Poetica* 39–40 (1994): 179–89.

Crane, Susan. "Story, History and the Passionate Collector." *Producing the Past: Aspects of Antiquarian Culture and Practice 1700–1850*. Eds Martin Myrone and Lucy Peltz. Aldershot and Brookfield, VT: Ashgate, 1999. 187–203.

Dahab, Elizabeth. "Théophile Gautier and the Orient." *CLCWeb: Comparative Literature and Culture* 1.4 (1999). 5 Dec 2004 <http://clcwebjournal.lib.purdue.edu/clcweb99=4/dahab99.html>.

Daniel, Glyn. *A Hundred and Fifty Years of Archaeology*. Cambridge, MA: Harvard UP, 1976.

Davie, Donald. *Ezra Pound: Poet as Sculptor*. Oxford and New York, NY: Oxford UP, 1964.

Davis, Whitney. "Winckelmann's 'Homosexual' Teleologies." *Sexuality in Ancient Art*. Ed. Natalie Boymel Kampen. Cambridge: Cambridge UP, 1996: 262–76.

Dellamora, Richard. "The Androgynous Body in Pater's 'Winckelmann.'" *Browning Institute Studies* 11 (1983): 51–69.

DeLaura, David. *Hebrew and Hellene in Victorian England*. Austin, TX: U of Texas P, 1969.

Denon, Vivant. *Travels in Upper and Lower Egypt*. Vol. 2. Trans. E.A. Kendal. London: Darf Publishers, 1986.

Derrida, Jacques. *Of Grammatology*. Trans. Gayatri Chakravorty Spivak. Baltimore, MD and London: Johns Hopkins UP, 1998.

———. *Writing and Difference*. Chicago, IL: U of Chicago P, 1978.

Dillon, Sarah. *The Palimpsest: Literature, Criticism, Theory*. London and New York, NY: Continuum, 2007.

Dobie, Madeleine. *Foreign bodies: Gender, Language, and Culture in French Orientalism*. Stanford, CA: Stanford UP, 2001.

Doolittle, Hilda (H.D.). *Asphodel*. Durham, NC: Duke UP, 1992.
——. *H.D. Collected Poems 1912–1944*. Manchester: Carcanet Press, 1984.
——. *Paint it Today*. New York, NY: New York UP, 1992.
——. *Tribute to Freud*. New York, NY: Pantheon, 1956.
Donato, Eugenio. "The Ruins of Memory: Archaeological Fragments and Textual Artifacts." *MLN* 93 (1978): 575–96.
Dresden, S. "Psychoanalysis and Surrealism." *Freud and the Humanities*. Ed. Peregrine Horden. London: Duckworth, 1985. 110–29.
Edwards, Amelia. *A Thousand Miles up the Nile*. London: Century Publishing, 1982.
Ellenberger, Herni. *The Discovery of the Unconscious*. New York, NY: Basic Books, 1970.
Epstein, Edna Selan. "The Entanglement of Sexuality and Aesthetics in Gautier and Mallarmé." *Nineteenth Century French Studies* 1.1 (1972): 5–20.
Espey, John. *Ezra Pound's* Mauberley: *A Study in Composition*. Berkeley, CA and London: U of California P, 1955.
Evans, Arthur. "Minoan Civilization at the Palace of Knossos." *Eyewitness to Discovery*. Ed. Brian Fagan. Oxford and New York, NY: Oxford University Press, 1996. 188–96.
Feydeau, Ernest. *Histoire des Usages Funèbres et des Sépultures des Peuples Anciens*. Paris: Gide, 1856–1858.
Finkelstein, Haim. *Surrealism and the Crisis of the Object*. Ann Arbor, MI: UMI Research P, 1979.
Finn, Christine. *Past Poetic: Archaeology in the Poetry of W.B. Yeats and Seamus Heaney*. London: Duckworth, 2004.
Flaubert, Gustave. *Salammbô*. Paris: Éditions de Cluny, 1937.
Foucault, Michel. *The Order of Things: An Archaeology of the Human Sciences*. Trans. Alan Sheridan. London: Tavistock Publications, 1970.
Fredman, Stephen. *The Grounding of American Poetry*. Cambridge: Cambridge UP, 1993.
Freud, Sigmund. "The Aetiology of Hysteria." Appendix B. *The Assault on Truth*: Freud's Suppression of the Seduction Theory. J.M. Masson. Boston, MA: Faber and Faber, 1984: 252–82.

———. "The Antithetical Meaning of Primal Words." *Writings on Art and Literature*. Trans. James Strachey. Stanford, CA: Stanford UP, 1997. 257–87.

———. "Civilization and its Discontents." *The Standard Edition of the Complete Works of Sigmund Freud*. Trans. James Strachey. Vol. 21. London: Hogarth, 1958. 64–148.

———. "The Claims of Psycho-analysis to Scientific Interest." *The Standard Edition of the Complete Works of Sigmund Freud*. Trans. James Strachey. Vol. 13. London: Hogarth, 1955. 176–89.

———. "Constructions in Analysis." *The Standard Edition of the Complete Works of Sigmund Freud*. Trans. James Strachey. Vol. 23. London: Hogarth, 1958. 255–70.

———. "Delusions and Dreams in Jensen's *Gradiva*." *The Standard Edition of the Complete Works of Sigmund Freud*. Trans. James Strachey. Vol. 9. London: Hogarth, 1955. 7–93.

———. "Fragment of an Analysis of a Case of Hysteria ('Dora')." *The Standard Edition of the Complete Works of Sigmund Freud*. Trans. James Strachey. Vol. 7. 1–122.

———. "Moses and Monotheism." *The Standard Edition of the Complete Works of Sigmund Freud*. Trans. James Strachey. Vol. 23. London: Hogarth, 1958. 7–137.

———. "The Moses of Michelangelo." *Writings on Art and Literature*. Trans. James Strachey. Stanford, CA: Stanford UP, 1997. 257–87.

———. "A Note Upon the 'Mystic Writing-Pad'." *The Standard Edition of the Complete Works of Sigmund Freud*. Trans. James Strachey. Vol. 19. London: Hogarth, 1961. 227–34.

———. "The Scientific Literature Dealing with the Problems of Dreams." *The Standard Edition of the Complete Works of Sigmund Freud*. Trans. James Strachey. Vol. 4. London: Hogarth, 1958. 1–95.

Gaimster, David. "Sex and Sensibility at the British Museum." *History Today* 50.9 (Sept. 2000): 10–21.

Gamwell, Lynn and Richard Wells, eds. *Sigmund Freud and Art: His Personal Collection of Antiquities*. London: Freud Museum, 1989.

Gaulmier, Jean. "Remarques sur le Thème de Paris chez André Breton de *Nadja* à *l'Amour Fou*." *Travaux de Linguistique et de Littérature* 9.2 (1971): 159–69.

Gautier, Théophile. *Émaux et Camées*. Ed. and trans. Madeleine Cottin. Paris: Minard, 1968.

———. "Leonardo da Vinci." *The Works of Théophile Gautier*. Vol. 9. Ed. F.C. de Sumichrast. New York, NY: The Athenaeum Society, 1901–1903. 253–80.

———. *Mademoiselle de Maupin*. Trans. Helen Constantine. New York, NY: Penguin, 2005.

———. *The Mummy's Romance*. Trans. G.K. Monkshood. London: Greening & Co., 1908.

———. *The Mummy's Foot. One of Cleopatra's Nights and Other Fantastic Romances*. Trans. Lafcadio Hearn. London: MacLaren and Co., 1907.

———. *Le Roman de la Momie*. Paris: Maxi-Livres, 2001.

———. *Théophile Gautier's Short Stories*. Trans. George Burnham Ives. Freeport, NY: Books for Libraries P, 1970.

Gilmartin, Sophie. "Transition and tradition: the preoccupation with ancestry in Victorian Writing." *Writing and Victorianism*. Ed. J.B. Bullen. London: Longman, 1997. 15–37.

Godfrey, Sima. "Mummy Dearest: Cryptic Codes in Gautier's 'Pied de la Momie.'" *Romantic Review* 75.3 (1984): 302–11.

Goethe, Johann Wolfgang von. *Italian Journey 1786–1788*. Trans. W.H. Auden. New York, NY: Pantheon Books, 1962.

Goldstein, Laurence. *Ruins and Empire: The Evolution of a Theme in Augustan and Romantic Literature*. Pittsburgh, PA: U of Pittsburgh P, 1972.

Green, André. "The Unbinding Process." *New Literary History* 12.11 (1980): 11–39.

Greene, Thomas. *The Light in Troy: Imitation and Discovery in Renaissance Poetry*. New Haven, CT and London: Yale UP, 1982.

Gubel, Eric. *Le sphinx de Vienne: Sigmund Freud, l'art et l'archéologie*. Paris: Ludion, 1993.

Halden-Sullivan, Judith. *The Topology of Being: The Poetics of Charles Olson*. New York, NY: Peter Lang, 1991.
Hake, Sabine. "*Saxa loquuntur*: Freud's Archaeology of the Text." *Boundary 2* 20.1 (1993): 146–73.
Harris, Wendell. "Ruskin and Pater – Hebrew and Hellene – Explore the Renaissance." *CLIO* 17.2 (1988): 173–85.
Harrison, John. "Pater, Heine, and the Old Gods of Greece." *Publications of the Modern Language Association of America* 39.3 (1924): 655–87.
Heidegger, Martin. "Hölderlin and the Essence of Poetry." *The Critical Tradition*. Ed. David Richter. Boston, MA: Bedford Books, 1998. 563–670.
Heine, Heinrich. *The Prose Writings of Heinrich Heine*. Trans. Havelock Ellis. London: The Walter Scott Publishing Co., 1887.
——. *The Gods in Exile*. Pasadena, CA: Castle P, 1962.
Hilprecht, H.V. *Explorations in Bible Lands During the Nineteenth Century*. Philadelphia, PA: A.H. Holman and Company, 1903.
Hines, John. *Voices in the Past: English Literature and Archaeology*. Cambridge: D.S. Brewer, 2004.
Hoskins, G.A. *Travels in Ethiopia*. London: Longman, 1835.
Hubert, J.D. "André Breton et le paradis perdu." *The French Review* 37 (January 1963): 200–5.
Hudson, Kenneth. *Museums of Influence*. Cambridge: Cambridge UP, 1987.
Huysmans, J.K. *Against Nature*. Trans. Robert Baldick. Baltimore, MD: Penguin Books, 1966.
Jacks, Philip. *The Antiquarian and the Myth of Antiquity: The Origins of Rome in Renaissance Thought*. Cambridge: Cambridge UP, 1993.
James, Henry. *The Beast in the Jungle and Other Stories*. New York, NY: Dover Publications, 1992.
——. *The Portrait of a Lady*. New York, NY: P.F. Collier & Son Company, 1917.
Janowitz, Anne. *England's Ruins: Poetic Purpose and the National Landscape*. Cambridge, MA and Oxford: Basil Blackwell, 1990.
Jensen, Wilhelm. *Gradiva: A Pompeiian Fantasy*. Trans. Helen Downey. Los Angeles, CA: Sun and Moon P, 1993.

Júdice, Nuno. *Meditation on Ruins*. Trans. Richard Zenith. Prague: Archangel, 1997.
Kenner, Hugh. *The Pound Era*. London: Pimlico, 1971.
King, Russell. "Émaux et Camées: Sculpture et Objets-Paysages." *Revue Litteraire Mensuelle* 1.84 (1979): 84–90.
Kuspit, Donald. "A Mighty Metaphor: The Analogy of Archaeology and Psychoanalsyis." *Sigmund Freud and Art: His Personal Collection of Antiquities*. Eds Lynn Gamwell and Richard Wells. London: Freud Museum, 1989. 133–52.
Lamartine, Alphonse de. *Souvenirs, Impressions, Pensées et Paysages pendant un voyage en Orient*. Paris: Pagnerre, 1856.
Lehman, Ulrich. *Tigersprung: Fashion in Moderity*. Cambridge, MA: MIT P, 2000.
Leppmann, Wolfgang. *Pompeii in Fact and Fiction*. London: Elek Books, 1966.
Levinson, Marjorie. *The Romantic Fragment Poem: A Critique of a Form*. Chapel Hill, NC: U of North Carolina P, 1987.
McFarland, Thomas. *Romanticism and the Forms of Ruin: Wordsworth, Coleridge, and the Modalities of Fragmentation*. Princeton, NJ: Princeton UP, 1981.
Malt, Johanna. "Archaeology, myth and the commodity: Walter Benjamin and *Le Paysan de Paris*." *Journal of Romance Studies* 1.2 (2001): 15–30.
——. *Obscure objects of desire: surrealism, fetishism, and politics*. London and New York, NY: Oxford UP, 2004.
Marinetti, F.T. "The Founding and Manifesto of Futurism." *Marinetti: Selected Writings*. Ed. R.W. Flint. New York, NY: Farrar, Straus, and Giroux, 1972.
Maud, Ralph. "Charles Olson's archaic postmodern." *Minutes of the Charles Olson Society* 42 (2001). Feb 1, 2007 <http://charlesolson.ca/files/archaic1.htm2007/02/01>.
Melville, Herman. *Moby-Dick, or, The Whale*. Ed. Harrison Hayford et al. *The Writings of Herman Melville Vol. 6*. Evanston, IL and Chicago, IL: Northwestern UP and the Newberry Library, 1988.

Merrill, Thomas. *The Poetry of Charles Olson*. Newark, DE: U of Delaware P, 1982.
Napoleon and Gilles Néret. *Description de l'Égypte*. (1809) Köln: Benedikt Taschen, 1994.
Nerval, Gerard de. *Journey to the Orient*. Ed. and trans. Norman Glass. New York, NY: New York UP, 1972.
Nicholls, Peter. "Pound's Places." *Locations of Literary Modernism: Region and Nation in British and American Modernist Poetry*. Eds Alex Davis and Lee M. Jenkins. Cambridge: Cambridge UP, 2000. 159–77.
Nietzsche, Friedrich. "On the Use and Abuse of History for Life." Trans. Ian Johnston. *Johnstonia*. Feb 20, 2005. <http://www.mala.bc.ca/~johnstoi/Nietzsche/history.htm>
Nora, Pierre. Introduction. *Realms of Memory: Rethinking the French Past*. New York, NY: Columbia UP, 1996.
Olson, Charles. *Additional Prose*. Ed. George Butterick. Bolinas, CA: Four Seasons Foundation, 1974.
——. *Charles Olson & Robert Creeley: The Complete Correspondence*. Vol. 7. Santa Barbara, CA: Black Sparrow P, 1980.
——. *A Charles Olson Reader*. Ed. Ralph Maud. Manchester: Carcanet, 2005.
——. *The Collected Poems of Charles Olson, excluding the Maximus Poems*. Ed. George Butterick. Berkeley, CA: U of California P, 1987.
——. *Collected Prose*. Berkeley, CA: U of California P, 1997.
——. "Definitions by Undoings." *Boundary* 2.2 (1973–4): 7–12.
——. *Human Universe and Other Essays*. New York, NY: Grove P, 1967.
——. *Letters for Origin 1950–1956*. Ed. Albert Glover. London: Cape Goliard P, 1969.
——. *Muthologos: The Collected Letters and Interviews*. Vol. 1. Ed. George F. Butterick. Bolinas, CA: Four Seasons Foundation, 1978.
——. "Notes for the Proposition: Man Is Prospective." *Boundary* 2.2 (1973–4): 1–6.
——. "Project (1951): 'The Art of the Language of Mayan Glyphs.'" *Alcheringa* 5 (1973): 94–100.
——. *The Special View of History*. Berkeley, CA: Oyez, 1970.

Oxford English Dictionary, on-line edition. Feb 23, 2005 <http://www.oed.com>.
Pater, Walter. *Appreciations. Walter Pater: Three Major Texts.* Ed. William Buckler. New York, NY and London: New York UP: 1986.
——. *Greek Studies.* London: Macmillan, 1910.
——. *Imaginary Portraits. Walter Pater: Three Major Texts.* Ed. William Buckler. New York and London: New York UP: 1986.
——. *Marius the Epicurean.* London, Toronto, New York, NY: J.M. Dent, 1934.
——. *The Renaissance: Studies in Art and Poetry.* Ed. Adam Phillips. Oxford and New York, NY: Oxford UP, 1985.
Pierrot, Jean. *The Decadent Imagination, 1880–1900.* Trans. Derek Coltman. Chicago, IL: U of Chicago P, 1981.
Pound, Ezra. *The ABC of Reading.* New York, NY: New Directions, 1960.
——. *The Cantos of Ezra Pound.* New York, NY: New Directions, 1993.
——. *Gaudier Brzeska: A Memoir.* Hessle: Marvell Press, 1960.
——. *Guide to Kulchur.* London: Peter Owen, 1938.
——. *Literary Essays.* New York, NY: New Directions, 1968.
——. *Personae: The Shorter Poems of Ezra Pound.* Revised ed. New York, NY: New Directions, 1990.
——. *Selected Poems.* Introduction T.S. Eliot. London: Faber and Faber, 1948.
——. *Selected Poems of Ezra Pound.* New York, NY: New Directions, 1926.
——. *Selected Prose of Ezra Pound 1909–1965.* New York, NY: New Directions, 1973.
——. *A Walking Tour in Southern France: Ezra Pound among the Troubadours.* Introduction and ed. Richard Sieburth. New York, NY: New Directions, 1992.
Rainey, Lawrence. *Ezra Pound and the Monument of Culture.* Chicago, IL and London: U of Chicago P, 1991.
Rand, Nicholas. *Le Cryptage et la Vie des Oeuvres.* Preface Maria Torok. Paris: Aubier, 1989.

Rauch, Angelika. *The Hieroglyph of Tradition: Freud, Benjamin, Gadamer, Novalis, Kant.* London: Associated UP, 2000.
Ray, John. Interview. *Black Athena.* Documentary. Dir. Christopher Spencer. San Francisco, CA: California Newsreel, 1990.
Read, Richard. *Art and its Discontents: The Early Life of Adrian Stokes.* University Park, PA: Penn State UP, 2002.
Reid, Donald Malcom. *Whose Pharaohs? Archaeology, Museums, and Egyptian National Identity from Napoleon to World War I.* Los Angeles, CA: U of California P, 2002.
Riffaterre, Michael. "The Surrealist Libido: André Breton's *'Poisson soluble, No. 8.'*" *André Breton Today.* Eds Anna Balakian and Rudolf Kuenzli. New York, NY: Willis Locker & Owens, 1989. 59–66.
Ruskin, John. "The Nature of Gothic." *Prose of the Victorian Period.* Ed. William Buckler. Boston, MA: Houghton Mifflin Company, 1958.
Said, Edward. *Orientalism.* New York, NY: Vintage Books, 1979.
Schliemann, Heinrich. *Troy and Its Remains.* Ed. Philip Smith. New York, NY and London: Benjamin Bloom, 1968.
Schnapp, Jeffery, Michael Shanks and Matthew Tiews. "Archaeology, Modernism, Modernity." *Modernism/Modernity* 11.1 (2004): 1–16.
Schuerewegen, F. "Volcans: Madame de Staël (Corrine), Gobineau, (akrivie Phrangopoulo) Gautier (Arria Marcella)." *Lettres Romanes* (1991): 319–28.
Schwyzer, Philip. *Archaeologies of English Renaissance Literature.* Oxford: Oxford UP, 2007.
Shanks, Michael and Christopher Tilley. *Re-Constructing Archaeology.* Cambridge: Cambridge UP, 1987.
Shanks, Michael. *Experiencing the Past.* London and New York, NY: Routledge, 1992.
Shelton, Allen. "The Mark on the Spade." *Cultural Studies/Critical Methodologies* 3.3 (2003): 287–303.
Smith, Stan. *The Origins of Modernism: Eliot, Pound, Yeats, and the Rhetorics of Renewal.* New York, NY and London: Harvester Wheatsheaf, 1994.
Spaas, Lieve. "Surrealism and Anthropology: In Search of the Primitive." *Paragraph* 18.2 (July 1995): 163–73.

Spence, Donald. *The Freudian Metaphor: Toward Paradigm Change in Psychoanalysis.* New York, NY: Norton, 1987.
Springer, Caroline. *The Marble Wilderness: Ruins and Representation in Italian Romanticism, 1775–1850.* Cambridge: Cambridge UP, 1987.
Stokes, Adrian. *The Quattro Cento.* London: Faber and Faber, 1932.
———. *Stones of Rimini.* New York, NY: Schocken Books, 1934.
Terrell, Caroll. *A Companion to The Cantos of Ezra Pound.* Berkeley, CA: U of California P, 1993.
Thomas, Julian. "Archaeology's Place in Modernity." *Modernism/Modernity* 11.1 (2004): 17–34.
Tiffany, Daniel. *Radio Corpse: Imagism and the Cryptaesthetic of Ezra Pound.* Cambridge, MA: Harvard UP, 1995.
Tremaine, Louis. "Breton's *Nadja*: A Spiritual Ethnography." *Studies in Twentieth Century Literature* 1 (1976): 91–119.
Trigger, Bruce. *A History of Archaeological Thought.* Cambridge: Cambridge UP, 1989.
Turner, Frank. *The Greek Heritage in Victorian Britain.* New Haven, CT: Yale UP, 1981.
Vives, Luc. "Les Poèmes de la Momie: Influence de l'imaginaire orientaliste et égyptisant de Théophile Gautier dans l'œuvre de Charles Baudelaire." *Bulletin de la Société Théophile Gautier* 21(1999): 53–70.
Wallace, Jennifer. *Digging the Dirt: The Archaeological Imagination.* London: Duckworth, 2004.
Ward, Anthony. *Walter Pater: The Idea in Nature.* London: MacGibbon & Kee, 1966.
White, Hayden. *Metahistory: The Historical Imagination in Nineteenth-Century Europe.* Baltimore, MD and London: The Johns Hopkins UP, 1973.
Wilkinson, John. *The Manners and Customs of the Ancient Egyptians.* London: J. Murray, 1878.
Williams, Carolyn. *Transfigured World: Walter Pater's Aesthetic Historicism.* Ithaca, NY and London: Cornell UP, 1989.
Woolley, Leonard. *Ur of the Chaldees.* London: Ernest Benn, 1929.

Index

Abraham, Nicholas 111–13
Altamira caves 181, 182
antiquarianism 10, 11, 107–8, 116
   as negative archaeology 13–14, 52, 81–3, 146
Apollinaire, Guillaume 5
Aragon, Louis 3, 157
   Paris Peasant 57, 160–5, 167
   see also surrealism
archaeological *mentalité* 2, 5, 9, 39, 62
   American poetry 172
   psychoanalysis 100, 106, 112–13
   surrealism 152
archaeology and writing, historical relationship 1–8, 9–36

Bachelard, Gaston 2–3
Baudelaire, Charles 41, 113, 122, 176
Belzoni, Giovanni 26, 28, 42, 43, 118
   Narrative of the Operations and Recent Discoveries in Egypt and Nubia 26–8, 40
Benjamin, Walter 45, 84, 113, 160
Breton, André 3, 54, 165–7
   Nadja 154–60, 165, 167
   "Sans Connaissance" 165–7
   see also surrealism
Bulwer-Lytton, Edward 19, 23, 29
   Last Days of Pompeii, The 23–5, 50, 138, 156

Carter, Howard 24, 135
   Tomb of Tut-ankh-amen, The 14–15, 16, 27, 89
cuneiform 13, 57, 162

Derrida, Jacques 95–6, 111, 112, 156
Doolittle, Hilda (H.D.) 3, 24, 35, 54, 58, 132–9
   Asphodel 134–5
   dream parallel 57, 156, 191, 192; *see also Asphodel*
   fragment, aesthetic of 133, 138
   gender subversion 7, 191; *see also Paint it Today*
   interiorized archaeology 88, 116, 135, 141, 186, 190
   Paint it Today 132–3
   synthesis 134–5, 165, 176
   Tribute to Freud 110–11
   "Trilogy" 135–9

Egypt 25–32, 37–40
elegiac tradition *see* Gautier, Théophile; Pater, Walter; Pound, Ezra
Eliot, T.S. 20, 115
Evans, Arthur 127, 128, 162

formal effects *see* Gautier, Théophile; Pater, Walter; Pound, Ezra
fragment, aesthetic of 20
   in postmodernism 192–3
   see also Doolittle, Hilda (H.D.); Freud, Sigmund; Gautier, Théophile; Olson, Charles
French surrealism *see* surrealism
Freud, Sigmund 3, 7, 87–114, 153, 169, 192
   "Aetiology of Hysteria, The" 102–3
   archaic heritage 100–1, 113, 159
   "Civilization and its Discontents" 91–3, 94

"Constructions in Analysis" 93–4, 107
"Delusions and Dreams in Jensen's 'Gradiva'" 103–10, 144
fragment, aesthetic of 101
interiorized archaeology 116, 130, 142, 186, 189, 190
"Moses and Monotheism" 97–100, 131
"Note Upon the 'Mystic Writing-Pad', A" 94–7, 110, 135
Freudian theory *see* Doolittle, Hilda (H.D.); hieroglyph; Stokes, Adrian; surrealism
futurism 115, 146–7

Gaudier-Brzeska, Henri 35, 115, 127, 183
Gautier, Théophile 3, 7, 24, 37–60, 88, 139, 145 189, 190
  archaeological romance 16, 29, 64, 102
  Arria Marcella 50–5, 155, 156
  desire 191, 192
  elegiac tradition 48–52, 120, 122, 155
  Enamels and Cameos 55–8, 124–7, 132, 136, 138
  formal effects 39, 55–6
  fragment, aesthetic of 41
  gender subversion 58–60, 132
  interiorized archaeology 81, 89
  Mademoiselle de Maupin 59–60, 132, 133
  Mummy's Foot, The 38, 43, 44–5
  Mummy's Romance, The 38, 40–4, 45, 46, 77
  paganism 148, 186
  romanticism 61–2, 70
  sculptural poetics 45, 73, 116, 130
  see also Egypt

gender subversion *see* Doolittle, Hilda (H.D.); Gautier, Théophile; Pater, Walter; Stokes, Adrian; Winckelmann, Johann

Heidegger, Martin 69, 83, 170
Heine, Heinrich 53–4, 62, 70–1, 72, 77, 148
Hermaphrodite Sleeping 58, 59, 132
hieroglyph 25–6, 31, 32, 145, 172–3
  as code 144–5, 159, 160
  and dream 57, 110, 156, 159, 192
  as mode of reading 57, 110, 150
  and writing 39, 43–4, 47, 111, 172–3
Howe, Susan 192
Huysmans, J.K. 49

interiorized archaeology *see* Doolittle, Hilda (H.D.); Freud, Sigmund; Gautier, Théophile; Pater, Walter; Stokes, Adrian; surrealism
Italian futurism *see* futurism

James, Henry 14, 104
Jensen, Wilhelm 54, 103–9, 144; *see also* Freud, Sigmund
Joyce, James 35, 167
Júdice, Nuno 192–3

Marinetti, F.T. *see* futurism
Michelangelo 99, 124; *see also* Pater, Walter
modernity
  and amnesia 190
  archaeology, relationship to 4, 6–7, 29, 52
  and colonialism 25
  definition of 50
  as negative force 4, 38, 45, 47, 120, 127, 136, 170
  and rationalism 169

Index

Nietzsche, Friedrich 82
Nora, Pierre 189

Olson, Charles 3, 7, 169–88, 192
   chronology 122, 138–9
   "Distances, The" 176–80
   fragment, aesthetic of 172
   "The Kingfishers" 183–7
   "La Préface" 181–3
   Mayan Letters 171, 173–5, 188
   and Melville, Herman 178–9
   post-modern 7, 169, 173, 185, 186, 190
   pre-rational 54, 173, 190
   social archaeology 170, 181–3
   see also time and space, treatment of

paganism *see* Gautier, Théophile; Heine, Heinrich; Pater, Water; Pound, Ezra
Pater, Walter 61–86, 88, 89, 122, 130, 189
   aesthetic criticism 17, 66, 131
   and Browne, Thomas 67, 81–2, 90
   classical revival 53, 62–4, 99, 119, 180
   and Coleridge, Samuel Taylor 62, 64, 67, 69
   elegiac tradition 23, 51, 78–80, 120
   formal effects 3, 63, 75–6, 77, 116, 191
   fragment, aesthetic of 68, 84–5, 101–2
   gender subversion 80, 116, 132, 191
   "Hippolytus Veiled" 68, 79
   interiorized archaeology 7
   and Michelangelo 62, 69, 72–4
   Mona Lisa 75–6
   paganism 54, 70–2, 76–7, 148, 186
   romanticism 7, 61–2, 70, 77–8
   science 64–8, 70, 86
   surplus 58, 62–3, 73, 125
   and Winckelmann, Johann 78–81
   and Wordsworth, William 62, 69, 83–4
   see also antiquarianism

Picasso, Pablo 87, 182
Pompeii 2, 11, 18–25, 29, 80, 129, 160
   in *Arria Marcella* 50–5
   in "Trilogy" 137–8
   see also Bulwer-Lytton, Edward; Jensen, Wilhelm
possession 63, 82–5, 121
Pound, Ezra 3, 7, 36, 58, 72, 115–40
   Cantos, The 35, 123, 128–30, 134, 174
   elegiac tradition 117–21
   fragment, aesthetic of 125, 133, 138
   formal effects 125–7
   "Hugh Selwyn Mauberley" 124–8
   paganism 54, 58, 74, 148, 189
   Provence 117–23, 124, 149, 150–1, 191
   sculptural poetics 73–4, 191
   social archaeology 88, 115, 130–1, 139, 140, 151, 190
   see also time and space, treatment

Rand, Nicholas 113
romanticism *see* Gautier, Théophile; Pater, Walter
Ruskin, John 85–6

Said, Edward 30–1
Schliemann, Heinrich 13, 33–4, 63, 89, 98, 172
   Troy and its Remains 34–5
   Troy, influence on writing 35–6, 102, 118, 119
sculptural poetics *see* Gautier, Théophile; Pound, Ezra
social archaeology *see* Olson, Charles; Pound, Ezra; surrealism
Stokes, Adrian 3, 16, 72, 130–2, 148, 156
   Freudian theory 7, 131, 139, 190
   gender subversion 116, 131–2, 191
   interiorized archaeology 88
   Stones of Rimini 130–2

surrealism 24, 58, 66, 141–68, 186, 190
  anthropology 147–9
  avant-garde and archaeology 146–7
  fragment, aesthetic of 149, 155, 156
  Freudian theory 88, 139, 41–5, 153, 159
  interiorized archaeology 7, 141, 147, 151, 190, 192
  science 145–6
  social archaeology 7, 141, 151, 153–4
  see also Aragon, Louis; Breton, André; hieroglyph; possession

time and space, treatment 35, 122, 172–5, 176, 190
Torok, Maria 111–13

vorticism 115

Winckelmann, Johann 20–1, 29, 51, 189
  gender subversion 21–3, 58, 62, 65, 132, 191
  see also Pater, Walter
Woolley, Leonard 1–2, 14, 23, 24, 27